EVE'S NEW RIB

EVE'S NEW RIB

Twenty Faces of Sex, Marriage, and Family

ROBERT T. FRANCOEUR

MacGibbon & Kee   London

Granada Publishing Limited
First Published in Great Britain 1972 by MacGibbon & Kee Ltd
3 Upper James Street   London   W1R 4BP

ISBN 0 261 10024 6
Printed in Great Britain by Fletcher & Son Ltd, Norwich

The author wishes to thank the following for permission to quote from
the works listed: Associated University Presses, Inc., for *Israel: The Sword
and the Harp* by Ferdynand Zweig, Fairleigh Dickinson University Press,
1969; The Clarendon Press, Oxford, for *The Allegory of Love* by
C. S. Lewis, 1936; Friends Home Service Committee, for *Towards a
Quaker View of Sex*, London, 1966; Herder and Herder, for "Marriage and
the Institutionalization of Sexual Relations" by C. Jaime Snoek, in *The
Future of Marriage as Institution*, edited by Franz Böckle, 1970; *The
Humanist*, for "Is Monogamy Outdated?" by Rustum and Della Roy,
March/April 1970; The Liturgical Press, for *New Dynamics in Sexual Love*
by Robert and Mary Joyce, copyright by The Order of St. Benedict, Inc.,
Collegeville, Minnesota; The New American Library, for *Honest Sex* by
Rustum and Della Roy, copyright © 1968 Rustum and Della Roy, and
for *You and I . . . Searching for Tomorrow* by Robert H. Rimmer,
copyright © Robert H. Rimmer 1971, both reprinted by arrangement with
The New American Library, Inc., New York, N.Y.; G. P. Putnam's Sons,
for *A Yankee Saint* by Robert Allerton Parker, copyright 1935 by Robert
Allerton Parker; Syracuse University Press, for *Oneida Community: An
Autobiography, 1851–1876*, edited by Constance Noyes Robertson, 1970;
The United Presbyterian Church in the U.S.A., for *Sexuality and the
Human Community*, copyright © 1970 Office of the General Assembly,
United Presbyterian Church in the United States of America.

Dedicated to our daemons,
    cosmic and earthly,
those maddening spirits which drove this
    book into print and drive all of us
    into the arms of the future.

Contents

viii   Contents

EVE'S NEW RIB

PROLOGUE

The Perversions of an Apocalyptic Age

FOR MORE THAN two thousand years Western civilization has wrestled to make the monogamous marriage not only *the* sole reality, but also the monolithic ideal of male/female relationships. This has been especially true in America, where the comforting myth of the faithful life-long marriage has squelched recognition of male/female relationships that deviate from the ideal monogamous family of husband, wife, and children.

Now, within the space of a few years, the technology of human reproduction has created a wide variety of alternatives which must appear to traditionalists as terribly shocking, even horrifying, perversions. Even if we are young enough to have encountered these alternative patterns before entering into serious relations with the opposite sex, very often they strike us as gross violations simply because in considering them as possible options in our own lives we must contradict our traditional images of man, woman, marriage, and family.

Try to imagine more radical deviations from our traditional images of man, woman, family, and marriage than the following alternative possibilities:

Today a woman whose husband is sterile can conceive a child by artificial insemination with her father-in-law's semen, thus retaining the genetic line of her husband and bearing a child with many of his hereditary traits.

Today a woman can conceive and carry a child by artificial

insemination using her deceased grandfather's frozen semen, or the semen of some famous male.

Today monitoring techniques such as intrauterine color television have opened up the heretofore sacred and private life of the fetus in the womb to public inspection and possible manipulation.

Today an unborn child can be removed from the maternal womb and operated on for an hour or two before being returned to its uterine nest to continue gestation.

Today a woman prone to miscarriage might conceive a child by natural intercourse with her husband or by test-tube fertilization of her egg, and then have her child transplanted to her sister's womb for a normal nine-month pregnancy.

Today a single girl can become a bachelor mother without having sexual intercourse by seeking artificial insemination with an anonymous donor's semen.

Today a prospective mother can choose the sex of her next baby with 85 to 90 percent accuracy.

Today's experiments with embryo transplants raise the possibility of surrogate mothers, both human and subhuman.

Today hundreds of humans have experienced the realities of living at one time as a functioning male and later in life as a sexually active and happy female, thanks to a transsexual operation.

The contraceptive-pill technology of the past twenty-five years has forced us to accept procreation and sexual intercourse as two distinct human actions, each governed by its own moral principles.

Within the next decade or two an artificial womb will be developed and a child will be "born" without spending a single day in the womb of a woman.

And the final "perversion," one that overshadows all the others, is that our children will face the possibility that a man, a normal male, will be able to reproduce, or procreate, his own identical twin (minus a few years of course) simply by culturing one of his skin cells in an artificial medium and womb, completely bypassing both egg and sperm, sexual intercourse, fertilization, and the previously universal dependence of humans on the womb of the female of the species.

Sociologists assure us that one of the surest signs that a culture and civilization have moved into a revolutionary new society appears when our traditional language is no longer adequate and we are forced to develop new words to express the realities of our new world. This happened with the advent of agriculture twelve thousand years ago, with the Industrial Revolution, with the computer and space technologies. And it is happening today in our sexual revolution.

To illustrate the total inadequacy of our traditional concepts and language regarding the male/female relation, and marital morality and the family, let me put some of the "perversions" listed above into a feasible situation: Consider the case of a Puerto Rican woman from the Bronx who is married to a young man of Polish ancestry from Pennsylvania. After several years without children, the woman learns that her ovaries are not functioning properly and that her only chance of having a child of her own is to accept an ovarian transplant. She agrees and an ovary from a Japanese woman in California is flown in from the Frozen Organ Bank in Minnesota. In a successful operation the wife is superovulated by hormone injection and a dozen of "her" eggs surgically removed for test-tube fertilization. Because her husband is sterile the eggs are fertilized with a donor's semen. The donor chosen by the couple is the husband's father, whose semen was frozen just before he died ten years ago. Then the wife learns that she is prone to miscarriage and cannot carry "her" child. A substitute mother is called in, perhaps her unmarried sister or an unmarried woman who is anxious to carry a child but does not want to marry. An embryo transplant is performed and the substitute mother carries the child for nine months in a normal pregnancy, delivers, and hands the child over to the couple. (Perhaps a few years from now the child might be transferred to the womb of a cow or to an artificial womb for the pregnancy.)

Now, try to apply our traditional concepts of morality and parentage to this situation. Who is the mother of this child? Does it have more than one real mother, that is, a genetic mother who donated the ovary, a biological mother who carried the child for nine months, and a social mother, the Puerto Rican woman, who raises it? Do we have to make a similar distinction in talking about the child's father(s), with a genetic father, perhaps several years deceased, a biological father responsible for the insemination, and a social father? In this context a child might have SIX real parents! And that is "perverse."

If our language of parenthood suffers in describing the "perversions" of our sexual apocalypse, what about our moral categories? In the situation just described what meaning and ethical value can we connect with such classic terms as adultery, incest, and virginity? Is the artificial insemination of the wife a violation of marital fidelity, and more, incest, since her husband's father donated the semen? If the husband's semen is used to fertilize his wife's egg in his sister's oviduct and the sister then carries the resultant child, is this incest? Will the unmarried sister who serves as substitute mother be considered a virgin after she delivers? Is an artificially inseminated single mother still a virgin? Does a priest violate his celibacy by providing semen for his sterile married brother? Would a nun violate her vows by providing eggs for her sterile sister, or by offering to serve as surrogate mother for her miscarriage-prone sister?

Our traditional images of man, woman, marriage, and family and the moral values and judgments flowing from these traditions may have been valid in past generations, but it is obvious from the options we face in human reproduction, the options we face in the emergence of woman as a person with rights of her own in our society and the resultant inadequacy of our traditional language that we have entered and will continue to experience in the 1970s all the tensions and conflicts and joys of an age which has gone beyond radical transition to apocalyptic discontinuity.

I titled this Prologue "The Perversions of an Apocalyptic Age" because what we deal with in this book will indeed be judged by traditional standards to be the immoral perversions of a decadent and decaying society. But I would like to use the term "perversions" in a creative and prophetic sense—as advancing a new configuration of relationships so stunning that only the term "perversions" can sum up the extent of their impact. By making possible some new options in the relationships between men and women, and for men and women as individuals, by creating new alternatives of parenthood, these "perversions" actually foreshadow a new world for mankind.

The term "apocalypse" has traditionally referred to the chaotic turmoil that precedes the death of an old way of life and the advent of a totally new order. We are in the midst of such an apocalyptic age, faced with a revolution in human sexuality. We face all the chaos, tensions, conflicts, and confusion that an apocalyptic age brings. The purpose of this book is to explore the sexual and reproductive "perversions" of our present apocalyptic age in the hope that we can discern some thread of evolution—Ariadne's thread, to adopt Teilhard de Chardin's usage —that will allow the reader to approach the coming decade with optimism and with some notion of where we seem to be headed. If I am correct in viewing the present "perversions" as prophetic of options in male/female relations tomorrow, then the historical, theological, and sociological insights in the pages that follow will serve the reader as a modest guide to human relations in the 1970s.

ONE

An Inventory of Babies Without Sex

MAN HAS SURVIVED a dozen revolutions. The discovery of fire and the invention of the wheel certainly changed man's way of living. The advent of agriculture and the domestication of animals triggered our earliest adventures into city life. The Industrial Revolution, the nuclear age, space travel—each of these has stirred turmoil in society. But, unlike our present revolution, these earlier convulsions touched only the periphery of human life.

The revolution to be probed in these pages affects our treasured and sacred images of ourselves as sexual persons and our most personal relations with other human beings. Any change that touches the relationship of men and women or the structure of family life is serious. Yet whether we like it or not, change does appear to be an essential aspect of a viable culture. Our society and its patterns of male/female relations are constantly changing and evolving, whether we like to accept this fact or not. What makes this constant change so upsetting today is the fact that we face a mountain of changes which affect practically every social, psychological, emotional, legal, and moral facet of our daily contact with people.

Why is it that suddenly, within a single generation, we find ourselves embroiled in a major storm of exploding changes on every side? What to my mind makes our situation today so radically different from the gradual changes and evolution of past generations is the sudden convergence and reinforcement of four major developments.

One obvious primer of our sexual convulsion is the exploding educational, economic, social, and legal emergence of women in our culture within the past century. As anthropologist Jessie Bernard points out in *The Sex Game,* the past century and especially the past few decades have demolished the traditional monoliths of masculine and feminine mystiques. A century ago three feminine sub-sexes were socially accepted: the "fair white maiden," sexless, passive, anti-intellectual mother of children; the pathetic and lonely spinster, living on the fringe of a marital-oriented culture; and the passionate "dark lady." Today a dozen different socially accepted options are open to women. Forty percent of all American women are now working outside the home, and over half of all the mothers with children in school also hold down jobs. The same explosion of freedom and choice has hit the male, including the acceptance of the bachelor-father sub-sex with an adopted family. Yet we are just beginning to appreciate the psychological and emotional impact of these new roles and sub-sexes.

A second and equally influential element boils to the surface because of our rapid medical advances in the control of both conception and birth: the contraceptive pills, the IUDs, the growing popularity of vasectomies and frozen-sperm banks, and the liberalization of abortion laws. By separating sexual intercourse from procreation, these advances have triggered psychological, emotional, legal, and moral complications.

The third factor is, perhaps, the grandchild of our contraceptive technology. Initially this reproductive technology was motivated by a desire to help childless couples. But now this remedial technology has become creative, providing us with a dozen options in addition to the traditional, "orthodox" way of conceiving and bearing a child, even with the potential of our designing the man of the future in a variety of molds.

We probably could handle these three developments without too much emotional stress and social shock *if* we did not have to contend with the fourth factor, which to my mind has turned the other developments into a critical mass far more explosive than any nuclear pile.

Until the advent of mass communications, social change was a gradual process thinly spread over several decades, often partitioned out among several generations. Furthermore, social innovations usually sprang up in some relatively isolated fringe community, or possibly in the heart of a culture, from which they could slowly reach out to transform the surrounding peoples village by village. Today this low-pain-level process of evolution has been churned into a constant revolution of overlapping, interwoven, and interdependent near-instant global changes. Communications satellites pick up the images of ubiquitous television and radio sensors to beam them into the largest metropolitan areas and the most isolated hamlet. News networks such as Reuters, Associated Press, and United Press International feed the news of the world to even the smallest weekly newspaper. Popular magazines, sold in local supermarkets, reach millions of isolated housewives to let them know about the latest happenings in women's liberation, the latest contraceptives, and new techniques of reproduction. Even syndicated columns such as "Ann Landers" and "Dear Abby" regularly deal with these developments. The film and stage media are slower in responding to these trends, but they also have their impact.

The mass media often report the sensational events, but the public reacts in an interesting way. As a group and as individuals they are far from being willing to go all the way in adopting the radically new, but, like the housewife reading *Vogue* or some other fashion magazine who adds an inch or two to her hemline or teases her hair a bit more into a modified version of the latest style, the general public is influenced and does slowly modify its images, opinions, and even behavior as a result of this reporting.

Technological breakthroughs are coming with a frightening acceleration, but without our electronic communications they would still require months, years, or even decades to influence the general populace. Set in motion by our electronic nerves, our mobile population is confronted with social innovations and scientific discoveries that reach and disturb the most remote inhabitants of our globe, often even before they become a reality. Escape from this barrage, retreat to some "primitive promised land of peace," is well nigh impossible today.

We are today in the midst of the most revolutionary convulsion in human history. I suspect that many will agree with me on the surface while remaining skeptical and indifferent in reality. For scholars and scientists in their ivory research towers, skepticism is inevitable unless we buttress this claim with some solid evidence. So let me proffer for your consideration some sample items taken from my inventory of technical and psychological developments in human reproduction: a brief survey of babies conceived and born without the benefit of normal sexual intercourse; and let us view the social impact of this technology.

INVENTORY ITEM ONE: A letter and response which appeared in the "Ann Landers" syndicated column on September 11, 1970.

"Dear Ann Landers: In your column recently there appeared a letter from a woman who wanted to bear a child through artificial insemination since her husband's tests proved him incapable of fatherhood.

"I was especially interested in her letter because I am facing a serious crisis as a result of the same problem. My husband has agreed to artificial insemination but only if I use his father's sperm. I was shocked at first, but his father insists on it and says unless we agree, he will not consider our child his legitimate heir.

"I have no real objections since I admire my father-in-law very much and the insemination would be artificial. But I do have some strange feelings. Will you ease my conscience and give me your blessings? Luana.

"Dear Lu: Since you have no 'real objections,' go ahead, but you do so without my blessings. Such an arrangement has endless possibilities for a lifetime of trouble. A father-in-law who makes such demands must be wildly egocentric, if not crazy. A husband who would agree needs to examine his relationship with his father. My guess is that he feels vastly inferior to Pa. The ultimate act of self-emasculation would be to allow his father to impregnate his wife. As for you, my dear, have you considered what it would be like to give birth to your own brother-in-law? I don't know how much money is involved here, but in my opinion there isn't enough money in the world to make this deal acceptable."

Fantastic? Incredible? Perhaps, even for our sophisticated and permissive society. But remember this: in a population where perhaps 10 percent of the people understand the possibilities of having a baby by artificial insemination, Ann Landers discussed this perfectly feasible proposal for an "incestuous" artificial insemination with millions of American men and women who devotedly read her column every day for the latest news about what is happening in their world.

INVENTORY ITEM TWO: An excerpt from the London BBC evening news, Monday, February 23, 1970.

"All I want in the world is to be a mother," Mrs. Sylvia Allen told the reporter. "I am as happy as any other expectant mother. People say I am being used as a guinea pig but if my experience helps other childless couples, then it will have been worthwhile."

The reporter interrupted to explain that Mrs. Allen, 34, and her insurance-salesman husband, Kenneth, 39, were childless after seven years of marriage and quite desperate to have a child of their own rather than just to adopt a child.

"I have no doubts or fears about going ahead," Mrs. Allen explained. "This is our last chance of having a child of our own."

Mrs. Allen had been unable to conceive because of blockages in both her Fallopian tubes. These tubes normally provide a suitable environment in which the egg can be fertilized by sperm coming up through the vagina and uterus, and also as a passageway for the fertilized egg to reach the womb for implantation. Through reports in the newspapers Mr. and Mrs. Allen had heard of experiments with test-tube fertilization of human eggs and the possibility of embryo transplants resulting from the research of three British scientists. They decided to consult two of these men about their problem and found Patrick Steptoe, a gynecologist at Oldham Hospital, and Robert G. Edwards, a reproductive physiologist at Cambridge University, most sympathetic with their desire to have a child.

The two scientists suggested a possible solution which would involve the first transplant of a human embryo. The experiment would entail triggering ovulation with hormone injections, collecting several eggs surgically, and fertilizing them in a test tube. After five to seven days' development in a special culture medium the doctors would then try to implant one of the resulting embryos in Mrs. Allen's womb.

Within twenty-four hours front-page stories in newspapers all over England were discussing the "Guinea Pig Mother of Test Tube Baby." British workmen at their pubs and housewives at home watched television panel discussions and listened to radio debates of this revolutionary prospect. The impact was immediate and nationwide. Within a week the debate had spread to factories, schools, offices, and homes in the United States and around the world.

In the fall of 1970, Dr. Edwards announced that forty-

eight other women with blocked Fallopian tubes had joined
Mrs. Allen at his Cambridge laboratory in hopes of having a
child by embryo transplant. Once again, the evening television
news and front-page newspaper accounts startled and stunned
people everywhere with the fact of this unbelievable prospect
for women and motherhood.

INVENTORY ITEM THREE: An American college student's experience with embryo transplants, November, 1970.

After a survey report on the latest developments with the
49 hopeful embryo-transplant mothers at Cambridge appeared
on the *New York Times* front page, I had a discussion with my
undergraduate class in experimental embryology. We talked
about the various complications and difficulties scientists and
physicians face in transplanting human embryos as well as about
the techniques of test-tube fertilization. The lively discussion
triggered a whimsical smile from a pert sophomore in the class
which aroused my curiosity because it gave no clue as to her
reaction or what thoughts this reproductive technique sparked
in her mind. After class I called her over and asked about her
reaction.

"Well, the whole thing just reminded me of last Christmas
Eve when our family gathered for the holiday. My older sister
and her husband were with us—they were just married. Sis
has a very serious blood disorder, somewhat like hemophilia,
which makes it impossible for her to have a child even though
she very much wants one.

"We were in the kitchen cleaning up after the dinner when
Sis mentioned that she had read an article in *McCalls* about
embryo transplants and the possibility that this technique might
soon be available for women who cannot carry their own
children. Sis explained—because at that time I knew very little
about embryology and these new developments—that a woman's
egg could be fertilized with her husband's sperm in the normal
way or artificially and then implanted in another woman's

womb. The article fascinated my sister no end, and she just came over and asked me whether I would be willing to carry her child for her if this kind of transplant were medically possible.

"My first reaction was sort of shock. My mother's reaction was even stronger. Like, what could I say: 'It's not my baby; it's my sister's'? But we did discuss the idea. My mother did not raise any moral or ethical objections, just the emotional complications, which sort of threw her and me both. We talked a good bit about how I might feel carrying a child for nine months knowing it really was not 'mine' and knowing also that I would be giving it up as soon as it was born. How would this affect me, my sister, her relationship with her husband, and my relationship with them, and how would all these emotions affect the child as it grew up?

"My brother-in-law had no idea that my sister had been thinking about this seriously. But he did not seem upset by the possibility. My main concern was whether I would be able to hand the child over to Sis and her husband and then go back to being just an ordinary aunt. Could I really react 'normally' with my new nephew or niece after all this?

"My sister was so serious about this, and about having a child with her husband, that she even talked about hiring another woman, outside the family, to carry her child if I refused But she really hoped I would agree, if the technique were safe and possible."

INVENTORY ITEM FOUR: From the January, 1971 issue of *Ladies' Home Journal* some interesting "Test Tube Baby News" in David Zimmerman's "Medicine Today" column.

The news of an ingenious if exotic alternative to the Edwards-Steptoe experiments in embryo transplants came from Australia. At Monash University in Melbourne, obstetrician Carl Wood has provided a woman with an artificial Fallopian tube to bypass blockages in both her tubes. First a silastic rubber bag was placed around one of the woman's ovaries. The small bag has two tubes, one connecting with her womb and the other emerging outside her body through the abdominal wall. Dr. Wood hopes the silastic bag will catch the egg when it breaks loose from the ruptured ovarian follicle. Semen from the woman's husband will then be introduced into her vagina as in a normal artificial insemination with the hope that some sperm may find their way through the blockage to fertilize the egg in the rubber bag. Since this is a fairly remote possibility, Dr. Wood will also introduce the husband's semen into the bag through the abdominal tube.

Ideally, the normal body fluids in the bag will provide a suitable environment for fertilization and development of the egg until it is ready for implantation in the womb. Some six or seven days after fertilization, when the womb is prepared for implantation, Dr. Wood plans to pump physiological fluids into the bag from outside, thus forcing the embryonic cell mass into the womb where it can embed in the lining and produce a normal pregnancy.

David Zimmerman concluded his brief news note with a very cautionary observation that several years may be needed before this test-tube-baby technique is successful and safe.

INVENTORY ITEM FIVE: From the author's domestic diary, Sunday, December 13, 1970.

"The phone rang in the kitchen and I pounced on it as is my custom. A bright feminine voice on the other end informed me that I was talking with a 29-year-old woman who had watched me on some television show and wondered whether I could help her solve a personal problem. She admitted to a certain pessimism about her prospects for marriage and yet very much wanted to have a child of her own, a girl, even if she did not marry. Could I tell her of some local doctor who would be willing to artificially inseminate her. A second question dealt with the possibilities of increasing the odds in favor of a female offspring."

INVENTORY ITEM SIX: A letter from the New York metropolitan area dated July 29, 1970.

"Dear Dr. Francoeur,

"Enclosed please find a clipping of Harriet Van Horne's column from the *New York Post* of 20 July '70. From it I deduced that you might be able to tell me how to go about getting an artificial insemination of frozen sperm *from a specific donor*, namely Dr. Linus Pauling who I believe teaches at Cal Tech. I should very much like to try for an August or at least September 1970 conception and seem at present to be running on a 25-day spacing of the menstrual cycle. We already have four healthy, attractive and intelligent children (ages six to 13). But they are all 'unplanned' and were conceived despite ample birth control. My wish is to have a very much PLANNED and *last* child, for I intend to have my tubes tied after this conception.

"Because I was 41 this month and a late maturer, time may be running out, but I do strongly wish it to run out in this very special way.

"Certainly we wish Dr. Pauling to be free of any legal implications in such an 'ethereal conception,' to use Miss Van Horne's phrase. Perhaps you know exactly how to go about this.

"We would wish the birth to take place locally, but, for discretion's sake, prefer the kind of conception described here to remain a private matter. . . ."

INVENTORY ITEM SEVEN: From an article in *Look* Magazine, April 21, 1970, on how to choose the sex of your next baby.

The authors of this article about a fascinating bit of do-it-at-home reproductive technology are David Rorvik, a respected science reporter, and Dr. Landrum B. Shettles, head of obstetrics and gynecology at Columbia Presbyterian Hospital in New York City.

The technique, claimed to be 85 to 90 percent successful,

is almost elementary in its simplicity. First, with the aid of a seven-dollar glucose fertility-test tape kit, the married couple tries to pinpoint as closely as possible the time of ovulation. If they want a girl, they refrain from intercourse for forty-eight hours prior to the monthly release of the egg. To increase the odds of conceiving a girl, the woman can douche with two table-spoons of white vinegar in a quart of water just prior to each intercourse, use the "missionary" or face-to-face position, avoid if possible having orgasm, and help her mate have his orgasm while very shallow in her vagina. For a boy the key to success appears to be limiting intercourse to within hours of the time of ovulation, immediately preceding intercourse with an alka-line douche of two tablespoons of baking soda in a quart of water, deep penetration at the moment of male orgasm, and vaginal penetration from the rear. It also helps tilt the odds in favor of a boy if the wife has an orgasm.

Simple enough? But who might be tempted to use this tech-nique? Apparently *Reader's Digest*, which has fifty million subscribers around the world, found it interesting, for they reprinted the article in several different language editions. Dodd, Mead & Company also decided to publish a slim volume with fuller details of this technique under the title *Your Baby's Sex: Now You Can Choose*.

INVENTORY ITEM EIGHT: From the *Detroit News* of July 24, 1971, a report from Rome.

"The 35-year-old wife of a Rome businessman miscarried with 15 fetuses Thursday, her doctor announced today. The woman is reported to be in serious condition.

"Professor Gennaro Montanino, a gynecologist at the Rome clinic Villa Flaminia, said there were 10 female and 5 male fetuses. He said their heads, trunks and limbs were perfectly shaped. Each fetus weighed 4.8 ounces and was about 4 inches long.

"He said the premature rejection, or 'spontaneous miscarriage,' three and a half months after conception, occurred because of lack of space for further development in the mother's womb.

"The doctor said that the woman had a child eight years ago, after the same fertility therapy. In both cases she had been taking a fertility drug."

The doctor had used the particular fertility drug over a hundred times previously and had always induced single births; not even one set of twins was induced. But on this occasion, 15 fetuses miscarried. Some months earlier an Australian woman gave birth to nine babies after treatment with a fertility drug.

INVENTORY ITEM NINE: In its unparalleled history as a best seller, David Reuben's *Everything You Always Wanted to Know about Sex . . . But Were Afraid to Ask* was reaching five thousand new readers each day. A sequel was imperative, and now the readers are devouring *Any Woman Can!* by the same Dr. Reuben. The book is meant for the "sexually marooned" woman, the single girl, the divorcee, and the widow. "For almost two hundred years the only socially acceptable alternatives offered to women have been marriage—on masculine terms—or spinsterhood on the fringes of society. It's about time that women were honestly presented with their six other choices. Some of these possibilities are legal bigamy, becoming a professional non-wife, and one fascinating choice that was impossible until a few years ago: the pseudoparthenogenetic family, which allows single women to become mothers."

If *Any Woman Can!* is half as popular as *Everything You Always Wanted to Know about Sex*, a lot of women and men will be very much aware of six options for the unmarried lady.

INVENTORY ITEM TEN: From the semi-annual convention of the Chicago Catholic Science Teachers Association, September 19, 1970, at Loyola Academy in Wilmette. This gathering brought together over four hundred elementary, secondary, and college science teachers as well as many educators from the humanities in the Chicago area. My task was to summarize in three lectures and discussion periods my views on "Teaching in 1971 for the Year 2000."

In the evening session my inventory of our biological revolution triggered a lively exchange of views on changing social patterns, sexual morality, and our emerging pluralism of male/female relations. The animated and serious dialogue was indicative of the awareness these science teachers had of their own responsibilities in preparing their students for life tomorrow. Perhaps it was the seriousness of our conversation that prompted one nun to interject a suggestion which, while perfectly in keeping with our discussion of changing social patterns, brought the house down with good-humored, if somewhat nervous, laughter. "Centuries ago Francis de Sales and others established religious communities of women to serve the sick and needy. I wonder if we might not update the charitable work of some religious communities and perhaps even establish a new order, a type of 'Sisters of Charity (or Mercy) for the Substitute Mother.' These women could in Christian charity offer to serve as surrogate mothers for women prone to miscarriage and unable to bear their own children." The suggestion immediately brought to my mind the image of my college student's dilemma about bearing her sister's child. But it also reminded me of a similar suggestion offered by Owen Garrigan, a priest and biochemist at Seton Hall University, in his book *Man's Intervention in Nature*. Father Garrigan had asked several years earlier whether a priest would violate his vow or promise of celibacy if he donated semen to a sperm bank.

INVENTORY ITEM ELEVEN: From a workshop on family law at the 1971 annual meeting of the Association of American Law Schools, in the Sheraton-Chicago Hotel.

Among the dozen possibilities of modifying our reproductive pattern none is more mind-boggling than cloning. A clone is an individual or a population resulting from asexual reproduction, and cloning is the production of a whole population of identical twins by asexual means.

Semi-cloning was achieved nearly two decades ago with frogs and other amphibians by transplanting nuclei from adult cells into eggs which have had their nuclei removed. The tadpoles thus produced are then identical twins, octuplets, or centuplets of the original donor of the transplanted nuclei.

Complete cloning would involve the use of isolated but intact adult cells, perhaps epithelial, or skin, cells, tricking these specialized and highly differentiated cells back into their embryonic state with artificial culture media, and then starting them over again developing into complete adult organisms. The result is identical twins, sextuplets, or centuplets of the original donor. Thus far true cloning has been accomplished only with plants and one-celled animals. But Nobel geneticist Joshua Lederberg maintains that we may well be cloning human babies within a decade or two, completely bypassing egg, sperm, sexual intercourse, and fertilization.

At this 1971 lawyers' gathering, Dr. Leon Kass discussed some of the possibilities offered by "Xerox" cloning, which he feels will be a reality by 1975, or at least by 1980:

Producing large numbers of genetically identical persons who could be used to perform special jobs, in the space program, for instance.

Permitting a man or a woman to reproduce himself, not just once, but many times over, if he so chooses.

Giving prospective parents the opportunity to have children who would be the identical twin, minus a few years, of their favorite famous person, provided of course that these people are willing to donate some cells.

Creating new family relationships, such as identical twins

with different social parents and different biological mothers, or identical twins spaced out over several generations or centuries.

Dr. Kass, the executive secretary of the Committee on Life Sciences and Social Policy for the National Research Council in the National Academy of Sciences, is very concerned about these possibilities, according to several reports in newspapers and on television. He asks, for instance, whether the individual has an inalienable right even before birth not to be manufactured. "I contend," he argues, "that we should not clone a man, not even once."

INVENTORY ITEM TWELVE: From a report by Victor Cohn in the *Washington Post*, January 28, 1971.

" 'Within a year,' a scientist will conceive a baby in a test tube and successfully place it inside a woman who will bear the child, a noted biologist told the House Science Subcommittee yesterday.

" 'Then all hell will break loose,' politically and morally, all over the world, Dr. James D. Watson of Harvard predicted.

" 'The United States,' he said, 'should take the lead now in forming an international commission to ask, "do we really want to do this?" and perhaps "take steps quickly" to make it illegal.'

"Watson is co-discoverer of the shape of DNA, the hereditary molecule, a Nobel Prize winner, and author of 'The Double Helix,' a best seller about the discovery of DNA. He spoke near the close of three days of testimony on international science policy.

"He is not the first scientist to warn of coming biological engineering. But the time has arrived, he emphasized, to speak not of mere theory but of a feat that could occur any day now in a British laboratory. . . .

"This means difficult 'decisions may soon be upon us,' Watson said. 'Thousands of infertile women,' once such an operation is successfully done, will want to have babies the same way, he commented.

"Then the next steps, as he sees it, could include:

"Hiring needy women as surrogate mothers to have a baby while the unharried biological parents look on.

"Determining while an embryo is still in the test tube whether it is a boy or a girl. If the baby were then unwanted, an unscrupulous doctor might wash it down the sink.

"Genetic engineering of various kinds, with many good purposes—like detecting and preventing hereditary defects but also, possibly, 'all sorts of bad scenarios.'

"The Harvard biochemist also emphasized that laboratory growth and fusion of human cells could have many good results. One might be understanding the genetic basis for cancer and other diseases, he said.

"But with laboratory growth of human embryos, he said 'the nature of the bond between parents and their children and 'everyone's values about [his] individual uniqueness could be changed beyond recognition.'

"Certainly, to many, our most sensible course would be to deemphasize all forms of research which would circumvent the normal reproductive processes."

But then on May 18, 1971, *Look* Magazine carried the full details of the first successful transplant of a human embryo from one woman to another. David Rorvik interviewed Landrum B. Shettles, who detailed the method for determining the sex of a child discussed above. Rorvik explained how eggs from the ovaries of a woman being operated on for urogenital complications were removed, fertilized *in vitro* with her husband's semen, and then implanted in the womb of another woman. When that substitute mother was operated on for a previously scheduled hysterectomy two days after the implantation, the embryonic cell mass was found embedded and developing normally in the lining of her womb. Watson's fear of a scientific development "just around the corner" is now a reality, waiting only for a normal nine-month pregnancy to make possible the complications he predicts.

INVENTORY ITEM THIRTEEN: From the December, 1970 issue of *Motion Picture* Magazine. I do not recall ever reading this magazine until one of my graduate students brought this particular issue to my attention in May, 1971. Maria was visiting the veterinarian with her cat and thumbing through some worn magazines in the waiting room when a cover story caught her eye: "After seven years of despair, Liz can now have Burton's baby! Read how the miracle happened. . . .

"From the time she became his wife back in March 1964, Elizabeth Taylor has lived with one dream—to have Richard's baby. Intellectually she knew it was an impossible dream. Emotionally she kept clinging to the hope that the impossible might someday be possible."

The impossibility stems from the fact that in giving birth to Liza in 1957 Liz came so close to death that Mike Todd insisted that she have her Fallopian tubes cut and tied. Then in 1968, amid rumors of possible cancer, Liz had a partial hysterectomy.

"But now—as unbelievable as it may seem, the chance [of Liz having Richard's baby] *still does exist*. The miracle that can make it exist is on the verge of a breakthrough. There are medical experiments now going on at Oxford University—the same Oxford where Elizabeth and Richard filmed *Dr. Faustus* —which, if successful, would enable Elizabeth and Richard to have their own child—without any risk to her health or life.

"These experiments may sound like science-fiction, but they are medical fact. And they were recently explained by Dr. Robert Francoeur, a Catholic priest and a professor of experimental embryology at Fairleigh Dickinson University and the author of an absolutely startling book called *Utopian Motherhood*."

The article went on to piece together quotes from my book

and television appearances in a quasi-interview, winding up with some comments exchanged with Phyllis Diller and Merv Griffin on the possibility of embryo transplants. After detailing the process used by Edwards and Steptoe at Cambridge and by Shettles in New York, I had joked with Miss Diller about the problem of a salary for the substitute mother: "It would be a 24-hour-a-day job, seven days a week for nine months, union scale and so forth."

Nell Blythe, author of the *Motion Picture* article, noted that "to a couple like the Burtons who don't think twice about spending a million dollars for a diamond, the financial aspects would be the least of it. They could certainly pay the going rates in addition to a sizeable bonus to whoever the third party might be in their case."

At the time I wrote *Utopian Motherhood*, Cambridge University—not Oxford as the article claimed—was the focus for embryo-transplant experiments. But Oxford would make the story more interesting, for Richard had just announced that he would be going there shortly to substitute for a professor friend who would be away on a sabbatical leave. "In his position as a don," *Motion Picture* suggested, "if not only as a worldwide celebrity, Richard will certainly be able to get all the information available on the subject, to view the laboratory experiments and to discuss whatever possibilities there may be of he and Elizabeth partaking in this startling technique of human reproduction."

This trite but widely read article wound up on a typical poignant note: "This may be Liz's only chance to have Richard's baby. Do you think she should take it?"

INVENTORY ITEM FOURTEEN: From the *New York Times*, August 13, 1971, this incredible report from a school district in north-central New Jersey.

"Basking Ridge, N.J., Aug. 12—The Bernards Township school board tonight suspended a 52-year-old music teacher who underwent a sex-change operation and wanted to return to class in September as a woman after teaching 14 years here as a man.

"The school board president, Paul F. Mallon, said the board would move to dismiss the teacher, Paul Monroe Grossman of Plainfield, although Mr. Mallon refused to discuss what grounds would be used in the action. The usual grounds for dismissing teachers with tenure is incompetence.

"Herbert Kestner, a lawyer representing the teacher, who now goes by the name Paula Miriam Grossman, called the board's move 'unfair,' since the teacher had not been allowed to teach 'in her new role as a woman.'

"The teacher, who is married and has three daughters—one 18 years old and 13-year-old twins—sat in the front row at the school board meeting at the Cedar Hill School, dressed as a woman. Also in the front row was Mr. Kestner and Mrs. Ruth Grossman, whom the lawyer identified as 'the wife of Mrs. Paula Grossman.'

"Mr. Mallon said the decision to try to dismiss 'Paul Grossman' came after the teacher rejected a school board request to resign the tenured position held under his male name, obtain a new teaching certificate as 'Paula Grossman' and accept a one-year appointment as a new teacher at the same salary, $14,300

"Mr. Kestner said there was no need for his client to give up tenure. 'If she proves incompetent,' he asserted, 'the statutes provide the machinery to remove her.'

"The operation was performed in March during the Easter recess, and the teacher finished the school year in male garb. But in May he informed School Superintendent Myron Headington of the operation and of his intention 'to assume a full female role' immediately after the close of school.

"The teacher submitted to two psychiatric examinations at the board's request since school closed, and while Mr. Mallon would not comment on the results, Mr. Kestner contended his client had passed 'with flying colors.'

"After tonight's meeting, Mrs. Ruth Grossman said her

family was going through a difficult period because of the controversy surrounding her husband's sex change.

" 'But I hope the board allows her to teach here,' she said. 'The twins have lived here all their lives.'

"Mr. Mallon said he expected a full hearing on the case to be scheduled by the State Education Commissioner's office within two weeks."

The story raises some interesting questions about legalities. Would Paula have a case against the school board for job discrimination on the basis of sex under the terms of the 1962 federal law? Would Paula and Ruth Grossman be allowed to continue filing joint "husband and wife" income tax returns? If Mrs. Paula Grossman has her new sex recognized in court, will the state continue to recognize her marriage to Ruth? Or can the state possibly annul the marriage or require a divorce? Or will the state simply ignore this unisex marriage if both adults consent to the altered relationship? How will the three daughters handle the social problem of having a biological father who is now a female but cannot be considered their mother? How should the daughters refer to Paula? Terms like "father," "mother," "aunt," etc. do not fit in a case like this. In the Prologue we mentioned the language problem as a clear indicator that we have entered a totally new world.

Bewildering, fascinating, intoxicating, and often mind-boggling as this inventory may be, the essential and extremely influential role played by the mass media should be very clear. The creative challenge and the specter of the man-made man are with us today in our technology of reproduction, our contraceptives, and our liberation of men and women, and they come to us with all the impact of instant world-wide communications.

TWO

Population Control and
the Sexual Revolution

AT FIRST SIGHT, there appears to be a major contradiction between the varied concern for infertility we noted in our inventory of babies without sex and our growing awareness of a population explosion. On one hand we appear to be fomenting and encouraging procreation for those who previously could not have any children of their own, even to the point of mass-producing humans in artificial wombs, while at the same time we are crying panic over an exploding population and pleading with people to use our contraceptive technology to limit their families to two children.

Discussions of the population-environmental crisis almost always stir a hopeful exploration of the latest contraceptives and related mass-education programs as if these were the sum and substance of population control. This is a quite natural, though simplistic, approach. Natural because the advent of a *practical* contraceptive technology after the Second World War gave us our first realistic hope for an effective, inexpensive, and commonly acceptable method of reducing the rate of human conceptions, but at the same time simplistic because it ignores the psychological revolution necessary to prime a public acceptance of this technology by the masses.

Before mankind can morally, psychologically, and emotionally accept any technological program for limiting the population, it has to experience and accept emotionally as well as intellectually a major and fundamental shift in our Western image of human sexuality.

For thousands of years mankind, especially in the West, has accepted a clear *equation* between sexual intercourse and procreation. While there was no scientific evidence for this connection, our inability to control procreation as a result of sexual intercourse made it logical to accept the connection as part of some law of nature, as the way the Creator established things in the beginning and the way he intended them to be throughout human history.

This equation was further reinforced in a variety of religious traditions, both Eastern and Western, which found it practically impossible to incorporate human sexuality and the seemingly irrational passion of sexual intercourse into the context of man's "spiritual" or "religious" life. To rule out completely the possibility of human sexual intercourse as being moral—even when engaged in solely to continue the human race, as the Albigensians, Cathari, Shakers, and others have done—never proved a popular solution to the perplexing passions of human sexuality. Thus most of the religious traditions, including those within the Judeo-Christian current, made accommodations by first tolerating sexual intercourse and then exalting its dutiful practice solely within marriage and solely for procreative reasons.

The history of this very unchristian attitude, which has been so dominant in our Western culture, is long and devious. Furthermore, it is a history which we Westerners are almost incapable of appreciating in depth because we are so much entwined in it subconsciously even today. The dualistic thought pattern which segregates in man a good, spiritual, sexless soul from our somehow not-so-nice sexed body flows not far beneath the surface of our philosophies, our laws, our literature, our politics, our economics, our psychology, and our everyday thinking. We have been brainwashed and nourished by this fragmented philosophical view primarily from early Greek thought, even though our religious roots germinated in the far more holistic and wholesome soil of the oriental Hebrew world. The story of this conflict has been explored in meticulous detail by many historians, philosophers, biblical scholars, and psychologists, but one or two aspects of it should be recalled here lest our backdrop for comprehending the sexual apocalypse suffer from serious sins of omission.

In *Sex and Love in the Bible*, William Graham Cole comes to the pungent conclusion that "modern Western man is an adolescent [in his understanding and appreciation of human sexual love] while the ancient Hebrew was grown-up, though such an idea will seem the quintessence of heresy to those who believe that a later arrival on the stage of history must always be superior to its predecessors." It is very hard for us, as sophisticated, cultured Westerners, to admit that the ancient Hebrew view of sexuality and morals in many ways far surpasses our contemporary images in maturity, basic humaneness, and moral depth. But the evidence appears very solid that this is indeed the case.

Two prime factors contributed to this anomaly. First, the Old Covenant Hebrews never tolerated any splintering in their view of love and affection. A man's love for his wife, his children, even for his concubine, could and should be as true and wholesome as his love for his Creator. The Hebrew simply could not set aside one part of his affections, emotions, will, and loyalty as some sort of sacred and pure love for his Creator and then retain a distinct arena for his profane, earthly love.

This first factor is closely interwoven with a second: the overriding reality of the covenant between the Hebrews and the Lord of History. Hence, everything in life had to be viewed within the context of the demands and promised rewards of that alliance. Every action of daily life was then sacred and holy. The profane simply did not exist, for nothing could escape the sacred dimension of the covenant.

Typically, the Hebrew language contained no word to express our Western concept of "religion." And in speaking of "love" the Hebrew used a single word with several cognates (*aheb*, the verb, and *ahabah*, a noun) to encompass a man's love for his God and every variation of human love including the sensual love of a man and woman.

This refusal to create two separate worlds carried over into many different areas. For instance, we often are tempted to view the sacred place where Abraham's bush burned or the Holy of Holies in the Temple as holy places like our churches, set apart from the profanities of the everyday world. But this is our Greek dualistic training coming to the surface. The sacred places, events, and holy people of the Old Covenant were especially holy, because of their more direct and immediate association with turning points in God's alliance with his chosen people. The Jewish Sabbath was quite the opposite of our modern Christian dichotomy between the Lord's Day when we worship and the other six days of the week when we are free to do as we like.

Understanding and appreciating this radical difference between the ancient Hebrew view of human love and our more current Western conception is vital to what follows in these pages. Therefore I would like to trace, in brief, this devious conflict between the Hebraic and Greek views over the past two thousand years, for I am convinced that most if not all of our problems in dealing with the sexual apocalypse and its "perversions" can be traced in one way or another to our insidious dualistic view of human nature and human relations.

Male, animating spirit, soul, logic, white, good, on one side; female, emotional, illogical, mother earth, body, dark and unpredictable, tainted if not evil, on the other side of the fence. The adolescent—or better, infantile—temptation to analyze by classifying everything into comforting, neat pigeonholes, preferably only two so that the choice is limited, seems to stem from the philosophical traditions of the Persians and Greeks. In the apostolic age of the Christian church her greatest and most dangerous rival was the Persian cult of Mithras, god of light and truth. The followers of Mithras offered the seductive view of a world divided into two camps, the realm of light, truth, and wisdom, and the domain of darkness and evil. Coupled with the Neoplatonic thought of Plotinus and others, early Christianity repeatedly had to contend with this dualistic view, which became quite prominent in the writings of Augustine in the third century.

The more wholesome, mature view of man held by the Hebrews was quickly supplanted by this reductionist, infantile view of man, and in the process human sexuality was relegated to the sphere of the earthly and profane and dirty. No longer could man's erotic and emotional nature be integrated into the "spiritual" life of the good Christian. This Gnostic view of man, reinforced by a belief in the imminent coming of Christ and the end of a profane, evil world, soon led theologians and religious leaders to exalt virginity as the ideal for all men and women. Marriage was not acknowledged as a sacrament until well into the Middle Ages because this dualistic view of human nature made it difficult if not impossible to find a place for physical, erotic, sexual love in man's "spiritual" life.

The expectation of an imminent golden age dominated Christian life through the Dark Ages and sustained the celibate tradition. But the failure of Christ to come on New Year's Day of the year 1000 and other factors prepared the way for a new appraisal of the male-female relationship in the early Middle Ages. The flowering of courtly love and the unexplained birth of sexual romance came unannounced into Western thought with the troubadours of Languedoc in southern France to spread like a passionate flame through the castles of medieval Europe.

Woman became an angelic person, the divine Beatrice eulogized by Dante in his Divine Comedy: beautiful beyond words and comprehension, endowed with inexhaustible wisdom and nobility. But despite the seemingly new image of woman we can easily find in the troubadour's lady a very Gnostic heart. Divine Beatrice was so beautiful, so wise, so noble, so ethereal, so angelic that she ceased being a member of the human race. Woman had been lifted from the low level of a sub-human object to an unattainable pedestal, beyond the reach of mere mortal men, and perhaps just as dehumanized and asexual as before. Beatrice drew Dante not to her boudoir, not to herself as a woman, but to God.

The birth of courtly love was midwifed by a number of known and unknown factors: by the discovery of such Moslem philosophers as Avicenna and Averroes, by a much misunderstood Roman poet, Ovid, whose satirical *Art of Love* achieved great popularity at the time; possibly by the emergence of a cult of the Blessed Virgin, possibly by the Teutonic image of woman, and perhaps even by a hedonistic element via Eleanor of Aquitaine.

Nevertheless, despite the recurring black-and-white world view of the Platonists and Gnostics and Persians, despite the berating of women as ill-formed males, courtly love did elevate and improve the image of woman, if only in a roundabout and unintentional way. It prepared the way, as we will see in Chapter Five, for the possibility of marriage based on love rather than parental choice, for the possibility of a man and wife truly relating to each other as persons, and for the possibility of extramarital relations based on love rather than mere sensuality for male enjoyment only.

In the seventeenth and eighteenth centuries, when most parents still arranged the marriages of their children and faithfully watched over the morals of their maiden daughters, romance was pretty much limited to engaged couples who might be allowed some private moments together before they married. But as with every generation of youth, the young people inevitably pushed this limited romance and freedom further, insisting on the right to choose their own mates and marry for love. Protestant historian Derrick Bailey notes that theologians in the mid-nineteenth century began to concede something unheard of for earlier generations of Christians: the possibility that sexual relations between a husband and wife might indeed be a joyful, pleasurable, emotional, and *morally good act*.

The next step, as we have already seen, involved many developments: our contraceptive technology, our reproductive technology, the accelerating emergence of women in society, the social and religious acceptance of divorce and remarriage, and others.

Progressive and optimistic as the above sketch may be overall, we would be distorting history and the realities of today if we did not indicate clearly that the black-and-white equation and justification of sexual intercourse we borrowed from the Near East centuries ago is still very much with us. It may be fading, but it is far from gone. It may be even too temptingly convenient to disappear at any time from human thought. It certainly is still very much in the minds and religious attitudes of many Christian clerics and laymen. I find it, for instance, very evident in the many statements by Vatican officials and in the behavior of many American Catholic bishops who intellectually and theologically defend and praise human sexuality and marriage, but emotionally and psychologically reject them.

The past half century has witnessed only the first move on the part of some Christian theologians to accept sexual intercourse as an interpersonal experience *whose value is distinct and separable* from its procreative potential. Beyond this distinction is the growing awareness that the social function of sexual intercourse is rapidly supplanting the previously primary function of reproduction, and is in fact making the procreative role a minor and very limited one.

In this context, one of my colleagues recently called my attention to an intriguing and illuminating shift now under way in our guilt mechanisms. Professor Irving Buchen, who heads Fairleigh Dickinson's experimental College of the Future, has approached futurology and our prospects for the years ahead by a rather unusual path: a serious study and analysis of perversion and decadence in literature. In his anthology, *The Perverse Imagination*, Dr. Buchen argues that all our concepts of individual sexual perversions and the moral decadence of societies are undergoing a very rapid evolution. So rapid that we can seriously ask whether perversion is still possible. If our society accepts the separation of human sexual intercourse and procreation as two distinct actions, then we must also recognize that the bohemian sexual behavior of a few individuals in the past (usually among the aristocratic and artistic communities), which society considered free-wheeling and perverse, is now a collective possibility for the masses.

One important result of this evolution, Dr. Buchen argues, is our lessening sense of guilt over non-reproductive sexual intercourse in all its variations, including homosexuality, and the simultaneous shifting of moral and psychological guilt to our reproductive capacities. Very often today a couple will feel more guilty about having more than two children than they would about living together in a non-marital relationship, having premarital intercourse, or accepting an alternative pattern of marriage besides the traditional monogamy. This new guilt is double-edged: those couples who decide to have more than two children are made to feel guilty by those concerned with our population growth while couples who refrain from producing more than two children are viewed as somehow decadent, morally perverse hedonists by those who have not yet accepted the distinction between sexual intercourse and procreation.

Many factors—social, cultural, political, economical, and technological—have worked together in bringing this new understanding of human sexuality to the fore in the minds of the average man and woman as well as the professional students of ethics, morals, and religious values. We have already mentioned some of these factors as catalysts for our sexual apocalypse, but there is one other factor that I want to mention briefly here: the shattering of our infantile understanding of human sexuality as being summed up in the reproductive function of the male and female genitals. (Reviewing this development reminds me of the judgment of Dr. William Cole, author of *Sex and Love in the Bible,* on the maturity of the ancient Hebrew image of sexual man and the primitivism of our own traditional Christian view.)

Until recently our Western culture has tried to pigeonhole human sexual relations into the same behavioral slot as the sexual functions of other animals, thus justified by God solely for reproduction, and by the devil for fun and perverse games.

Until the turn of the century, biologists were ignorant of the intricacies of reproduction and the radical differences that exist in the estrous and menstrual cycles of the female. Hence their observations only confirmed those of the farmer, the hunter, and the animal breeder that bulls and cows, stags and does, rams and ewes—in fact all the lower animals—seem immune to the lure of the opposite sex until the warming spring, lush food, or lengthening hours of day trigger the madness of compulsive mating, sexual heat. Normally these females, on an estrous cycle, could not care less about the wandering and indifferent males. Only when she is ready to ovulate a fertile egg will the female trigger the mating instinct of the male and openly respond. Not understanding that females on an estrous cycle behave quite differently from those on a menstrual cycle, theologians, hanging over the shoulders of biologists, drew the following conclusion: the Creator wisely provided Adam and Eve with sexual organs so that like other animals they might reproduce their kind. Sexual intercourse equals procreation.

But then the students of animal behavior—ethologists by trade name—came on the scene to throw this equation into complete jeopardy by noting that, unlike the lower animals on an estrous cycle, the higher primates—monkeys, chimpanzees, apes, and humans—are not nearly so circumscribed in their sexual attractions and interactions. Among the latter, sexual behavior has evolved into a far less instinctual and more socially oriented menstrual cycle which permits and even encourages male/female interactions outside the fertile period.

Man and his near cousins, we have learned, are the only sexual animals known to mate regularly during pregnancy, nursing, and after menopause—times when conception is either impossible or highly unlikely. Then, as if to reinforce this budding awareness of the primary social function of human sexual relations, reproductive biologists uncovered several other interesting facts. For instance, the availability of males for mating at times does not coincide with the most favorable time for pregnancy and birth. To solve this dangerous conflict natural selection has favored the evolution of structures such as seminal vesicles in bats, insects, and even cows, which permit the storage of semen and insure normal fertility. In women we find the exact opposite, with the evolution of a barrier at the opening of the womb and chemical secretions in both the womb and vagina which are lethal to sperm except during the few fertile days in the monthly cycle. In terms of female behavior the human has moved even further along the path to social sexuality, for the average woman experiences peaks in her sexual desire just before or after the menstrual period when conception is most unlikely. As a Benedictine friend once remarked to me, "Animals have season and no reason; man has reason and no season."

Even more revolutionary in terms of our growing understanding of human sexuality has been our sudden disillusionment with a black-and-white division of human sexuality into male and female on the basis of genital structures. Every day we function, for the sake of convenience, with an "operational definition" based on the simplism of testes and ovaries, penis and womb. But more and more we are becoming aware that while anatomy is a very important base for dealing with sexual persons, it is at best tentative and provisional, an incomplete criterion.

We now have at least six criteria on which to appraise an

individual's sexuality and/or gender. Most basic of these is the genetic or chromosomal sexuality, which ordinarily falls into the convenient arrangement of two female chromosomes for women (XX) and one female and one shorter male chromosome for men (XY). But we also know of dozens of variations that can and do occur in this basic hereditary pattern. One in every 200 white Americans suffers a variation from the normal genetic sexuality. Among the more common variations are "super-males" with an additional male chromosome (XYY) and the sexually underdeveloped female who has male muscular development resulting from a mosaic with two types of cells in the body, some bearing a "supermale" XYY pattern and others having a single X chromosome. Equally puzzling are other genetic mosaics and intersexes.

As yet we do not know how this genetic code is translated into the development of ovaries or testes from the undifferentiated reproductive glands or primary gonads, but the translation is usually accomplished without a hitch.

In terms of the kinds of hormones produced by the ovaries or testes and by the cortex of the adrenal glands situated on top of the kidneys, every man and woman is a hermaphrodite, a dynamic balance of masculine and feminine hormones. In the male, the testes produce two male hormones, androgen and testosterone, while the outer layers of the adrenal glands produce cortisone, some of which is converted into estrogen, one of the female hormones. In the female, a similar dynamic balance is maintained between the ovarian hormones, estrogen and progesterone, and the adrenal production of cortisone, some of which is converted into testosterone. Thus we are all a combination of male and female hormones.

The hormones, in turn, affect the development of the undifferentiated internal and external reproductive systems: the oviducts, womb, vagina, clitoris, and major and minor lips in the female; and the *vas deferens*, penis, and scrotal sac in the male.

For the first ten weeks of human embryonic life it is impossible to distinguish a male from a female embryo on the basis of either external or internal anatomy; both sexes are almost identical in their development up to this stage. Only when the fetus is starting its fourth month of life in the womb is it possible to distinguish the sexes, and then sometimes with considerable hesitancy.

The most controversial and disturbing facet of our sexuality is the behavior patterns that are imprinted on our subconscious minds just before and just after birth by the male hormones. A number of experimental psychologists, among them Seymour Levine, Charles Phoenix, John Ruskow, and Alan Fisher, have uncovered evidence of a basic female orientation in the oldest portion of the mammalian brain, the hypothalamus. This means that in much of our basic psychosexual behavior *we all*, males and females alike, *start with a radical female orientation*.

Only the presence of the male hormones at the proper time and in the proper proportions in the weeks just before and after birth enables a genetically male fetus to superimpose masculine behavioral patterns on the innate female patterns. In terms of assuring the survival of the species this is perfectly logical, for mammals must care for their offspring after birth; they must nurse and protect them. And this task is usually left by nature to the female. Hence the simplest type of female or maternal imprinting is advisable, one free from the vagaries of hormonal control. There are always enough males around to insure fertility for the females, and an occasional or even frequent deviation in the normal male behavior would hardly be noticed. But even a few females deviating from their normal maternal behavior could work havoc for the species, especially if the deviation were regular and inheritable.

Small wonder Dr. John Money of the Johns Hopkins Gender Identification Clinic remarked that "in view of the alleged higher incidence of psychosexual pathologies in males, it is conceivable that masculine psychosexual differentiation is more difficult to achieve than feminine, and is more vulnerable to error." In simple terms, it is much easier to be a psychologically normal female than a normal male.

The complexities of the genetic, hormonal, and psychological facets of human sexuality underline very clearly how simplistic a sexual ethics based only on the functioning of the external genitals in reproduction really is.

Considering these same complexities, it is no small wonder that most humans grow up without major sexual problems. Consider what is involved in the process of becoming a male or female! A normal egg must be fertilized by a normal sperm so that the single microscopic zygote ends up with millions of genes—coded information precisely laid out along the 22 pairs of body-controlling chromosomes and the one pair of sex-determining chromosomes. This single cell then must duplicate its millions of hereditary units *a billion times over without flaw* to produce a normal body for the newborn. Even if the embryo manages to surmount this initial hurdle without becoming a genetic mosaic or intersex, those same genes must then be translated into properly differentiated and functioning ovaries or testes, producing just the right dynamic balance of male and female hormones. These hormones in turn must activate the undifferentiated internal and external systems, these tissues must respond properly. Then there is the crucial psychological imprinting surrounding birth that will permit normal sexual behavior in later life. Finally, we face the fact that we are never fully developed in our sexual personality. *We are always sexual persons in the process of becoming male or female throughout our lives, as we grow and interact with other sexual persons.*

There are countless risks in this process of becoming a sexual person. An embryo can begin life in one sexual channel and for some unknown reason be shifted into the other pathway. Some men have started off as genetic females and ended up with normal male anatomy, behavior, and psyches. The reverse is also possible. More unfortunate is the person who ends up with a conflict between his anatomy and his psychological orientation, the transsexual.

The natural, and more recently the experimental, reversal of an animal's sexuality is a fascinating possibility. Some clams and other shellfish, along with some bony fish, are known to begin life as females and then change into functional and normal males as they age. A classic example of natural sex reversal is found in populations of a small fish from the Red Sea, *Anthias squamipinnis*. Usually the females outnumber the males in this species by eight or nine to one. However, when the percentage of males drops below roughly 10 percent, some of the females will simply mutate into males. Dr. Lev Fishelson, a biologist from Tel-Aviv University in Israel, has duplicated this natural process in the laboratory and has found that ten to twenty females are quite content if they have one or two males in the tank with them. But when Fishelson removes the males, one of the twenty females will quickly mutate into a normal functioning male. And the process of transsexual change can be induced several times simply by removing the new male. Complete and totally functional reversal of human sexuality is impossible today, but we do face the reality of partial success in plastic surgery and hormone therapy at several gender clinics around the world.

Human sexuality and the varieties of human sexual behavior and relationships are far more complex than the simple black-and-white concept of sexuality we have so long accepted as fact without question.

This brings me full circle to my opening thesis that today's sexual apocalypse has been triggered not only by the emergence of women and the advent of a mobile world-wide community created by the electronic media, but also by our contraceptive and reproductive technologies, by mounting concern about our growing population, by a reappraisal of human sexual mores within the more mature biblical context, and by the scientific realities outlined here.

In the sexual apocalypse, certain facts already stand out as inescapable:

1. Reproduction and sexual relations are two distinct areas of human behavior, each to be guided by its own newly evolving ethic.

2. Unlimited, chance human reproduction is no longer a blessed event.

3. The traditional models of parenthood and the orthodox, "natural" way of procreating are now complemented by a variety of options open to everyone.

4. Sexual relations that are non-procreative or that occur outside the marital bond can no longer be automatically damned as unnatural and immoral.

5. Finally, a paradox: continued separation of human sexual love in Western thought from the love of the absolute involves more risk for God than for man or woman.

In the following chapters I will discuss some new patterns in reproduction/parenthood and in the male/female relationships. Two new ethics will emerge from the discussion, along with some pros and cons of these new patterns.

THREE

The Single Person—A New Species of Human

Not too long ago Robert H. Rimmer, a long-time student of human relations, introduced me to some of the first graduates of an exciting experimental college just outside Cambridge, Massachusetts. Beth, Jack, Sheila, Harry, Valerie, and Stan were typical of many young people I have known on college campuses, perceptive, enthusiastic, intelligent, a bit naïve about the world and life, but very much concerned with the course of today's society and their future.

But there was something unusual about them that I could not pin down at the time. Only recently, reflecting back on that informal and friendly weekend, does it strike me that their uniqueness is that between 1962 and 1966 these young people were tackling a very serious problem of today's society in a surprisingly creative, prophetic, and forthright program of action. I suppose what threw me off guard more than anything else was the fact that they looked like the average middle-class college student. I realized that these young people had somehow made up their minds ten years ago that they could not be satisfied with the fearful, hesitant, backdoor approach of so many parents and educators even today. For them honesty and openness were essential to life. Their attendance at this experimental college was rooted in that conviction.

Before I tell you any more about the program at Harrad

College, I shall introduce the six students I met through Bob Rimmer.

Stanley Cole was every girl's dream of a hip guy—long wavy brown hair, sideburns, suave and poised. Stan confided that his father had changed his name to Cole from Kolasukas shortly after coming to this country.

Sheila Ann Grove was a quiet plain Jane, prim and proper at all times, I suspected, the daughter of a self-made multi-millionaire in oil. Sheila had graduated *summa cum laude*— "Ugh!" as she put it—from Brightwater Academy and came to Harrad a "physical virgin, but mental unvirgin." She summed up her life to this point as "pretty fouled up. Mother divorced Daddy when I was twelve. She couldn't stand two things about him: his desire to get richer no matter what . . . and the richer he got the more women he thought he could go to bed with."

Beth Hillyer's family and relatives could have staffed a small medical clinic. Natural blonde, blue eyes, a turned-up pert nose, brains and beauty combined.

Harry Schacht was tall, skinny, very self-conscious of himself as "the Beast" and very uneasy in the company of girls. I do not recollect Valerie and Jack too clearly, except that Val was interested in sociology and had left graduate work at Case Western Reserve to work in the inner city. Jack, as I recall, was in graduate work in economics at Wharton after graduating from Harrad.

In one short weekend these young people tried to explain to me the rhyme and reason behind their attending such an experimental college as Harrad and the philosophy behind its program. They decided that the best way to introduce me to the Harrad way of life would be to let me read the diaries and personal journals they had kept with meticulous care during their four years at Harrad. And so I spent the weekend sharing the very personal thoughts and reactions of these six young people to their years at Harrad.

These diaries let me into the skin of these young people,

they let me see their growth as persons—which is really the important story of Harrad—but they also exposed me to some of the philosophy and history of Harrad.

The college was organized in 1962 by two sociologist-psychologists, Margaret and Philip Tenhausen, who were convinced that "in order to survive, Western man must take the long step away from the primitive emotions of hate and jealousy and learn the meaning of love and loving as a dynamic process. Such a program would counteract the decadence that is slowly infiltrating our society."

The 400 Harrad students, evenly divided between boys and girls, lived on the former Carnsworth Estate. Their more conventional college courses were taken at nearby schools, but everyone was required to take an active part in the weekly seminar on "Human Values" and to study an extensive reading list which included the key utopian novels of Huxley, More, Campanella, and the like, a strong dose of modern psychology, and a thorough survey of documented sociological studies of utopian experiments in this country during the nineteenth century—the Oneida Community of upstate New York and the Harmony Communities of Ohio and Indiana, among others.

This academic program would not mark Harrad College as anything unusual among colleges of the day. What *was* unusual about the school was the living arrangements in the dormitories and the philosophy behind them. The Tenhausens had published a proposal for this experiment in human living in a paper for the *North American Journal of Sociology* a few years before the college was established. The paper met with considerable negative reaction, but in 1962 an unexpected and substantial grant from the Carnsworth Foundation allowed the Tenhausens to launch their experimental program with four hundred students.

Phil Tenhausen summed up the purpose of Harrad with candor when he told me that the new college was designed to "provide the blueprint for a new sexually oriented aristocracy of individual men and women who are free of sexual inhibitions, repression, and hate, and are thoroughly educated in the meaning and art of love as distinguished from the purely sexual relationship. This program," he assured me, "is in sharp contrast to our present system of segregating boys and girls of seventeen or eighteen, when they are at a high point of their emotional interest in each other, and forcing them into abnormal or premature living patterns during their college days. Social pressure for prolonged sexual continence often creates fear, anxiety, and actual repulsion between the sexes, or it drives them into bed before they are ready. The results are too obvious: a premature marriage ending in divorce, unwanted children born out of wedlock, sexual frustration before and continuing into marriage, and a sex-obsessed society with little or no knowledge of what dynamic love is."

Phil was inclined to go on theorizing, and would have if Margaret had not interrupted him to clue me in on some of the practical aspects of Harrad. "During their four years here, our students live together, not only under the same roof, but after some careful psychological tests to sort out compatible pairs, heterosexual couples share the same suite, a joint study, a common bathroom, and a common bedroom with twin beds.

"Since our program encourages premarital relations among our student body, we make a complete study of contraception very early in our course on Human Values. Roommates can live together with or without sexual intercourse as they themselves choose, and with the possibility, if they desire, of changing roommates at the end of each semester. There is a certain amount of discipline, we find, in requiring the couples to share the same suite for at least a full semester. Any marriage commitment is strongly discouraged, though we assume that the students who live together in this program will ultimately find a spouse among their fellow students, because they have become so conditioned by the program that they cannot relate easily with less mature young people who have not been exposed to this program.

"The Human Relations seminar runs every week for two hours over the four-year college course. It is required of every Harrad student. Its content and purpose is to explore every aspect of man's attempt to deal with his own sexuality, and society's attempts to organize or institutionalize that sexuality religiously, economically, and politically. Most of the students relate very well to the program, despite an initial shock—most of them do come from a liberal background. The course is designed not to inculcate any particular or predetermined values, religious or otherwise, but rather to open the door for each student to evolve his own philosophy, his own values, and his own orientation of his 'self' to the world."

Most of the students in this four-year program will, the Tenhausens feel, end up in healthy monogamous marriages. But some of the graduates have already found that the close and lasting friendships they formed during college years lead them into alternative forms of marriage, particularly communal or group marriages. This, as it turned out, was exactly what happened with Sheila, Val, Beth, Harry, Jack, and Stanley, who, after graduation, bought a large home and formed the "InSix." Margaret's impression of InSix came right to the point, I think, when she suggested that "they realized the many advantages of an informal group marriage as a result of their experiences together here at Harrad. Without fear, jealousy, repression, or inhibition they recognized their need, not only for sexual varietism, but, even more important, for the stimulus of living together which adds depth, meaning, and breadth to the intel lectual crosscurrents of life."

There are many illuminating passages I would like to quote at length from the journals that touch on the personal reactions of six students to their unique education and living arrangements, but interested readers can get a much fuller impression by studying Robert Rimmer's novel-essay from the journals, *The Harrad Experiment.*

Whether or not Harrad College actually exists outside

Cambridge is irrelevant to our concern here. What is relevant and vital for us is the fact that *The Harrad Experiment* has been for more than six years an extremely influential underground book on college campuses. We must also realize that *much of the basic philosophy and a good bit of the coed living encouraged at Harrad are today a common, if informal, reality in many* colleges and universities around the country. Coed dorms and off-campus accommodations, the availability of contraceptive counseling, and other developments have created informal situations closely approximating those recorded by Rimmer in *The Harrad Experiment*. Harrad exists under hundreds of different names around the country. Of course, both educators and parents are most reluctant to admit this reality.

Why do many people still view Harrad's as such a radical and revolutionary program? I tend to think that much of the hesitation can be traced to the fact that the Harrad proposal *forces us to recognize a totally new species of human being: the mature, sexually active single person.* In terms of human society the single person is a relatively recent sub-species.

Consider for a moment the following statistics. The median age for the first marriage of young Americans today is 21.4 years. Yet we know that American girls generally mature sexually at about 12½ years. A 1934 study of 250 Jewish orphans in New York City placed their puberty at 13½; an 1820 survey of working-class girls in Manchester, England, placed puberty then at 15½, while 250 years earlier girls from rural Austria were maturing sexually only in their 17th, 18th, or even 20th years. As for the young men, medical evidence indicates a similar situation. Two examples come to mind: the eighteenth-century records of the Bach Boys' Choir in Leipzig note that on an average the boys stopped singing soprano at about the age of 18, while the voices of boys in London choirs in 1959 dropped out of the soprano range usually in their thirteenth year.

To complete the picture of our new human sub-species, one also must consider the average age at which young people married and moved out on their own. In Shakespeare's England, childhood ended at the age of 7 when lads were apprenticed to the local smithy, cooper, or tradesman and girls entered domestic service as maids. By 14 a young man was considered an adult with adult responsibilities. He was often married by 15. And the same held true for girls. In this situation sexual maturity came several years after a person married and was accepted by society as an adult. Today we have quite the opposite situation, and this is why we can speak of a new human sub-species, the single person.

Traditionally, all of us are thought of as single persons with unique rights in all areas of study, vocation, work, and devotion, with one major exception, our sexuality. Sexuality outside the marital bond cannot be moral. Thus friendships between men and women are always oriented to give way to love and marriage, unless it is the safe, surface friendship existing between married couples as couples, or between a married and a single person where the single person of the opposite sex is somehow asexual. Even the single monk bargains for his brotherhood within the monastic family, as does the single nun. One of the unique elements in the Harrad experiment is that deep heterosexual friendship does not have to yield to love. At Harrad, friendship serves as a companion to love, if love so develops. Psychologists have been emphasizing for some time that in the long run it is better to like the person you are married to than to "love" him in the romantic tradition. In simple terms, when the single person claims not only study, vocation, work, and devotion, but also sex as his individual province, the intimate relationships existing between friendship, love, marriage, and sex are completely rearranged. An extreme but common example of this rearrangement is the friendship, love, and even marriage that exist among some homosexuals.

The advent of this new type of human has hardly been noticed by those moralists and religious leaders responsible for offering guidelines in human behavior.

The controversial study document *Sexuality and the Human Community*, adopted by the General Assembly of the United Presbyterian Church in the United States in May, 1970, was among the first formal statements to admit frankly the problem created for Christian moralists by the growing number of single persons in our society: "[We are greatly disturbed by] the emphasis we have found on marriage and the family as the exclusive model for ordering all sexual activity. By understanding sexuality primarily in terms of its place in the orders of creation, we emphasize its procreative function still, admitting the relational functions of sexual expression but subordinating them to those concerned with child-bearing and nurture. We feel that Roman Catholicism has suffered in its understanding of sexuality by emphasizing the religious superiority of the virginal state. But Protestantism has, in reaction, suffered from an equally single-minded preoccupation with marriage and the family, and by their silence have left the impression that the single estate is a deficient one, requiring more explanation and apology than guidance. So, less by intent than by omission, Protestantism has left the unmarried in the shadow of an ethical structure designed to serve another manner of life than theirs."

This, the Presbyterian document admits, "has meant that the church has made less pertinent ethical statements than it might have to the not yet married, to those who are single by vocational choice or statistical accident, to the homosexual, to the widowed, the divorced, and the many others who do not live in the 'normal' estate of marriage."

The task-force document, which I will quote frequently in this book, was accepted for publication and recommendation to the churches for study and appropriate action at the 182nd General Assembly of the United Presbyterian Church in the United States by a vote of 485 affirmative to 259 negative.

"This action is not to be construed as an endorsement of the report." A motion from the floor was subsequently passed, 356 to 347: "We, the 182nd General Assembly (1970), reaffirm our adherence to the moral law of God as revealed in the Old and New Testaments, that adultery, prostitution, fornication, and/or the practice of homosexuality is sin. . . ."

This document is a bold statement for a church whose official policy on sex opposes adultery, prostitution, fornication, and homosexuality. But even more interesting and significant for our creative age is a sentence in the opening portion of that document which notes that "the Christian community encompasses a wide diversity of racial, ethnic, and cultural groups, and therefore a wide variety of assessments of sexuality and sexual behavior." The authors of the Presbyterian document had the courage to admit something most religious people refuse to accept, namely, *the ethical validity and social acceptability* of widely different conceptions of human sexuality and sexual behavior in different racial, national, and cultural groups. But the authors go beyond this basic insight and implicitly accept the fact that sexual ethics continually evolve at very uneven paces on several different planes among the unmarried, the married, and the post-married with any national, racial, or cultural grouping.

It is quite easy to document this insight with data from the research of cultural anthropologists for other societies and races. But sometimes it is not so easy to document a basic revolution within our own culture, especially when we are sitting on top of it. Most casual observers of our society would concede that we have witnessed a major shift in our appraisal of what is morally acceptable in the sexual behavior of single people. The contraceptive pill, liberalized abortion, the mobility of the automobile, the motel, the emergence of women— these are events we all experience. Their impact on the sexual ethics of the single youth is fairly evident, even if we cannot document precisely the increase of premarital sexual intercourse among today's youth as compared with that of their parents or grandparents. Even so, some clear indications might be worth noting here.

It is a fact that fully one-third of all the first births in the United States between 1964 and 1966 were conceived outside of marriage. Fifteen percent of these first babies were conceived and born out of wedlock while 18 percent were born after their parents married. This "conservative" estimate comes from Mary Grace Kovar, a leading analyst for the U.S. Division of Vital Statistics, who studied the data on the first births to married women detailed in the June, 1970 *Monthly Vital Statistics Report.* This means that nearly 400,000 of the over 1 million first births in each of the years 1964, 1965, and 1966 were conceived by premarital intercourse, with slightly more than half of these being legitimized by their parents' subsequent marriage. Forty-two percent of the babies born to women between 15 and 19 years old were conceived out of wedlock; for women 20 to 24, the percent was 14.5; for the 24- to 29-year-olds, 3.7 percent; and for older women, slightly under 2 percent.

Broken down according to racial groups, the statistics indicate that 20 percent of all white wives and 42 percent of all non-white wives in the United States have their firstborn child within eight months of their marriage. Among married and unmarried white women, 27 percent of *all* first births were conceived outside wedlock; among non-white women, the percentage is 68 percent of all first births.

These statistics, of course, do not take into account the availability and extensive use of abortion among the different racial groupings or on different economic levels. Thus 37.5 percent of such births were to women whose family income was under $3,000 a year. The percentage fell to 8.2 when the family income was over $10,000. Education is another important factor: 32 percent of the girls with one to three years of high school had their first baby within eight months of marriage;

but this percentage decreased as the amount of formal education increased: 21 percent of the high-school graduates, 18 percent of the women with one to three years of college, and 7 percent of the college graduates had their first baby within eight months of marriage.

More dramatic is the evidence recently made available as a result of a May, 1970 Gallup Poll of students from fifty-five colleges and universities around the country. The survey sought an over-all view of how today's college students feel about premarital sexual intercourse and virginity. The results were not surprising for those who work with college students: three out of four students said it is not important to them that the person they marry is a virgin. Interestingly, the opinions of men did not differ significantly from those of women on this question.

How does this compare with the views of the "older generation"? A similar survey by Gallup a few months earlier indicates that 68 percent of Americans over twenty-one believe premarital sex is morally wrong. This is a complete reversal: from nearly three-quarters of the older generation opposed to premarital sexual intercourse to three-quarters of the younger generation saying it is unimportant to them whether or not they marry a virgin.

Even more interesting is the breakdown according to the liberal/conservative image. Seventy-nine percent of the students who consider themselves liberal feel virginity is unimportant for marriage, while a solid 58 percent of the conservatives agreed with this untraditional view. Eighty-five percent of the students for whom religion is not a relevant part of their lives do not worry about virginity, but 58 percent of the religious-oriented students again agree with the untraditional view.

Breaking the statistics down according to attendance at state, private, and public colleges versus denominational and church-affiliated colleges, nearly the same statistics hold true. Three-quarters of the first group were unconcerned about the virginity of their future spouses and 56 percent of the students at religious-affiliated colleges also were unconcerned about virginity. The over-all percentage of students who believe that lack of sexual intercourse before marriage is unimportant rose from 68 percent among freshmen to 80 percent among seniors and 83 percent among graduate students.

Then there is the survey "Heterosexual Cohabitation Among Unmarried [Female] Students" at Cornell University reported by Dr. Eleanor Macklin at the May, 1971 Groves Conference. Dr. Macklin, who heads the Department of Human Development and Family Studies at Cornell, made an in-depth study of the female students on campus in the academic year of 1970–1971, with retrospect questions going back to 1966 for senior students. She was very careful in defining her terminology, so that when a quetsion asked if a student was living or had "lived with a man," it was clearly understood that this meant "spending four nights a week with the same male for three consecutive months." When the female students were asked how many of them were presently living with a man in these terms, over 30 percent answered in the affirmative. And when the survey was extended over four years, it was found that at any one time approximately 30 percent of the girls were spending at least four nights a week with one man for three months. In the same four-year period, from 1966 to 1970, Macklin believes that 75 to 90 percent of the girls on campus had lived with at least one man during their four undergraduate years. A good number had lived with more than one man. This survey did not even attempt to find out how many girls had serious relations with men that did not last at least three months, though these undoubtedly would be more frequent than the defined "living with a man at least four nights a week for three months" asked about in the survey.

In the Prologue I noted the very practical problem created by our continued use of traditional terms to describe the realities of a totally new culture. This problem turns up here when we try to describe sexual intercourse among today's youth as "premarital." Traditionally we have divided sexual relations into three temporal pigeonholes: premarital, marital, and extramarital. But, as the Reverend William Graham Cole, author of *Sex and Love in the Bible,* has noted, "this ignores the fact that a very considerable number of individuals never marry, but do, nevertheless, engage in sexual activity." Actually there are only two kinds of sexual relations: those occurring within a marriage and those outside the marital bond. We can only use the term "premarital" in hindsight after the couple are married since there is no guarantee that even engaged couples are having truly premarital relations. We really need a new word to indicate what we mean.

It would be very easy to attribute the changing patterns of premarital ethics and behavior among today's young to the decadence of a leisure-pampered society which caters to its offspring. But that would do a serious injustice to the sincerity of the younger generation, to the forceful impact of reproductive technology, and to social currents which are molding our ethics and our society much more than we are willing to admit. While avoiding the temptation of deducing our sexual ethics from statistical behavior, it seems much more reasonable to take the present situation at face value and try to situate it within a historical context of social evolution, as Snoek and others have tried to do, however briefly and tentatively.

In terms of strictly premarital sexual intercourse, there appears to be a new wholesomeness emerging among many young people. They are beginning to take human sexuality in a much broader context than the genital reductionism of earlier generations. As McLuhan and Leonard remarked in their *Look* study, "The Future of Sex," young people are beginning to integrate sexual intercourse into the broad scope of sensual experiences, taking it off the pedestal of sacredness and thereby making it more human and personal. This allows them to work free of many of the compulsions and restrictions which have traditionally surrounded our "high-intensity genital sex."

The pace of social and cultural change since the Second World War has reached such a peak of acceleration that the younger generation hardly knows what stability and permanence mean. They live, breathe, and think change, evolution, process, without even being conscious of it. It is the only world they know. As a result they view marriage as a process, not a product. They find it impossible to deal with the male/female relationship in terms of a fixed philosophy of nature. That primitive, pre-Darwinian image had three discrete stages: random dating with the opposite sex; then serious engagement with one person—both of these relationships being very tightly restricted to a good-night kiss, holding hands, and other "safe" expressions of affection; and then marriage until-death-do-us-part when, having pronounced their vows publicly, the couple was suddenly permitted what had previously been forbidden.

The Presbyterian statement on sexuality notes that today, "as the pattern of our society moves away from the larger family unit and relies more and more exclusively on the immediate family, there is a tendency for courtship patterns to take on the form of sequential and increasingly intense monogamous relationships. This pattern has developed along with a steady postponement of the age of economic independence and a steady lowering of the age of the onset of puberty." Thus, the Presbyterian statement concluded, "the standard of premarital virginity, which was once expected to be maintained during a relatively short period of two to five years (or less than a year in the Middle Ages), is now more difficult to maintain during the ten or more years that commonly elapse between puberty and marriage in our time." According to Rabbi Borowitz, a professor at Hebrew Union College, the Jewish tradition was even more restricted, for the period of courtship, during which the father usually arranged the espousal for his daughter, lasted only during the period of maidenhead (*naarah*), from the age of twelve to twelve and a half. By the time a Jewish maiden became a *bogeret*, a "mature free woman," at twelve and a half, she was espoused and under the protection of her husband.

Most young people today would agree with the statement offered by a British group of Friends, "It is right and proper that many boys and girls and young men and women should fall in and out of love a number of times before they marry— and this *process* will involve emotional heights and depths." (In the mid-1960s this unofficial committee of Quakers, under the direction of Alastair Heron, of the Friends Home Service Committee, produced a monograph, *Towards a Quaker View of Sex.* A number of the conclusions from this Quaker statement will be mentioned in the course of our discussion.)

I italicized the word "process" in the previous sentence because I am convinced that today's youth, conditioned to change, are really the first generation capable of viewing marriage as a process of personal and mutual growth within the total context of one's lifelong development as a person. Premarital behavior must thus be integrated within the context of personal growth. Such an extended process of deepening relations makes it extremely difficult, if not impossible, to continue accepting the black-and-white dichotomy which prohibits all sexual intercourse prior to an official marriage.

In this respect youth may be more traditional than we suspect. We can go back a couple of centuries to the great moral theologians Sanchez and Cajetan, who also viewed marriage as a process. They called it *matrimonium in fieri*, pointing out that every marital relationship is a process of becoming that begins with espousal and does not end until death. In their legal approach to marriage they divided the essential process of marriage into three phases: the exchange of marital vows by the couple, the witnessing of the church, and the consummation in sexual intercourse. The process could be interrupted, aborted after the first step, and, with a church dispensation, even after the second step. Updating this concept, C. Jaime Snoek, a German Catholic moralist, asks, in Böckle's *The Future of Marriage as Institution*, whether, considering "the greater continuity felt today to exist between engagement and marriage . . . in some circumstances it would not be permissible for the partners to place the consummation before the assent of the Church." Both Sanchez and Cajetan would, Snoek feels, reply yes.

Père Lagrange, the great Dominican pioneer founder of L'Ecole biblique in Jerusalem at the turn of this century, pointed out in his 1927 commentary on the Gospel of Luke that the Jewish tradition, at least in certain areas, allowed an engaged or espoused couple to have sexual relations. He added that it is highly unlikely that these same Jews would be required to renounce this custom when they converted to Christianity. Snoek, in fact, implies rather clearly that the frequent occurrence of premarital sexual intercourse and its informal "institutionalization" in a formal "trial marriage" would be merely updating the Jewish custom of espousal.

The Judaic tradition contains an interesting paradox which Borowitz sums up this way: "Judaism considers sex God's gift and procreation His command. It considers marriage the proper context for intercourse and makes it a prescribed religious duty. With such a high value given to marriage, Judaism would thus seem to side with those who see it as the necessary condition for sexual intercourse. Yet neither the Torah, the rest of the Bible, the Mishnah, nor the Talmud contains a law prohibiting premarital sexual relations."

The eighty-five-year-old Anglican Archbishop of Canterbury, Lord Geoffrey Francis Fisher, is quite concerned about the prevalence of premarital intercourse. In a recent book, *Touching on Christian Truth*, he argues that the churches should revive the old Jewish custom of espousal as a ritual celebrated in church. By making engagement more serious in the eyes of the church and recognizing it by a sacramental rite the Archbishop believes that the moral guilt often associated with premarital intercourse would be removed. I think that this custom would benefit the parents more than the young couple, but there are many young people who would value such a recognition rite by the church. The espousal ritual suggested by the Archbishop would in effect sanctify the trial marriage.

"Since," according to the Presbyterian document, "the chief goal of marriage is the perfection of interpersonal relationship, a courtship which has helped a couple develop profound sensitivities to each other, and tenderness in response to each other's needs and desires, can prepare them for a healthy adjustment of their sexual energies in the marriage that follows. If in the course of such a courtship, a couple has taken a responsible decision to engage in premarital intercourse, the church should not convey to them the impression that their decision is in conflict with their status as members of the body of Christ. If they are Christians, whatever joys and sorrows, doubts and delights, attend the development of their relationship are part of their experience as Christian persons, moving towards marriage, and are elements of human experience as susceptible as any others to that reconciling ministry to which the church is called."

In almost every discussion of premarital sexual intercourse and trial marriages, a basic problem is posed by the fact that many, perhaps most, of these relationships will not develop into formal marriages. This makes conception a definite hazard and a complicating risk. In the past this posed a real problem for any discussion of trial marriages and premarital sex; today, with inexpensive and effective contraceptives available to almost anyone, the problem may be minimal. However, it is still one that must be considered.

If a child is born out of wedlock, society still labels it illegitimate, however that label may be fading. And again our traditional language shows its inadequacies in describing the present situation. Una Stannard has neatly dissected the fallacies behind our continued use of the term "illegitimate" in a fascinating study titled "Adam's Rib, or the Woman Within." For centuries in our Western culture, she points out, men were considered to be the sole progenitors, with women providing only the nursery bed or incubator for the male semen (seed). In this context, men regarded the virginity of women highly because it was the one way they could be sure the child that a woman bore was their own. Thus men severely restricted woman's sexual and social life, demanded that their brides be virgins, and made marriage the only legal situation in which a woman could have a child.

Legitimacy, it turns out, was man's way of validating parenthood. In societies where women are thought to be the sole progenitors of children, there are no illegitimate offspring since every child has a legal mother and the father's identity is unimportant. But where the male is believed to be the sole generator, a child without a legally acknowledged father becomes taboo, and worse than taboo, a child of no one, *filius nullius*, as church law puts it. Legally the woman has no right to bear a child out of wedlock, especially if, as Napoleon said, women are merely the machines in which children are manufactured. In a patriarchal society a child born out of wedlock has no known creator; he has no legal right to exist. Centuries ago even a child born in wedlock might be declared illegitimate by the father. When a child was born, it was brought in and laid at the feet of the father. If the father reached down and raised up the babe, he acknowledged it as his legitimate offspring, whence our expression about raising children.

Una Stannard recalls some other interesting history about the illegitimate child in her article for *Trans-Action*. "Since the woman who bore an illegitimate child made both herself and the child social outcasts, it should not be surprising that many a mother destroyed her illegitimate children. The sewers and rivers of medieval Rome used to be clogged with their bodies. In 1633 an act was passed in England 'to prevent the Destroying and Murthering of Bastard Children,' apparently to no effect. In 1713 Joseph Addison commented that 'there is scarce an

assizes where some unhappy wretch is not executed for the murder of a child.' In 1777 Frederick the Great wrote to Voltaire
that the largest number of executions occurring in Germany
were of girls who had killed their illegitimate infants."

Woman's maternal instinct, according to Stannard, was apparently not great enough to withstand the taboo of a patriarchal society that forbade a woman to have a child of her own.
Yet that same patriarchal prohibition enabled men to manifest
their maternal instinct, after the women, their victims, had been
forced to give up their offspring. The male maternal instinct and
compassion came to the surface in the countless orphanages
established by men over the centuries. In 787 Archbishop Da-
theus of Milan was so revolted by women throwing their illegitimate offspring into the sewers and rivers that he opened a
foundling hospital where the children could be left without risk
of the mother being charged legally for her crime. In 1204,
Pope Innocent was likewise appalled by the number of dead
infants fishermen found in their nets and opened a section of
the hospital in Rome to care for illegitimate children. In eighteenth-century London, Thomas Coram was upset on his frequent walks to the city by the sight of abandoned infants on the
dunghills or on the sides of the road, some alive, some dead,
and some dying, and he too established a foundling hospital,
like countless other men over the centuries.

But let us return to the question of trial marriage, which
has come some distance since 1890, when Miss Mona Caird
wrote some articles on the subject for Karl Pearson's *Ethics of
Free Thought*. Miss Caird, a young lady of very modest intellectual ability, created a literary sensation in England with her
plea for the acceptance of trial marriage. Her articles were widely
reprinted in the States, and years later, in the 1920s, they
prompted Judge Ben B. Lindsey of Denver to recommend
"companionate," or trial, marriages again. The judge triggered a
national uproar, was denounced from thousands of pulpits, and
quickly lost his seat on the bench.

The basic thesis behind a trial marriage is twofold: first, to allow a young couple to test their compatibility; and second, to provide the opportunity for them to adjust to living with each other without adding the heavy responsibility of a newborn infant to their problems. Eliminating the possibility of illegitimate children, even considering the history and legal fiction of legitimacy, is a worth-while effort. So also is the psychological and emotional benefit to be derived from legitimatizing premarital intercourse. Archbishop Fisher suggests several psychological and moral benefits to be obtained by institutionalizing a form of trial marriage. "It would have to take place with the full consent of the two families. It would, in fact, be a sacramental act, made, as indeed marriage itself is, essentially by the two persons themselves. After that, sexual intercourse between them would not be regarded as, in the moral sense, fornication." Thus, much of the guilt, tension, and emotional turmoil of courtship and engagement could be reduced or eliminated. Marriage and children could follow when and if the two parties decided they were ready for them.

Although we are leaving the particular ethic of premarital intercourse for later discussion, we can explore some of the social and psychological issues raised by Margaret Mead in her 1966 proposal which appeared in *Redbook*, "Women: A House Divided." These issues have been commented on favorably by such diverse thinkers as Siegfried Keil, a German theologian at Marburg University, and the Canadian Jacques Lazure, a Catholic priest and sociologist. In her article, Margaret Mead asked two questions: how can we invest marriage forms with a new meaning, and at the same time move to reconcile our beliefs and our practices in a way that is consonant with our understanding of good human relations?

Dr. Mead answered these questions by calling for a "serious commitment, entered into in public, validated and protected by law and, for some, by religion, in which each partner would have a deep and continuing concern for the happiness and well-being of the other." In this individual marriage, "the central obligation would be an ethical, not an economic, one. The husband would not be ultimately responsible for the support of his wife; if the marriage broke up, there would be no alimony or support. The husband would not feel demeaned if he was not yet ready, or was not able, to support his wife. By the same token, husband or wife could choose freely to support the other within this partnership."

Dr. Mead argued that the individual marriage, requiring use of an effective contraceptive, would allow two young people a chance to know each other with an intimacy not available in even a prolonged courtship or furtive love affair. If they learned from their relationship that they could not live together compatibly on an emotional, psychological, intellectual, and/or sexual basis, the lack of children and economic dependence would allow them to separate without "the burden of misunderstood intentions, bitter recriminations, and self-destructive guilt."

The individual marriage, with its potential for maturing into what Dr. Mead calls a parental marriage, would also give greater reality to the belief that marriage and the choice of a lifelong partner is the result of a decision freely and maturely made by the couple without pressures from parents, relatives, friends, or society to legitimize their liberal premarital courtship, and without the fear of an extramarital pregnancy which often precipitates a premature wedding.

In contrast to the individual trial marriage, the parental marriage would be explicitly directed toward founding a family. "It would not only be a second type, but also a second step or stage, following always on an individual marriage, and with its own license and ceremony and kinds of responsibility. This would be a marriage that looked to a lifetime relationship with links, sometimes, to many people [a point we will take up in the remaining chapters]."

Dr. Mead hopes "that we would hold on to the ideal of a lifetime marriage in maturity. No religious group that cherishes marriage as a sacrament," Dr. Mead maintains, "should have to give up the image of a marriage that lasts into old age and into the lives of grandchildren and great-grandchildren as one that is blessed by God. No wholly secularized group should have to be deprived of the sense that an enduring, meaningful relationship is made binding by the acceptance, approval, and support of the entire society as witnesses."

But how, in a democracy as complex and pluralistic as ours, where we must always deal with a great diversity of religious, regional, class, and national styles—how can we effect such a radical change in our marriage customs? Certainly a major educational program, touching on all levels and in every possible way, is essential. We need discussions in the press, from church pulpits, on television, in government agencies, in the theater and in community organizations, on every level of the schools, with some pioneering experiments being put into motion. The experimenting, as we found above, is already quite real and extensive, even if society withholds its approbation out of fear. We will touch on the other elements in this education program in Chapter Ten. Dr. Mead is optimistic that eventually a consensus can and will evolve in our society, and that it will then be possible for legal, social, and religious groups to give full approbation to this two-step pattern of marriage.

FOUR

Virgin Wives and the New Dimensions
of "Premarital"

INVARIABLY in discussing premarital sexual experience some gad-
fly will ask whether virgins or non-virgins make better wives.
Sociologists and psychologists have booted this question all over
the globe and have come up with conflicting answers, often
much conditioned by scarcely hidden a priori assumptions. I
will make no attempt to answer the question except to offer an
opinion that it depends very much on the unique individuals
involved before and after marriage. However, one report turned
up in my research so irritated me with its assumptions and bias
that I decided to use it here and draw from it a suggestion that
the authors, three clinical psychologists, might find surprising.

Dr. David Shope, marriage counselor, clinical psychologist,
and director of the Psychological Clinic at Lock Haven State
College in Pennsylvania, collaborated in this study of unmarried
college girls between seventeen and twenty-three years old, "Virgins Make Happier Marriages," with Drs. Carlfred Broderick
and Clifford Adams. The girls were in an undergraduate marriage
course at Pennsylvania State University and several other colleges. All of them were contemplating marriage. Eighty virgins
and eighty non-virgins were matched in age, religious affiliation,
undergraduate grade level, number of terms in school, health,
and socio-economic status.

In tests of their childhood happiness, their relationships with their fathers, the strictness or permissiveness of their upbringing, no significant differences appeared between the girls in the two groups. Some minor differences were found. Non-virgins often considered their parents at times unnecessarily harsh, and while they attended religious services about as often as the others, they did not feel as strongly about their religious beliefs or about the religious training of their future children.

Real differences, however, did appear in two areas: prejudice and personal stability. Virgins scored much higher in dislike and intolerance of almost any unconventional behavior in their associates. They disliked "smelly" people, people who indulged in profanity, permissive girls, know-it-alls, cheaters, anyone who deviated from the accepted norm. Non-virgins, on the other hand, were, as a rule, more moody and changeable in their dispositions. Girls who regularly achieved orgasm outranked others on this point, indicating perhaps that, as Shope suggests, "while moodiness may be helpful to sexual responsiveness, it is not an aid to overall marital happiness."

The conclusions of this study are far more vital in their implicit assumptions than in their actual objective statement. Shope states that "a virgin will be a better wife not because she is technically a virgin, but because the very qualities that kept her a virgin are also those qualities that give her a greater chance for marital happiness." The crucial phrase here is "marital happiness." What does it *imply*? Apparently the underlying principle of the three-hundred-item Adams Marital Happiness Prediction Inventory is that "individuals who follow socially approved ways of behavior have the best chance for marriage success." In simple terms, conformers are more content, happier, and more tranquil in their marriages because they expect nothing more than what society has said they should expect.

Apparently some sociologists prefer to view the marital state and the happiness of married couples in terms of a fixed pattern where conformity means happiness/contentedness, and any restlessness or resistance to the roles imposed by society is interpreted as unhappiness. When a woman does the things society expects of her as a wife, she is fulfilling her "role." And, as Shope suggests, "the woman who accepts society's definition of a good wife has the best chance for marital happiness." Of course, since we learn about social roles from our family and parents, the assumption is that the girl who follows her mother's traditional pattern of wifely behavior will make the happiest wife. One major danger of this assumption is that the mother's conforming pattern of behavior will likely not fit the very changed environment the daughter will meet as a wife.

The common assumption of happiness via conformity is undoubtedly what leads some sociologists and critics of family life to a very negative view of that institution. For instance, David Cooper, British psychotherapist, argues that the family is basically a destructive force. In *The Death of the Family* he claims that the family tends to produce children who conform at all costs—the well-conditioned, endlessly obedient citizen. This rather extreme view of what undoubtedly does occur in many families ties in with the degree of prejudice and intolerance found by Shope in his virgin group. Cooper describes the childhood of many such individuals pungently: "One is instructed in great detail to disown one's self and to live agglutinatively, so that one glues bits of other people onto oneself and then proceeds to ignore the difference between the otherness in one's self and the selfsameness of one's self."

The Shope study highlights a basic question that every one of us must answer for himself. The question runs through every chapter of this book in a variety of guises: should I conform to the role and mores that society has set for me, or should I risk the creative instability and tensions involved in making my own place in society? From a different angle: will I find more personal fulfillment and contribute more to the good of others by conforming, or by creating?

While I would not disparage the innocence of the conforming virginal wife, my personal impression in an age of constant and radical change is that such people may have very smooth sailing for some years, but inevitably the turmoil and change of life does catch up with them. And then the reality of a changed world hits them far harder and with greater pain than it does the restless and discontented individual who accepts the adage of John Henry Newman: "In a higher world it is otherwise, but here below to live is to change, and to be perfect is to have changed often."

All of us find change somewhat disconcerting, both emotionally and intellectually, but there is really no way to escape it. The stagnant conformist-oriented wife is playing with explosive delaying tactics, blissfully or wistfully unaware of the time bomb already fused and burning. "It is safe to generalize," as Brian Boylan does in his book *Infidelity*, "that the more intelligent and curious a wife is, the less happy she will be as a full-time mother and housekeeper." This does not mean that she totally rejects or does not enjoy motherhood, merely that she is not content to make kitchen and diapers her whole world.

The prejudice, coupled with a certain inflexible naïveté, found by Shope in his virgin group is typical of what I frequently encounter in lecturing around the country. There is a very common adjunct of this inflexible naïve prejudice which assumes the absolute value of a monolithic but unreal image. People tend to picture things not as they are, but as they would like them to be. Let me illustrate this.

In discussing trial marriages and premarital sex, I usually get some very disturbed reaction when I point out that our monolithic image of dating, courtship, and engagement in terms of a 1900 Victorian pattern is not universal, and never has been, even in our American culture. The reaction becomes even more disturbed when I point out the history of Jewish and early Christian espousal, which often allowed premarital sex to test the prospective bride's fertility. And when I touch on a similar custom prevalent in such traditionally Catholic areas as Bavaria or Protestant sections of Europe, the reaction is even stronger.

In such situations I find it helps to contrast the variety we find in basic moral and religious practices within very traditional denominations. For instance, a good contrast can be drawn between the sexual patterns of Bavarian and Irish peasants, both staunchly traditional Roman Catholic cultures.

Among the Bavarian villagers there is a well-known custom of *Fensternl*, which roughly translates as "windowing." Bavarian girls of marriageable age commonly leave their bedroom windows open, with lights in them, so that their boy friends or fiancés can slip in and spend the night with them. Eventually, when the girl becomes pregnant, the marriage will be announced, either before or after the birth. It is not uncommon for a woman to have her first-born child by a man other than the one she finally marries. Such a child is accepted in the family, but is often assigned the Cinderella role. In the Bavarian community a high premium is placed on the wife being able to produce offspring, particularly a male, who will inherit the father's farm as well as work on it. So, very few Bavarian girls are asked to marry until their fertility is in evidence. The local parish priests and certainly the parents and community are well aware of this custom. And everyone accepts this form of premarital sex, this trial marriage of sorts, as no problem morally. This is even true in a devout village such as in Oberammergau, where the great Passion Play is held every ten years.

Contrast this Catholic custom with the sexual customs of the Catholic Gaeltacht community anthropologist John C. Messenger calls Inis Baeg. This Irish folk community has been studied by many anthropologists and ethnographers over the last hundred years. Messenger found that courtship is almost non-existent, and most marriages are arranged even today with little concern for the desires of the young people involved, despite the fact that the men marry at an average age of thirty-six and the women around twenty-five. Conjugal love is extremely rare, for the family serves only an economic and reproductive function, with a sharp dichotomy existing between the sexes.

Men, both before and after marriage, associate almost exclusively with other men, and the same holds for the women, who are restricted by custom to visiting other women, attending a few neighborhood parties in the winter, and sharing in church-associated activities. Many women, Messenger found, leave their cottages only to attend mass, wakes, and funerals, or to make an infrequent call on a relative.

Among the Irish of Inis Baeg female orgasm is either unknown or considered a deviant response. The men feel that sexual intercourse is debilitating. *Time* and *Life* magazines are considered pornographic and have prompted lively denunciations from the pulpit. Males and females swim at separate sections of the beach. Premarital intercourse is unknown and marital intercourse very brief. Only the "missionary position," face-to-face, is known. Night clothes are not removed and foreplay consists of some kissing and rough fondling of the buttocks. Nudity is such a taboo that fathers are not allowed to see their children of any age bathe, and they seldom consult the village nurse because it would entail baring their chests. So much for the inhabitants of Inis Baeg.

Variations just as extreme as those between the Bavarian and Irish Catholics can be found in other religious groups. Compare, if you will, the well-known sexual mores of the Swedish, where Lutheranism is the state religion, with those expressed in the very conservative social statement "Sex, Marriage, and Family," adopted at the Fifth Biennial Convention of the Lutheran Church in America, or similar conservative positions taken by the Lutherans of the Missouri Synod.

Or consider the plight of Jacob Minline and Sarah Tuttle, a New England couple, who were censured by the Puritan church and by the civil court because while courting they had "sat down together (in public), his arm being about her, and her arm upon his shoulder or about his neck; and he kissed her and she kissed him, or they kissed one another, continuing in this posture about half an hour" (Ferm, *Responsible Sexuality Now*).

Jacob was found innocent, but Sarah was fined for being a "bold virgin." Yet in several of the Puritan settlements an engaged couple was considered as good as married and the betrothal period served as a trial period during which the couple could get to know each other better. Premarital sexual intercourse was divided into two types: that engaged in by two ordinary single people, which the Plymouth Statutes of 1671 punished with a ten-pound fine, and that of engaged couples, who were fined only five pounds. As could be expected, the fines did not prevent the deviant behavior. In Groton, Connecticut, the local church records indicate that of its two hundred members between 1761 and 1775, sixty-six publicly confessed to fornication before marriage.

It is impossible to maintain belief in some absolute, unchanging code of sexual behavior within any religious or cultural boundary unless you care to restrict your vision to a single generation and then even further to a very narrow and homogeneous ethnic group within that generation.

There is, nevertheless, a much broader prejudice or blindness common among liberals, conservatives, Christians, Jews, and others alike, which comes down to the blunt assumption that the Old and New Testaments prohibit as totally immoral any and all use of sexual intercourse outside the marital union.

But is this true?

Rabbi Borowitz says that "yet neither the Torah, the rest of the Bible, the Mishnah, nor the Talmud contains a law prohibiting premarital sexual relations." Many leading Christian biblical scholars today agree with this appraisal of the Old Covenant tradition.

"The New Testament," according to the Presbyterian document, "contains no record of Jesus' teachings concerning most matters of sexual behavior. It would be proper to assume that his concern for particular expressions of human sexuality would have been based on *the way they might serve or injure human communion, whether with God or with other persons.*" This last phrase, which I italicized, raises the crucial question of

moral principles and guidelines: how are we to judge the morality of a particular expression of human sexuality if on the specific issue of premarital intercourse there is no black-and-white
prescription from Christ and the Old Testament? We will take
up that serious question in Chapter Ten. Meanwhile let me
pursue this biblical assumption.

What about Paul and the other apostles, especially Paul,
for he appears very scathing in his denunciations of fornication?
Snoek points out that "placed in the situation of having to
reflect on what attitude the Christian should take to a pagan
ethos, [Paul] included *porneia* among the works of the flesh
which excluded one from the Kingdom. But recent authorities
cast doubt on the absolute nature of this prohibition. Furthermore, just what does St. Paul mean by *porneia*? [Incest? Sacred
cultic prostitution? Ordinary prostitution? Exploitative sex? Or
every form of sexual relations outside marriage?] And on whose
authority does he condemn it—is it in virtue of a precept of the
Lord's, or the apostolic interpretation of the gospel ethos for
that time and place, or a personal interpretation? Without a precise reply to these questions [which we cannot provide at the
present], it is difficult to evaluate the exact import of Paul's
pronouncement." What Snoek, the Presbyterian authors, and
others indicate is that most, if not all, of the denunciations of
fornication in the Old and New Testaments may very well refer
to exploitative and depersonalizing acts since they appear in "the
context of lists of antisocial and personally destructive forms of
conduct which characterize 'the unrighteous.' " *Porneia* seems
very much focused on the risk of being enticed into idolatry—
a risk that an Israelite or Christian ran by consorting with the
sacred prostitutes of Baal, Canaan, and the Greeks. The antisocial aspect of *porneia* is also evident in the injustice imposed
on the father of a maiden who is deprived of a proper bride-
price if his daughter is not a virgin, and on the husband, who
then cannot be certain that his wife's first-born child is his
legitimate heir.

This does not exhaust the question of true premarital intercourse and the advisability of trial marriages, but since many of
the sexual relations that occur among single people are not truly
premarital, we must deal with this facet.

In discussing dating, the authors of the Presbyterian statement highlight some helpful insights into the problem. They
note, for instance, that the pattern of dating has changed radically in the last half century. Today dating is a form of courtship only incidentally related to marriage and it is certainly
carried on largely in isolation from the older generation.
Dating begins earlier today than ever before in human history,
while today's youth are maturing sexually far earlier. Their parents, infatuated with the myth of marriage, and worried about
the popularity of their offspring, push them into dating and
even courtship long before they are emotionally mature enough
to handle this human relationship. Even worse, they are sent
off with "appropriate parental admonitions"—appropriate in the
parents' minds, but hardly relevant to their offspring. Often
without even a basic understanding of the facts of life, the youth
of today are "left to their own and their peer group's resources
to weave an acceptable ethical pattern for themselves. Not surprisingly, many adolescents manage this badly, with results that
perplex and sometimes anger their elders." This pressured dating pattern then frequently results in early experiences with
sexual intercourse "badly out of phase with developing emotional maturity," in an increased incidence of venereal disease,
and in out-of-wedlock pregnancies.

Courageously, the Presbyterian document moves on to the
gut question, asking whether "abstinence or sublimation [is] the
only advice the church will have to give to single persons. . . . Our
standards and teachings about premarital sexual conduct *assume
that the practices and restraints which are being recommended
are justified in terms of their value in preparing the couple for
successful adjustment to marriage* [italics mine]. But what of the
person who never marries, or who, having been married, is once

again single?" The answer reached is simple but cutting: "Sexual expression with the goal of developing a caring relationship is an important aspect of personal existence and cannot be confined to the married and the about-to-be-married."

Since we are limiting ourselves here and in the next two chapters to the pertinent conclusions of various theologians and of religious statements, and not delving into the moral and ethical guidelines behind these conclusions, let me move on to a conclusion offered in the Quaker statement, Towards a Quaker View of Sex. "The Christian standard of chastity should not be measured by a physical act, but should be a standard of human relationship, applicable within marriage as well as outside it." Condemning exploitation in any form, this group of Friends agree that "wherever the most transient relationship has, as it may have, an element of true tenderness and mutual giving and receiving, it has in it something of good." Furthermore, "it is right and proper that many boys and girls and young men and women should fall in and out of love a number of times before they marry."

At its April, 1964 meeting the British Council of Churches appointed a working committee "to prepare a Statement of the Christian case for abstinence from sexual intercourse before marriage and faithfulness within marriage, taking full account of responsible criticisms, and to suggest means whereby the Christian position may be effectively presented to the various sections of the community." The Working Party, headed by the Reverend Kenneth Greet, chairman of the British Council of Churches Advisory Group on Sex, Marriage, and the Family, did not "affirm as Christian the rule that sexual intercourse should be confined with the married state." Despite this contradiction of their mandate, their report was accepted by the Council because it "has much to contribute of value to the contemporary discussion of moral questions by both Christians and non-Christians." This ambivalence of the British Council of Churches echoes the contradiction which emerged in the Presbyterian General Assembly when its task-force document was accepted and then contradicted by a motion from the floor.

Dr. Michael Valente is one of the first and still very few laymen to serve as chairman of theology at a large Catholic university in the United States, Seton Hall University in New Jersey. Thus his bold and at times acerbic conclusions in *Sex: The Radical View of a Catholic Theologian* are critical to our summary here. Noting that "sexual activity is tied to one's total development as a . . . person," Valente concludes that "if human sexuality can have a non-procreative purpose to fulfill, then it is at least questionable that this purpose is fulfilled exclusively in marriage. . . . The separation of human sexuality in itself from human sexuality as procreative," Valente argues, "leaves open the possibility that where it is made non-procreative—whether in circumstances that are marital or non-marital, heterosexual or non-heterosexual, inseminative or not—it does not have to be surrounded by the kinds of restrictions hitherto placed on it. If human sexuality is made non-procreative, then it must be judged on its own merits, by what it contributes in a particular situation to the growth and mutual . . . creativeness of the two persons involved."

In a similar vein, the Reverend Eugene Kennedy, a highly respected Catholic psychologist, accepts premarital intercourse as part of the human growth process, "as a growth problem, and the moral question, as I see it, is whether we deal intelligently and sensitively with this or not." Father Kennedy's book is interestingly titled *What a Modern Catholic Believes about Sex.*

Rustum and Della Roy, the authors of *Honest Sex: A Revolutionary Sex Ethic by and for Concerned Christians,* have been very active in Protestant church communities and programs. More to our interest here, they have helped form the novel Christian Community experiments Koinonia, for students, and the Sycamore Community, for adults. Their book grew out of discussions in the Sycamore Community over a period of years.

"To sum up: Christians should immediately desist from putting so much emphasis on the occurrence or nonoccurrence of premarital coitus as such. The word *virginity* should be de-emphasized, since its reclamation in the near future is hopeless. Rightness or wrongness has nothing, absolutely nothing, to do with whether or not physical juxtaposition of sex organs has occurred."

Disillusionment with the institution of marriage as they have experienced it in the nuclear family and in frequent broken or unhappy homes has led an increasing number of young people into more or less stable but informal non-marital relations that go under the labels of "living together" or the more traditional "common law marriage," which some states recognize legally.

Snoek points out that the Christian churches have always recognized both in their legal structures and in their theology a whole series of "marital states" which approach but do not attain the fullness of the Christian ideal, the indissoluble monogamous sacramental marriage. So he finds no grounds on which to reject the moral acceptability of a couple living together without benefit of church and/or state legitimization as long as the Christian ideal is upheld and encouraged. But the casualness of cohabitation without legal marriage bonds so common today has upset not a few Americans. This upset is likely the reason behind the introduction of a bill in the New Hampshire State Legislature in 1971, stipulating that "unattached" couples living together for thirty days "shall be deemed to be married" as far as "all the obligations of support" are concerned.

In some afterthoughts on her proposal for trial marriage, Margaret Mead argues forcefully that merely living together will not work.

Public reactions to Dr. Mead's proposal for the two-step system of marriage were very negative. Dr. Mead has found that most people "want to reserve the word 'marriage' for a commitment that they can feel is permanent and final, no matter how often the actual marriages fail." She notes, however, that there has been some recognition of the need for change: the growing awareness of the population problem, an increasing availability of effective contraceptives, and a clamoring of young people for a new morality "that will put some kind of seal of approval on premarital sex relations."

This last element is important to any overview of the problems of young people today, especially of those in college. The crucial and positive aspect of the situation is that the young are seeking a new set of relevant *standards*, not some utopian license to do as they please. Instead of implicitly threatening their parents with an illegitimate pregnancy, they are taking the opposite tack and demanding the right to a full sex life without the threat of pregnancy and without marriage. "Why get married when we are not ready? Why can't we just live together? With the Pill there will be no illegitimate children. No one's reputation will be ruined. No one will be trapped into marriage and besides we can finish our education."

On college campuses all over the country there is more than enough freedom for students so inclined to do whatever they like in the way of sex. With such freedom, why should good students push their parents, the dormitory directors, and deans for approval of their premarital sex by opening the dormitories to twenty-four-hour unrestricted visiting? This is not rebellion! Far from it. These students want the approval of society and their parents. In some way they want to be told that their appraisal and their solution of the situation is valid and moral. They have learned that sexual relations are an important factor in their growth as persons. They also know how disastrous early marriage can be to their education and its financial prospects. They are willing to wait for marriage but honestly wonder why this also means they must wait for full sexual expression.

Is living together the only solution, tolerated by parents because they cannot or will not offer a positive solution of their own? Will living together, as it is now understood by society,

solve the problem? Or must we in some way socially and formally recognize living together as a true trial marriage? Margaret Mead is firmly convinced that a tolerated form of living
together will not work, even if it appears to be the only practical development on the horizon. A tolerated living together
has definite social risks, because it is only tolerated. Students
living together are still subject to suspension or even dismissal
from many schools. Even when school officials and dormitory
directors close their eyes and parents do not object to their
children living together in coed dorms, the local community
can become very irate about "immorality on campus." Parents
who allow their sons or daughters to enter into a serious and
responsible relationship with another person, whether they are
engaged or not, are likely to be severely censured by neighbors
and friends who still adhere to the old standards. More important, though, is that this toleration is not what the young
people are seeking. They want a new set of socially acceptable
standards for their behavior.

Given the dilemma of resistance to any official acceptance of
trial marriages and the serious drawbacks of tolerated informal
premarital relations, where do we turn? Dr. Mead was not at
all optimistic about the immediate prospects in her *Redbook*
article. "I believe we have to say at present: If you want the
experience of full-time companionship with someone you love
—and this is what you should want . . . you had better get
legally married, use contraceptives responsibly and risk divorce
later. You are risking even more if you don't."

I do not feel quite as pessimistic about the situation. I admit
the dangers and risks of informal living together today, but
these are lessening with every day. And the mass media are
playing a major role in this transition on many levels.

I wonder, for instance, how many devotees of television have
noticed a subtle shift in the image of family programs over the
past decade or so. With increasing frequency premarital relations are being dealt with openly and frankly in the "soap

operas." And even a new form of single life is cropping up: the single-parent family, which carefully beats around the bush of a new option for single people but at the same time is psychologically conditioning us for the social acceptance of a pattern of life society commonly rejected even through the Second World War.

Consider the following television shows: *Bonanza* with its champion bachelor-father, Ben Cartwright; *The Rifleman* with his son, Mark; *Bachelor Father*; *My Three Sons* which moved out of the category when Fred MacMurray married a widow with a daughter; *The Courtship of Eddie's Father* with another bachelor-father.

And the single mothers: Doris Day, the champion widow finishing among the top-ten shows several years; *The Big Valley*; Diahann Carroll, a black widow; Loretta Young; Lucille Ball, a widow with two different sets of offspring, friends, and bosses; Hope Lang's double-Emmied *The Ghost and Mrs. Muir*; *The Brady Bunch* which spawned the movie *Yours, Mine and Ours* with widower Henry Fonda; *The Partridge Family* and Shirley Jones, the singing widow with five kids to raise. A very real message about family life is being conveyed by these shows, and their popularity indicates that the message is not too alien to the American public, for reasons that are mostly subconscious.

In Sweden one child in every ten under the age of sixteen is living in one-parent families. Denmark is becoming increasingly worried about the rising number of single-parent families. In the United States figures from the Federal Census Bureau indicate that almost one in ten white families and three out of ten black families are headed by women in single-parent households.

So far the television message has been limited to the socially acceptable widow and widower as a single parent. No television series has yet dealt with a divorced father or mother as a theme, yet millions of such single parents together with those contemplating separation provide a high popularity for these shows, however subliminally.

The single-parent phenomenon is further complicated today by the increasing number of young people who decide to have a child even though they are not married. It was not too long ago that an unwed mother who kept her child was a social outcast, left to her own means by her family and by society. Even the extreme popularity of Ingrid Bergman suffered severely when she bore a child out of wedlock to Roberto Rosselini.

But today our nationwide illegitimacy rate is 9 percent, which means that over a third of a million babies are born each year in this country to single mothers. Large urban centers have an even higher rate; San Francisco, for instance, has a rate of 16 percent.

Recently this factor has been coupled with a reversal of the Ingrid Bergman reaction, for today a celebrity's decision to have a child without being married is often a boost to fame and career. By mid-1971, well-known happily unwed parents included Vanessa Redgrave; Maureen O'Sullivan's two daughters, Mia and Tisa Farrow; Keith Richard, one of the Rolling Stones; singer Tony Bennett; and two of the Jefferson Airplane, Paul Kantner and Grace Slick.

Miss Slick explained some of her reasons for having a baby without marrying its father, Paul Kantner, in a press interview. "It's something I felt I should experience as a human being. If my mother tried it, she'd have problems. Her friends would give her a lot of garbage and they wouldn't come around to play bridge. But my friends don't care what I do."

In July, 1971, Northern Ireland's militant civil-rights leader and the British Parliament's youngest member, Bernadette Devlin, announced that she was pregnant. A Roman Catholic representing a very traditional Irish constituency, Miss Devlin declined to identify the father, adding, "My moral position on abortion is such that I would not be able to justify it to myself." Several members of Parliament called for her resignation without effect, and when Miss Devlin gave birth to a six-pound girl in August, 1971, she noted that her "situation is of no great significance when compared against the problems we all face in Ireland."

She, and most political commentators with her, was uncertain whether her pregnancy would cost her support in Ulster.

These, of course, are celebrities, but the filtering process has already begun so that an increasing number of single women are considering the possibility of deliberately having a baby even though they are not married. The twenty-nine-year-old woman who called me on a Sunday morning in December, 1970 is far from unique.

In large cities the response to the single mother has not been moral indignation so typical of past generations, but rather the introduction of special high-school programs for unwed mothers. In New York City, where unmarried mothers in grades seven through twelve doubled between 1962 and 1969, five special schools have been opened solely for pregnant students. Courses in infant care, health, and birth control are integrated into the regular courses, and a realistic manual for school administrators and teachers has been issued. In Atlanta, Washington, D.C., and the whole state of Maryland, unwed pregnant students are expected to remain in the regular classes. About 175 programs were in operation around the country by mid-1971 to meet the special educational, medical, and psychological needs of single mothers.

The shift in social atmosphere is evident even in changes in our sloth-like legal structures. In the summer of 1968, the Supreme Court ruled unconstitutional a Louisiana law which stated that an illegitimate child could not claim damages for the wrongful death of a parent. Since then other courts have modified age-old laws limiting the rights of illegitimate children. In many states illegitimate children can now inherit from their acknowledged parents, recover workmen's compensation for the death of a parent, and claim legal parental support. Both the U.S. Navy and Air Force have been charged in court with unfair discrimination for trying to discharge unwed pregnant servicewomen.

New York City is an anomaly in many ways, but it is perhaps still significant that a 1970 in-depth study revealed that 90 percent of the unwed mothers in that city in 1964 kept their children and have blended well into society. Most of the children who were not kept by their mothers were living with relatives, usually the maternal grandparents. About 50 percent of the mothers had married, half of them marrying the child's father. Half of the mothers were receiving public assistance, but only a third of the whole group had been on public assistance for over a year.

In Bonn, Germany, where illegitimate children were automatically assigned to the state for custody and their upbringing and education were in the hands of state juvenile workers, a new law was passed in July, 1970 granting custody to the unwed mother. Inheritance rights for legitimate and illegitimate children were equalized. And acknowledged fathers, who in the past made up the difference between what the child needed and what the mother could provide, are now assessed according to their own means.

When the problem of single parents has been faced by the state and educational systems, however, it has been very one-sided on the female side. The responsibilities and the psychological, emotional, and educational needs of the male responsible for the pregnancy are simply and universally ignored. This policy probably will change as the phenomenon of the single father becomes more prevalent.

In 1965 in Oregon, a 38-year-old bachelor musician, Tony Piazzam, became what is likely the first male in the United States to legally adopt a child. And in Mill Valley, California, a 34-year-old bachelor teacher liked kids so much he hated to see them go home each day. His solution was to adopt a hard-to-place 2-year-old boy, David, from an interracial background.

Other bachelor-fathers have joined these two, relying on their landladies, girl friends, aunts, and friends to provide a feminine and maternal influence in the raising of their "progeny."

At the same time the attitude of the law and the courts as to custody in divorce cases has been slowly changing. In London, 20-year-old Michael Cooper won the right to raise his infant son when his short-lived marriage terminated in divorce. With no desire to remarry, Cooper expressed an interesting thought: "I wish you could just ask beautiful women to have babies for you. Or any woman you liked, or who had something you admired. Ideally, I'd like a big house full of children—all different colors, shapes and sizes." Commenting on this in *Future Shock*, Alvin Toffler asks: "Romantic? Unmanly? Perhaps. Yet attitudes like these will be widely held by men in the future."

Ten years ago I gave a weekend retreat in the Washington, D.C., area for Young Christian Workers, the American version of the Jocists of France, and found that many of the young ladies were pessimistic about their chances of finding a mate in the female-dominated Washington area. Many of them openly spoke of having a baby if they were not married by the age of 30. More recently I have found this attitude more common, and the reasons expand beyond the scarcity of gentlemen. One prominent reason is the experience of many young women with men of their own age who are unwilling to accept the integrity of what I would call moderately liberated women. The men want to marry an intelligent, educated, charming, sophisticated girl, but they want her to stay at home, even if that means a three-room apartment with one or two children. If young men continue to react negatively to the emergence of women as persons with equal rights, we can expect more and more single mothers.

The problems faced by a single parent are fairly obvious; most of them focus on the task of providing a normal balance of male and female influences for the child, and on the social acceptance of the situation, so that the child is not a victim of unnecessary prejudice at school or around home. But the economics of this choice are a very real, if often overlooked, problem. This is particularly evident with divorced women who have the custody of their children and yet must work full or part time to supplement an insufficient amount of child support and alimony from the father. The increasing popularity of social groups for single parents is an indication that some effort is being made to help these people in their problems, whether the role of single parent was forced on them or whether it was their own deliberate choice.

There is one final group of single people we must discuss if our chapter is to be complete. Like all the others, this group is experiencing great turmoil over questions of identity. But I think the religious communities of nuns and brothers are suffering more than other single people because their image was so clearly stereotyped and because their whole training conditioned them to think of themselves as somehow asexual.

Years ago Owen Garrigan, biochemist and priest at Seton Hall University, asked whether a priest would violate his vow of celibacy if he donated a semen sample to a sperm bank. More recently I have asked in public lectures whether a religious sister would violate her vows by supplying an egg for fertilization in a test tube with her brother-in-law's semen and subsequent implantation in her sterile sister's womb. Or whether serving as a substitute mother, via embryo transplant, for her sister's child would violate these same vows. These questions are beyond the point, but by going far beyond the issue they tend to highlight that issue in a way we could not do otherwise. Also, as theologians continue to remove the dualistic, black-and-white philosophical overtones that have colored our thinking on celibacy and our understanding of the religious life from the days of the ascetics and anchorites in the desert down to the present, the basic issue is sharpened into two questions. First, is there any true Christian value that can be attributed to the totally celibate life, simply because it does not involve sexual intercourse, whether or not such would deliberately exclude procreation? And second, with today's religious communities moving farther and farther out of the convent, both psychologically and physically, is there any real difference between the member of a modernized religious community and a very dedicated single woman not in such a formal community? If not, it is logical to ask whether the ethical conclusions touched on in this chapter apply equally to members of religious communities as well as to the ordinary single man and woman.

In the past, celibacy has been defended as a prophetic, eschatological witness to the state of things to come, to the virginal life after death. This, I believe, is tenuous and risky theology. The value of celibacy and virginity, I am convinced, must rest on their witness to the fact that men and women can share a deep personal intimacy and a deep emotional relationship without these necessarily being expressed in sexual intercourse.

Future shock can be toned down by anticipating the changes before they fall on us. But the young people of Harrad College are already with us, exploring, so perhaps the best we can hope to do today is ride into tomorrow with our eyes fixed on Marshall McLuhan's rearview mirror. This is the focus we shall use in the next six chapters.

Our rearview mirror should provide an insight into what is happening today and tomorrow and why. It should also give us a historical perspective that will help us understand why these changes are so shocking for an older generation. The young adults in the Harrad experiment may find this report of what is happening, its historical setting and shock value, all irrelevant, for they live psychologically in a timeless, ahistorical, instant world, in which the present alone exists. Perhaps our rearview mirror will break through this atemporal world of the younger generation with a new dimension even as it brings a maximum spanning of vision from a different angle to the older generation.

So far our rearview mirror has turned up some interesting options for the new species of human being—the sexually mature single person—some new challenges and some new responsibilities. Most basic is the choice young people and our society face in continuing to tolerate an increasing amount of informal living together or in working toward a social and religious acceptance of some form of trial and parental marriages. Social, moral, and religious guidelines and responsibilities have to be worked out to help young people handle the freedom and growth potential of the casual "non-premarital" relation. The same can be said for the new phenomenon of the single parent and his or her family, whether this results from widowhood or divorce and deliberate choice. Finally, in our furiously overmarried culture, we must give some serious thought to making this a more humane and fulfilling world for the single person who freely chooses to remain single, celibate or otherwise.

FIVE

Serial Polygamy, Infidelities, and Modern Affairs

MANY social institutions in American life are under attack, not just the institution of marriage. The trade unions, our educational system, the inflexible and monstrous corporate conglomorates, our capitalistic economy, all face serious challenges. In most cases, as with our institution of marriage, the main trouble stems from the fact that an environment very gradually created and molded a particular social structure to meet the specific needs of that environment, and then suddenly, often unexpectedly, just when everyone was content with the institution, the environment changed so drastically that the once effective structure is totally antiquated and inadequate. Traditional, sexually exclusive monogamy evolved in our Western society as an adaptation to a unique patriarchal agricultural and industrial environment. It reduced sexual tensions to a minimum, kept the family stable, and met the needs of the majority of the population. Today, the patriarchal and pastoral culture is fast expiring. Even the traditional individualistic industrial culture is changing radically. Result: traditional monogamy can no longer function as it once did so effectively.

Rustum and Della Roy, two dedicated and astute advocates of modifying and improving the present monogamous marriage, have highlighted four particular problem-causing elements in our changed environment which make a basic modification of traditional monogamy imperative.

1. Our eroticized environment, coupled with prosperity, mobility, and contraceptives, has made it infinitely more difficult to retain monogamy's monopoly on sex.

2. We face a vast increase in the number and variety of men/women contacts after marriage with no guidelines except that we are allowed only one spouse, one sex partner, and thus only one heterosexual relationship of any depth at all at one time.

3. Traditional monogamy is in trouble because it has failed to adjust to the possibility that marriages based on and judged by the satisfied interaction of two persons rather than on parental arrangement and economic slavery may years later become unlivable. Divorce was inconceivable in the past; today it is common. In 1969 there were 660,000 divorces in America. Yet society imposes a very heavy price for the "privilege" of being "let off the hook." This heavy price, however, may owe more to society's desire to protect happily married couples from the distinct danger posed by an abundance of "sex-starved divorcees" than to any desire to nurse and salvage unhappy marriages. A divorced woman, in particular, frequently finds that married women with whom she and her husband had been close and dear friends now treat her with a definite reserve and coolness. In the past many bantering jokes were safely exchanged by the couples about their mutual affection. Now, after the divorce, these same jokes suggest a real threat.

4. Traditional monogamy is also in trouble because it has denied a new and expanding segment of our population both a voice and a role in society. What voice or place do the single adult, the widowed, and the divorced have in much of our society? They are taxed far more heavily than the married. Companies judge them a risk in hiring because they are not "settled down." At formal dinners and other occasions where couples dominate, the single person throws everything out of whack.

They are at least subconsciously feared by the happily married. And most inhumanely, our monogamous culture has ruled that tens of millions of its members shall have no socially acceptable way of obtaining sexual satisfaction. As the Roys note in "Is Monogamy Outdated?" "Because sexual intimacy is potentially associated with all heterosexual relationships of any depth, [the single person] must also be denied such relationships." And this is no small minority we are speaking of! A society cannot survive monogamously unless it recognizes and adapts to the fact that only one third of the single thirty-five-year-old women, one in ten of the forty-five-year-old single women, and one in fifty of those over fifty will obtain a marriage license and permission to achieve sexual fulfillment.

To these problem-causing elements in our cultural environment, the Roys add four near-parallel characteristics of the modern American marriage which have helped speed its obsolescence.

Most basic of these is the very romantic myth of the "one and only love" which believes and demands that two persons can and should provide all the intimate companionship and fulfill all the needs of one another in an exclusive relationship for half or three-quarters of a century. This might have been feasible at least for women a few centuries back when they knew no other possibility save their estate as chattel without rights and as voiceless baby factories. But today life expectancy is nearly doubled, so that the "boredom and routine potential" is at least quadrupled. In addition, the liberation of wives has suddenly thrust them into the very unrealistic rat race of trying to be an efficient housekeeper, assistant school teacher of the new mathematics and other new subjects, chauffeur, active participant in the local P-TA, League of Women Voters, and church societies, lover and mistress, gourmet cook, part- or full-time employee in some outside business, social hostess, pediatrician, mother, and *bon vivant* companion for her husband. This variety may relieve boredom but it can become an impos-

sible frustrating task. In past generations the needs and responsibilities of both husband and wife to each other were minimal
in terms of human relations. Today husbands and wives face a
two-edged sword. The men, confronted with an ever more impersonal and cold world around them, turn to their wives for
warmth, understanding, companionship, and sexual communion.
But the wives, increasingly liberated from patriarchalism and the
kitchen, demand respect, egalitarian treatment as persons, enjoyment in their sexual relations, and the right and opportunity
to develop their personal talents fully.

A second damaging characteristic of today's monogamous
marriage is the belief that there should be no sex outside marriage, either before or after the ceremony. Yet premarital sex is
commonly practiced and at least silently tolerated by this same
culture. More serious as a contradiction, though, is the reduction
of fidelity to a very simplistic but nicely black-and-white prohibition of coitus with anyone other than one's spouse.

Most married persons define infidelity as adultery and nothing more. But as Brian Boylan rightly notes in the opening paragraph of his study, *Infidelity*, unfaithfulness "as it actually is
practiced by married men and women is much more extensive
and involved than simple adultery. In addition to sexual infidelity, there is emotional infidelity and psychological infidelity,
plus many lesser forms. A more accurate definition of infidelity
is that it takes place whenever a married person repeatedly has
to look outside the marriage for a need not fulfilled by the
person's spouse. *Need* is the key to this definition, for it indicates the importance of certain needs in everyone's life. It is the
rare couple who can be all things to one another. The gratifications which people expect from marriage are so varied and
demanding that the absence or denial of just one can send the
deprived partner stumbling into infidelity—that is, looking for
this need from another." Some of these expectations may be
unrealistic and grossly immature, but many of them can be
both realistic and reflective of a mature need which traditional

monogamy is not designed to meet. Defined in this context, today's monogamous marriage is in far deeper trouble than the data on adultery might indicate. Marriage experts commonly estimate that 60 percent of the married men and a third of the married women today engage in adultery sometime in their married lives. How realistic then is our image of the sexually exclusive monogamous marriage? And how common is its achievement?

Rustum Roy, in "The Obsolescence of Marriage, American-Style," reveals another dangerous characteristic of marriage today that is seldom mentioned by the experts, namely, the familial egotism so prevalent in our culture. "The family in many eras and especially in contemporary America has been in the majority of homes a noxious shield against the reality of Christian community. Only in a minority of homes has it been what Paul Tournier once called '. . . the school of the person,' the seed-bed for developing concerned, loving citizens." Each nuclear family, it seems, takes on an absolute priority on all demands for one's time, money, affections, and concern. To hell with all others, to put it bluntly. "It is just damned difficult to be any kind of a committed Christian with a family in the suburbs! . . . The rule is that the institution of marriage— American-style, as practiced by the majority—encourages selfishness, possessiveness, and exclusivity instead of a wide open sharing and openness. True, the marital contract should be understood to restrict exclusivity to [relationships and] sexuality, but the symbolic damage is done. Our culture says by its ideals: Marriage is sacred—the deepest interpersonal relationship is an exclusive one! If you share it you destroy it! Is *that* the Biblical message? How does that square with the battle cry of Christian evangelism from the early Church down to the missionary ideal: share everything for the cause?"

Phil Tracy, columnist for *The National Catholic Reporter*, has commented on another aspect of this familial egotism in terms of interpersonal relationships rather than the lack of social involvement suggested by the Roys. "If from more or less the time your sexual instincts blossomed, you have been sleeping with members of the opposite sex as either a prelude or encore to any serious attempt to get to know them, fidelity to one person comes to be much more than the limiting of your sex life to one partner. It becomes an insurmountable block to any kind of serious relationship with any member of the opposite sex."

The final defective myth that the Roys dissect for our inspection is the fantasy that divorce is somehow a failure and hence shameful. Vance Packard, in *The Sexual Wilderness*, sums up the most recent major survey of marriage thus: "In other words, a marriage made in the United States in the late 1960s has about a fifty-fifty chance of remaining even nominally intact." Clifford Adams, formerly head of the Child Development and Family Relations Center at Pennsylvania State University and an expert on family life, argues that the *real* divorce rate is somewhat worse: "Seventy-five percent of marriages are a 'bust.'" With California's new divorce law, nearly two out of three marriages terminate peacefully in divorce.

One out of every four bridegrooms in America has been to the altar before. One does not have to turn to the Orthodox tradition where a man is allowed three marriages to find a defect in our myth about marriage "until death do us part." As Jessie Bernard noted in *The Sex Game*, "Plural marriage is more extensive in our society today than it is in societies that permit polygamy—the chief difference being that we have institutionalized plural marriage serially or sequentially rather than contemporaneously." Our American tradition is not monogamy, but *serial polygamy!* Toffler labeled this fact "the best kept family secret of our Age of Transience."

Morton Hunt, in "The Future of Marriage," argues that since divorcing people are actually marrying people, "divorce is not a negation of marriage but a working cross between traditional monogamy and multiple marriage." Far from being a wasting illness, Hunt maintains that divorce and remarriage is a healthful adaptation, along with infidelity, which enables monogamy to survive in a time when patriarchal powers, privileges, and marital systems have become unworkable. Divorce in his view is not a radical change in the institution of marriage, but a "relatively minor modification of it and thoroughly supportive of most of its conventions."

In *Future Shock*, Toffler suggests that "rather than opting for some offbeat variety of the family, [most people] marry conventionally, they attempt to make it 'work,' and then, when the paths of the partners diverge beyond an acceptable point, they divorce or depart. Most of them go on to search for a new partner whose developmental stage, at that moment, matches their own. As human relationships grow more transient and modular, the pursuit of love becomes, if anything, more frenzied. But the temporal expectations change. As conventional marriage proves itself less and less capable of delivering on its promise of lifelong love, therefore, we can anticipate open public acceptance of temporary marriages." Toffler suggests a series of marriages, beginning with a trial marriage which may mature into a parental marriage of some type, giving way when the children leave home to a more *real* marriage of maturity which may well last until death of one of the partners, and finally a retirement marriage, possibly polygamous in character.

I cannot help but agree with Toffler that sequential polygamy is already a common feature of our marital scene. But beyond this I question his projection. As we move into a pluralism of male/female relations, and particularly as we come to accept more flexible forms of monogamy, a development I will deal with shortly, I believe that serial polygamy will become less popular than it is now. I also believe that flexible monogamy, which allows for occasional sexual relations with persons other than one's spouse within the context of a lifelong marriage, will be more popular than serial polygamy because it adapts better to the present pressures within a more stable framework.

"Fidelity" clearly appears to be a keystone to any discussion of the future of marriage and male/female relationships. Our classical definition is obviously inadequate. The debates over whether artificial insemination is legal or moral adultery, whether embryo transplants violate marital exclusivity, and similar totally new complications created by reproductive technology make this inadequacy painfully clear.

The question of marital fidelity becomes even more disturbing if we look at the anthropological data available on different cultures that are very much alive in our world today. Professors Ford and Beach of Yale University have studied the patterns of marriage and fidelity in 185 distinct cultures. Their conclusion is that our American mythic pattern of lifelong monogamy with sexual exclusivity is really an anomaly. Only 29 of the 185 cultures restrict marriage to one mate, and of these 29, only 9 completely disapprove of both premarital and extramarital relations. More significant is the fact that 72 of the 185 cultures actually approve of specific types of extramarital relations. In most of these, given the patriarchal orientation of most cultures, women are more restricted than men in their extramarital affairs. Even so, 10 percent of our known societies place no restrictions on extramarital sex for women, and 40 percent, according to Kinsey, allow it with special persons such as a brother-in-law or an honored guest or on special occasions such as seasonal festivals or even the wedding night. Until not too long ago various forms of the *droit du seigneur* were accepted by European society, with the bride being deflowered by the local prince, lord, or even the pastor.

Is it possible—considering today's mass communications and the intermingling of widely divergent customs, our mobility, the challenge of technology, and our information explosion— is it just possible that the image of monogamy and fidelity in our Judeo-Christian culture might be silently evolving? Not too long ago the Protestant churches began to accept divorce and remarriage; Roman Catholics are changing on birth control as the Protestants did earlier; premarital sex is tolerated, if not accepted openly. I am convinced that the evolution has reached the threshold of a revolution, both on the grassroots level of American life and in, of all places, theological circles, both Protestant and Roman Catholic. Evidence?

ITEM ONE: From a discussion between Jesuit theologian Thomas Wassmer and Professor Joseph Fletcher, well-known advocate of "situation ethics," in their book *Hello, Lovers: An Invitation to Situation Ethics:*

Wassmer: "I would not call an act adultery if it's an act done with loving concern."

Fletcher: "Why not, for heaven's sake? Adultery means an act of sexual intercourse with someone who is not one's spouse."

Wassmer: "I agree that this is the usual meaning of the term, and that the term *adultery* as so defined already has moral overtones, given to it by the legalists, but I don't think that we should accept this legalistic notion of adultery. I say that the mere presence of a man in the bed of a woman who is not his wife is not necessarily adultery."

Fletcher: "Then what would you call it?"

Wassmer: "I don't know precisely, but I would much rather describe an act of this kind done out of loving concern by some term other than adultery, some kind of circumlocution."

Some time later, their discussion turned again to the question of adultery and Father Wassmer objected to the term: "I'm not going to use their [legalistic] language."

Fletcher: ". . . I say that the morality of adultery depends on the situation."

Reporter: "Adultery in the sense of exploitative sexuality is intrinsically evil for you, is it not?"

Wassmer: "No, because adultery defined in terms of exploitative sexuality is not an act, it's a disvalue. But whether any given act embodies this disvalue is simply something that we cannot determine. I am questioning the existence of intrinsically evil acts [such as adultery has been labeled by the legalists]."

Do you recall that first statement of Father Wassmer's, "I *would not call an act adultery if it's an act done with loving concern*"?

ITEM TWO: Methodist theologian Edward C. Hobbs is professor of theology and hermeneutics (the interpretation of scriptures) at the Graduate Theological Union and the Church Divinity School of the Pacific and the author of a dozen books on theology. In his essay "An Alternate Model from a Theological Perspective," Hobbs offers a pungent two-sentence prophecy of marriage in the near future.

"Marriage would be, as in all societies, the institution whereby men and women are joined for the purpose of founding and maintaining a family; the special kind of dependence, however, would be limited to reproduction of offspring by the couple. *Sexual relationships would not be limited to the marriage bond in any special way whatever, except of course that pregnancy-control would be utilized at all times outside the marriage and always within it except when children are planned as a result* [italics mine]."

ITEM THREE: From the United Presbyterian statement on human sexuality: "Sexual fidelity is important because it both symbolizes and supports the total fidelity of the marriage relationship, which in turn has always been suggestive to Christians of the fidelity of God to his people and of Christ to his church.

"We recognize that there may be exceptional circumstances where extra-marital sexual activity may not be contrary to the interests of a faithful concern for the well-being of the marriage partner, as might be the case when one partner suffers permanent mental or physical incapacity. But an exception is an exception and not a new rule. Such judgments finally have to be made by and of the responsibility of the person who takes the exception. Our concern for the church is that it might see the question of marital fidelity in broad enough terms to understand that faithfulness in marriage and coital exclusivity are not synonymous. It is quite possible to be coitally monogamous yet maritally unfaithful. [An equally interesting and important question, I think, is whether the inverse of this statement is also true: can one be faithful and yet have extra- or co-marital relations?] In any case, the church must not leave the Christian who finds himself in an exceptional circumstance with nothing more reliable than his own rationalizations to fall back upon as an ethical resource."

ITEM FOUR: From *Towards a Quaker View of Sex:* "It can be said that the Society [of Friends] has recognized recently that love cannot be confined to a rigid pattern: '. . . For some, there is a monogamy so entire that no other love ever touches it; but others "fall in love" time and time again, and must learn to make riches of their affection without destroying their marriage or their friends. [In Charles Williams' *Religion and Love in Dante,* "falling in love" is taken to mean seeing the image of God, a type of beatific vision. It should lead one to God, but when the object of love is not one's wife, Williams feels that the vision should be accepted gratefully but with "hands off."] Let us thank God for what we share, which enables us to understand; and for the infinite variety in which each marriage stands alone.' [An extract from the 1960 statement, "Christian Faith and Practice."]

"Some Friends were disturbed by this statement, fearing that it condoned extra-marital relationships, but one of those primarily responsible for the drafting made it clear that the reference to falling in love was intended to be 'a statement of observed fact' and that the statement about 'making riches of their affection' recognizes that 'there is a problem; that it involves responsibilities to others beyond themselves; and that there may be various ways of tackling it—not the same way for everybody.' "

ITEM FIVE: In preparing their statement *Sex and Morality*, the committee members for the British Council of Churches asked themselves several very hard, and crucial, questions. Some of the more basic ones are included with responses in one section of the report devoted to major objections that their report might easily stir up. One objection was the following:

"But you will surely agree that in one important matter you are out of step with the main body of Christian judgment, namely in your refusal to endorse the view that chastity consists in obedience to an invariable rule which forbids sexual intercourse outside marriage."

"It may be so, but we do not wish our position to be misrepresented. We have not said that all rules are valueless. We have tried to show that rules by themselves are an inadequate basis for morality. No rule can cover all the varied and complex situations in which men and women find themselves. Moreover, an action which is in outward conformity to a rule may nonetheless be immoral because the motive and spirit behind it are wrong. Our reluctance to spell out the meaning of chastity in terms of basic rules is not due to any lack of conviction about the value of chastity, but rather to a desire to give adequate content to the word."

ITEM SIX: John A. T. Robinson, dean of Trinity College, Cambridge, former Bishop of Woolrich, and author of *Honest to God*, offers an unusual insight in his latest book, *Christian Freedom in a Permissive Society*: "The decisive thing in the moral judgment [of extramarital sexual activity] is not the line [of the marriage bond] itself, but the presence or absence of love at its deepest level."

ITEM SEVEN: Deane William Ferm, dean of the College Chapel, and lecturer in religion at Mount Holyoke College, is an ordained minister. After contributing many articles to major religious publications and secular magazines, Dr. Ferm decided to spend his sabbatical in Sweden studying the relationship between the churches and the developing moral standards of that country. Out of this experience came a book, *Responsible Sexuality Now*, from which we borrow the following conclusion:

"There may be, for some couples, another alternative to divorce. This is the matter of extramarital relationships. We can state unequivocally that for most couples extramarital affairs are probably a dangerous alternative, primarily because most people have been reared to have guilt feelings about such 'illicit' encounters. Moreover, fidelity is such an important value to a successful marriage that anything that subverts fidelity should be discouraged. . . .

"We must give consideration, however, to some couples who can either save their marriage or strengthen an already existing happy marriage through extramarital experiences. Are such extramarital relationships morally wrong? Once again we should answer that question in terms of the total context and not in terms of the sex act itself. If extramarital sex harms the already existing human relationships, then it is morally wrong. If extramarital sex enhances the human dimension, then it may be morally proper. As Erik Erikson has suggested: 'Fidelity without a sense of diversity can become an obsession and a bore; diversity without a sense of fidelity, an empty relativism.' We are not suggesting here an empty relativism which has no sense of fidelity and perspective; this is morally wrong. But we are suggesting that a sense of diversity is not always improper."

Coping with the techniques, both practical and theological, whereby our traditional marriage pattern can evolve within the Christian tradition toward a more realistic balance between the tensions of modern life, the male/female potentials, and the social requirements of family life is a colossal task. *The task is especially difficult when a solution obviously involves modifying the very taproot of our modern image of marriage, the conception of fidelity.* Each piece of evidence offered above in some way orbits this conception of fidelity, emphasizing the urgent need to modify it some way. All the theologians, except Wassmer and Hobbs, appear perplexed and somewhat ambivalent on this issue, which is understandable, and perhaps even unavoidable at this point of the discussion.

Normally, in theological discussions as disturbing and revolutionary as this, one can turn to the scholarly and unemotional German theologians, who usually can tackle even the most sensitive issue with a much envied objective tranquillity. This makes the response of at least one German theologian, the Redemptorist C. Jaime Snoek, even more interesting. Snoek has no difficulty handling the morality of premarital sex, polygamy, and common-law or trial marriages in an open, creative way. But when he comes to deal with the question of extramarital affairs and "fleeting amorous encounters," Snoek's staid, scholarly approach evaporates into a series of poetic, sharply punctuated observations and questions: "It seems as though a cosmic force, held back for centuries, has now burst the old dam, and is flooding everywhere like a tidal wave. Perhaps it is the historical destiny of man in the last part of this century to channel this force once more into service of the new man. A new era is certainly coming upon us, and is going to affect all our institutions, even marriage, the basic institution of our present civilization. Humanity is entering on a new and awesome adventure. It is as though we were setting foot for the first time on a new planet, not knowing what we are likely to meet. . . .

"How will the man of tomorrow live his sexual life? Will he have won greater inner freedom? Will he have destroyed the tyranny of genitality and replaced it by a more discreet form of eroticism, more widespread, more communicative, permeating all human relationships?"

This is not answering the question at hand, except in a circular way implicit in the positive and creative tone of Snoek's observations and questions. The question disturbs him, and this is obvious. Nevertheless he admits, "It remains to be seen whether the institutionalization of sexuality in the sacrament of marriage excludes any other sexual activity as being incompatible and immoral."

The ambivalence of Snoek and other open theologians may very well stem from a certain schizophrenic element in the history of Western man's image of the extramarital relationship. During the past two thousand years Western man appears to have been sharpening his focus and rising to confrontation over two contradictory codes of behavior. One is the common Christian tradition which allows (or tolerates) sexual relations only in marriage and abhors all extramarital relations as the mortal enemy of monogamy. The other code is the more liberal tradition, with faint roots in the Greek, Roman, Teutonic, and Celtic cultures, which came to flower unexpectedly and inexplicably after the advent of courtly love. This double current has resulted in some intriguing schizoid behavior, especially in the United States. To illustrate my point let me complement the brief history of Western man's approach to sexuality that we sketched in Chapter Two with a brief outline here of Western society's understanding of the extramarital affair.

Outside the Hebrew tradition the love between a man and woman as we understand it simply did not exist until well into the Middle Ages, or even the Renaissance. First of all, women were not considered fully human, but chattel at worst and unformed misbegotten males at best. Hence true interpersonal love was impossible: the female was not really capable of such a human reaction. Thus, as C. S. Lewis indicates in his classic *The Allegory of Love*, the relationship between men and women seldom rose above "mere sensuality or domestic comfort, except to be treated as a tragic madness . . . which plunges otherwise sane people (usually women) into crime and disgrace. Such is the love of Medea, of Phaedra, of Dido; and such the love from which maidens pray that the gods may protect them. At the other end of the scale we find the comfort and utility of a good wife acknowledged: Odysseus loves Penelope as he loves the rest of his home and possessions, and Aristotle rather grudgingly admits that the conjugal relation may now and then rise to the same level as the virtuous friendship between good men. But this has plainly very little to do with 'love' in the modern or medieval sense."

This is a point which Morton Hunt, Robert Rimmer, and others apparently miss in the reading and interpretation of the love poetry of the ancient Greeks and Romans, particularly that of Ovid. In the piping times of the Roman Empire, about the time that Christ began preaching and before the dark figure of Tiberius crossed the stage, C. S. Lewis informs us, "Ovid sat down to compose for the amusement of a society which well understood him an ironically didactic poem on the art of seduction. The very design of his ART OF LOVE presupposes an audience to whom love is one of the minor peccadilloes of life, and the joke consists in treating it seriously—in writing a treatise, with rules and examples *en règle* for the nice conduct of illicit loves. It is funny, as the ritual solemnity of old gentlemen over their wine is funny. Food, drink, and sex are the oldest jokes in the world; and one familiar form of the joke is to be serious about them. From this attitude the whole tone of the ARS AMATORIA flows. In the first place Ovid naturally introduces the god Amor with an affectation of religious awe—just as he would have introduced Bacchus if he had written an ironic ART OF GETTING DRUNK. Love thus becomes a great and jealous god, his service an arduous *militia*: offend him who dares, Ovid is his trembling captive. In the second place, being thus mockingly serious about the appetite, he is of necessity mockingly serious about the woman. The real objects of Ovid's 'love', no doubt, he would have ordered out of the room before the serious conversation about books, or politics, or family affairs began. The moralist may treat them seriously, but the man of the world (such as Ovid) certainly does not. But inside the convention of the poem they are the 'demnition charmers', the mistresses of his fancy and the arbitresses of his fate. They rule him with a rod of iron, lead him a slave's life. As a result we find this sort of advice addressed to the 'prentice lover:

> Go early ere th'appointed hour to meet
> The fair, and long await her in the street.
> Through shouldering crowds on all her errands run,
> Though graver business wait the while undone.
> If she commands your presence on her way
> Home from the ball to lackey her, obey!
> Or if from rural scenes she bids you, 'come',
> Drive if you can, if not, then walk, to Rome,
>   and let not Dog-star heats nor drifted load
>   of whitening snows deter you from the road.
> Cowards, fly hence! Our general, Love, disdains
>   your lukewarm service in his long campaigns."

No one who has caught the spirit of Ovid, C. S. Lewis maintains, will misunderstand this irony. The adulterous conduct Ovid recommends is in his mind both shameful and absurd. It is a kind of comic confession of the depths to which this ridiculous appetite of love can bring a man. It is also shrewd advice in the art of fooling the latest wench to catch your fancy. As Ovid sarcastically but wisely recommends: "Don't visit her on her birthday, it costs too much."

It was not really until the advent of courtly love in medieval southern France that anything close to what we understand by adultery as an extramarital love affair came into being. The early angelic character of courtly love did not endure long, as we noted in Chapter Two, and as it disintegrated the poetry of Ovid and others in the Greco-Roman-Teutonic-Celtic tradition gained a new popularity but in a grossly misunderstood version. As C. S. Lewis notes with his own touch of irony, "the very same conduct which Ovid ironically recommends is now somehow seriously recommended by the courtly tradition."

In the age of courtly love two things still prevented men from connecting their ideal of romantic and passionate love with marriage, and hence from considering the possibility of an extramarital love affair as we know this today. The first was the actual practice of feudal marriages that had nothing to do with love. All matches were matches of interest, and worse, of an interest—political, social, economic—that would surely change before long. Sooner or later the alliance no longer served its original need, and then the husband's object was to get rid of the lady as quickly as possible. C. S. Lewis rightly points out that "marriages were frequently dissolved. The same woman who was the lady and 'the dearest dread' of her vassals was often little better than a piece of property to her husband. He was master in his own house. So, far from being a natural channel for the new kind of love, marriage was rather the drab background against which that love stood out in all the contrast of its new tenderness and delicacy. The situation is indeed a very simple one, and not peculiar to the Middle Ages. Any idealization of sexual love, in a society where marriage is purely utilitarian, must begin by being an idealization of adultery."

The second factor that prevented love and marriage from mixing in the Middle Ages was the universal belief that passionate love itself was wicked, whether the object of one's passion was one's wife or not. The man who loved his wife too ardently was obviously guilty of adultery according to the moralists of the day. It was not so much the act of sexual intercourse, however, as it was the immorality of the desire that accompanied the act. The medieval view of love, according to Lewis, does find "room for innocent sexuality: what it does not find room for is passion, whether romantic or otherwise." But the newly emerged reality of courtly love does mark something very new, something unique in human history. Courtly love, in the opinion of C. S. Lewis, is one of the rare, one of the three or four real changes in human sentiment to occur in man's history. In the courtly-love tradition adultery and the extramarital love affair as we know it first became possible.

The troubadour's ladylove, like Dante's Beatrice and Lancelot's beloved Guinevere, was invariably the aristocratic wife of another man. How natural in a castle filled with bachelor knights, troubadours, a few wenches, serfs, and one or two noble ladies to rhapsodize the unattainable, especially when everyone was convinced that to endure, the new romantic love between a man and woman must remain free of the contamination of sexual intercourse, and hence of marriage also.

In the early days of courtly love, very little if any sexual expression was permitted. Everything, in keeping with the black-and-white Persian/Greek world view, was quite platonic between a man and his lover. Lancelot, for instance, was quite content to visit Guinevere in her chambers and nobly listen to her confess, "I loved you once in silence, but now that we have expressed our love openly in words, dear, all is ended." But despite the puritanism, tenderness and affection did enter the male/female relationship, and this was a major development.

As the courtly tradition emerged into the Renaissance, love as we know it became more and more mingled with human sexuality and with sexual relations, even in the attitudes of the new class of wealthy businessmen.

By the fourteenth century angelic courtly love had touched earth somewhat and a lady might well reward her lover's undying devotion by allowing him to spend the night with her, provided he not try to seduce or rape her. Naturally, such an arrangement was not too practical and the extramarital affair based on love began to win practical acceptance.

The Reformation and the rise of a bourgeois middle class, especially those of Calvinist persuasion in northern Europe, trimmed romantic love to fit within the marital boundary. The Calvinists were too hard-working and righteous to spend time and money on illicit love affairs. So they took the best of the affair—the tenderness of courtly love, its idealism and its romance, the poetry and the idolization of woman—to incorporate these into the Christian ideal of monogamy.

By the seventeenth century romantic love had begun to percolate down from the upper classes of society into the culture and consciousness of the new middle-class merchants, although the more open and formal acceptance of adultery as a reward for love still caused many nobles and most of the conservative middle class serious concern. To relieve this tension somewhat, society arranged a convenient shift in the identity of the beloved lady, from the married woman to the single woman. (This shift in turn gradually led to the affirmation of a young lady's or gentleman's right to marry out of love rather than parental dictate.)

In the past two or three centuries the European consciousness of the extramarital affair has developed an intriguing dichotomy between the North and the South.

"In the northern European puritan-bourgeois tradition," Morton Hunt states in The Affair, "marriage came to be viewed romantically and idealistically as the most intense, most meaningful of human relationships and the only one in which sex, love, and parenthood were socially and morally acceptable. Any outside emotional or sexual involvement was seen as directly competitive with some part of this synthesis, disruptive of it, and therefore evil." When divorce became somewhat acceptable to the Protestant culture, the extramarital affair became even more intolearble. Psychologically this invidious and lethal virus was kept in check by the widespread message that one could not possibly truly love his or her spouse and be beautiful, and, conversely, that infidelity was a sure proof that one did not really love one's spouse. The common acceptance of this message forced the extramarital relationship into a very definite garb of guilt, conflict, secrecy, and the choice between a purely physical, fleeting encounter or a deeply emotional relationship that would inevitably supplant the marriage.

In the countries of southern Europe the highly modified pagan-courtly tradition has remained the stronger of the two codes. Marriage was, and still is in many cases, a practical arrangement concerned with property, children, and the stable comforts of life. Sexual pleasures are involved, both for procreation and simple release, but as the French love to say, "If there is nothing better, a man sleeps with his wife." For the Mediterraneans, emotional and romantic pleasures, along with the ecstatic exuberance of sexuality, are to be found outside marriage and without jeopardy to it. This pagan-courtly tradition has also invaded the North to some extent, but primarily among the aristocracy and royalty.

In America the puritan-bourgeois tradition prevails, and it certainly is the only one acceptable for the masses. In a few enclaves, among the jet-set, the aristocratic rich, recent immigrants, and the "bohemian artists," the pagan-courtly tradition is openly accepted but without unnecessary publicity, as Cuber and Harroff observe in their study of sexual mores, *The Significant Americans.* Yet, beneath the surface, as Hunt suggests, the unacceptable pagan-courtly tradition "fits too well the emotional needs of many adults to go unused and unappreciated." The result is a mythic image of lifelong exclusive monogamy coupled with a quite different unadvertised and often subconscious practice for many Americans.

Morton Hunt labels this our schizoid character and blames it on the fact that we are offered "an approved model of marriage which, for all its value and its beauty, is suited to the needs and emotional abilities of only some—perhaps a minority—of us; [and] simultaneously offers us a deviant, disapproved model which, for all its disadvantages, is suited to the needs and emotional abilities of the rest—perhaps even a majority—of us."

The approved model has some distinct practical advantages in our Age of Transience. In our fragmented, impersonal culture, romantic and faithful marriage provides an island of emotional stability and security for both husband and wife. But, on the other hand, lifelong monogamy seems to be ill-adapted to our increasing life span. Boredom can easily come from a narrowed relationship which outlaws any in-depth alliance with the other sex for both parties. There is a constant need to revivify the physical relationship and to keep open the opportunities for full personal development without risking any intimate heterosexual relationship.

The disapproved model, on the other side of the fence, in Hunt's view, "seems better suited to the emotional capacities and requirements of many people, particularly men. It offers renewal, excitement, and the continuance of experiences of personal rediscovery; it avoids the demands and challenges of intimacy; it is an answer to the boredom of life-long monogamy; it solves the problem of the ever-present temptations of modern society by yielding to them. But again, those who choose this alternative may have to pay for it: infidelity is expensive and time consuming, it conflicts with the home-based habits of middle-class society, it is socially and professionally hazardous, it may be psychologically traumatic to one's self, wife, and children if discovered—and even if not discovered." And yet Hunt concludes that while the increasing life expectancy is likely to make fidelity a bore and increasingly more difficult, the secretive affair becomes less and less practical as one grows older.

Unlike its European counterpart, the American practice of infidelity has little recognized social status. Except among men and some women in the upper class, where the discreet love affair is considered an essential component of marriage, and among lower-class men, who have always considered an extra-curricular romp in the hay essential to one's peace of mind, the affair in America remains "cheating," it is illegal and punishable in most states by heavy fines, and grounds for divorce; it is secretive and thus isolated from the rest of one's life. There are other differences between the European and American conception of extramarital relations. Hunt finds that Americans by and large do not have affairs that last for years, nor do they engage in a continuous series of minor liaisons. The American pattern seems rather to boil down to an occasional brief affair now and then, so that most married couples, despite the prevalence of infidelity, spend most of their married life being faithful.

Some interesting conclusions can be distilled from the many recent books on infidelity and affairs. Among these are the strong impression that men, perhaps the majority of unfaithful spouses, are not seriously dissatisfied with their marriages or with their mates. A fair number in fact appear to be quite happily married. Only about a third, perhaps less, seek an extramarital relation for neurotic motives. Finally and very important in terms of an apparent shift in our conception of the affair, men, perhaps even a majority of unfaithful spouses, do not feel that their outside relations are harmful to themselves, their mates, or their marriages. Some in fact feel that the outside relations are beneficial to their marriage relations.

In Hunt's earlier studies of extramarital affairs, one gets a definite impression that both he and his interviewees consider these usually harmful and negative. His more recent writings, and those of other observers, seem to indicate a new appraisal evolving in the United States as a result, perhaps, of the new openness in discussing marriage and its problems. The compulsiveness and possessiveness which so dominated extramarital affairs in the past often thrust the parties into an escape mentality and the frantic, romantic, and unrealistic pursuit of a greener pasture elsewhere. The affair then was prelude to divorce and remarriage. It became an escape hatch from one monogamous marriage to another, forbidden by society because of our dedication to the myth of lifelong monogamy that the affair inevitably threatened in this context.

It would appear that this compulsiveness and possessiveness are fading with a new appreciation of the affair. Marital infidelity is becoming for more and more couples something positive, an alternative to divorce that will probably continue to increase, all the more so as women come to share more in the traditional freedom, mobility, and privileges of the liberated male. "Within another generation," according to Morton Hunt in "The Future of Marriage," "based on present trends, four of five husbands and two of three wives whose marriages last more than several years will have at least a few extramarital involvements." One question I have about this straight-line extrapolation is this: *if* much of the popularity and allure of infidelity can be traced to its "forbidden fruit" character today, will it still be as attractive and prevalent in a society of tomorrow that takes the comarital relation for granted within the practice of monogamy? For many reasons, which will become evident as we move through the sexual apocalypse, I very much agree with Hunt's projection of an increasing prevalence for the comarital relation in our American marriage pattern.

Morton Hunt is one of the very few commentators to approach the crucial issue at stake here in our projection of future patterns of male/female relations: the issue of fidelity and intimacy. But he does skirt the issue, no matter how close he comes to it. The comarital or satellite relationship is *the* issue, as I see it, and no one has stated this in a sentence or two except the Roys in *Honest Sex:* "To sum up: we find that sexual relations with persons other than a spouse are becoming more common. When other criteria of appropriateness are fulfilled, such relations do not necessarily destroy or hurt a marriage, nor do they inflict an unbearable hurt on the partner not involved. Indeed, when human need is paramount, such relationships can serve as the vehicle of faithfulness to God."

SIX

Comarital Concubines, Bigamy, and
the Obsolete Mistress

OVER THE CENTURIES the extramarital relation has had many
faces in our Western heritage. One venerable experience is
found in the Jewish tradition of concubinage. The early Judaic
culture placed great value on sex, children, and family, and so
adultery was considered a fearful sin. But adultery was defined
in a very limited, strict way to mean only a married woman
having sexual intercourse with anyone not her husband, or any
man, married or not, having intercourse *with a married woman*
not his wife.

To reduce the tension between the value placed on children,
the monogamous but childless marriage, and the temptation of
divorce, as well as the more liberal practices of their neighbors,
the Jewish law allowed a man to take a concubine. Abraham
had Hagar; Jacob had Bilhah and Zilpah; Saul had at least one
concubine; David had ten, one to warm his feet in his old age;
and King Solomon was encircled with three hundred concubines
and his seven hundred wives. Lesser biblical figures also had
concubines as the Book of Judges indicates.

The Judaic distinction between a wife and a concubine, according to Rav Judah, is "that wives have a marriage contract
and were taken by the accepted rabbinic rites. Concubines have
no contract and came to live with their man without benefit of
ceremony." In the Middle Ages when the great lawgiver Moses

Maimonides tried to restrict the right to take a concubine to royalty, the Jewish rabbis and scholars quickly challenged his interpretation and with success restored the ancient tradition that if the Bible had permitted concubines at all, it allowed them for all Jews.

In most cases, a Jewish man took a concubine in order to obtain an heir. This was the case with Abraham: "And still Abram's wife Sarah bore him no children. But she had an Egyptian maid-servant, called Hagar; and now she said to her husband, The Lord, as thou seest, denies me motherhood; betake thyself to this maid of mine, in the hope that I may at least have children through her means. So Abram consented to the wish of his wife, and she brought this Egyptian maid-servant of her, Hagar, and gave her to her husband as his mate. . . . Abram, then, had knowledge of her, and she, finding herself with child, began to look on her mistress with scorn" Gen. 16:1–4.

The situation of Sarah and Hagar is not much different from that portrayed in a recent movie, *The Baby Maker*. The "baby maker," or concubine in this modern case, is Tish, a happy, healthy young woman of twenty-two. Having a baby is beautiful, and the unmarried Tish has already had one child, whom she gave up for adoption. Suzanne and Jay Wilcox very much want a child, but Suzanne recently learned that she is sterile. Would Tish be willing to sleep with Jay and carry a child for them? An agreement is worked out, and a legal-style document outlining the obligations of each party is prepared. The three take a vacation in the mountains and Suzanne leaves Jay and Tish to spend several nights in a cabin while she stays at a nearby motel. The movie follows the trio for the next nine months, focusing on their conflicts, tensions, jealousy, and eventual understanding until, beaming with joy, they emerge from the delivery room, where all shared in the natural birth of a healthy boy. Despite Hollywood's propensity for mangling a theme as delicate as this, the movie is a perceptive story of a temporary concubine.

There are many areas of the world, in the Philippines among others, where peasant girls are still occasionally hired as temporary concubines—baby makers—by well-to-do but childless couples. A year ago I met a charming switchboard operator who has had a dozen children. She had read my book *Utopian Motherhood* and wanted to know where she could volunteer as a surrogate mother. She said she was never happier than when pregnant and that she would love to have five or six more children to help out some childless couples.

Given this past history of a schizoid practice of monogamy and an evolving theological perspective, we still face the dangerous dichotomy between theory and practice, as noted by Charles A. Reich in *The Greening of America*. Applied to monogamy today, Reich's critique might be modified as follows: the American society is trying to solve the radically new and very practical problems of the 1970s with the consciousness of an nineteenth-century romantic Victorian of the bourgeois class. This is an impossible task. The solution will come only when individuals work out new modifications and models. In the end, two or three decades from now, the custodians of our legal, religious, and social structures will painfully admit that a revolution has occurred in marriage and that it might as well be accepted by all.

Of the three areas—the legal profession, our social consciousness, and our religious thought—the religious area seems the closest to a real awakening, as the evidence above indicates. One would hardly expect this prophetic openness to occur first in religious circles, given the dogmatic and legalistic approach to morality that has dominated in Christian thought for centuries. But this is where that action is today, not in the official voices of society and jurisprudence, but among the theologians and in some of the churches.

The modern roots of this prophetic spirit stem primarily from the writings of the British philosopher and theologian John Macmurray. In 1936 Macmurray broached the subject of a new approach to ethics and moral judgments based not on the application of universal immutable laws, but rather on the Christian demands and responsibilities arising in the unique concrete situation each person finds himself in when acting as a rational and moral agent. In the chapter "The Virtue of Chastity" in his book *Reason and Emotion.* Macmurray rejected the traditional base of ethics in Christianity, the "natural law," and its various guises. This legalistic approach to ethics he traces more to pagan Stoicism than to the New Testament. The Stoics viewed man and morality as a conflict between reason and emotion in which the rational will must rule over the irrational emotions. This victory is achieved, the Stoics and later Christians argued, by applying the logic of immutable laws of nature to individual situations. This has been the predominant (but not exclusive) basis of Christian ethics for centuries. It was also the basis of Roman civil law, of the influential moral system of Immanuel Kant, and of all canon or church law.

Macmurray rejects this traditional approach, arguing that "what Jesus did was to substitute an inner and emotional basis of behavior for an external and intellectual one." In the past, using what Bishop John T. Robinson calls the deductive approach, beginning with marriage as a given datum of nature, traditional morality has said that all sex outside of marriage is evil and sinful, and any sex within marriage is perfectly proper and good, provided it is procreative. But even Thomas Aquinas admitted it would be difficult to condemn extramarital sex if it could be rendered non-procreative. Yet the legal deductive absolutes have remained as the basis for our morality. Against this external intellectual morality, Macmurray proposed what he saw as the true essence of Christ's teaching, an ethics based on emotional integrity. In his 1953–1954 Gifford Lectures, Macmurray pointed out that a prime error in the thinking of Descartes and many ethical systems is the false assumption that the individual can be abstracted from his social context and that this same person is reducible to his intellect. The individual, for Macmurray, is inseparably intellect/emotion, and this dynamic personality exists only in a unique situation in relation to other whole persons. Thus it is just as immoral to act in violation of one's emotions or to pretend to feel otherwise than one in fact does as it is to act or speak contrary to what one's intellect knows to be true. Emotional lies are just as immoral as intellectual lies.

Dr. William Graham Cole sums up Macmurray's thought on marital morality quite nicely in Gerhard Neubeck's study *Extramarital Relations:* "Sexual relations that spring from mere erotic attraction to another are immoral, both within marriage and outside of it. This is to use and exploit another human being. But sexual intercourse based on genuine love, on sincere mutuality, requires no other justification to validate it, not even marriage. Macmurray carefully defined his terms in an effort to render rationalization difficult, if not impossible, circumscribing his concept of love so as to exclude sentimentality and mere physical arousal. But he was persuaded that real love, understood in the Christian sense of *agape*, made sex pure and fulfilling for both persons without regard to their marital status. He knew that his position was dangerous to conventional morality and that it would arouse much anxiety and hostility, but he felt compelled to assert it."

The ethical approach taken by Macmurray in 1936 has since been more fully explored by a number of leading theologians, often totally independent of his inspiration. Dietrich Bonhoeffer, the German pastor whose writings are very popular among college students, started out as a staunch advocate of absolutist moral law. But his experiences in a Nazi concentration camp persuaded him that the moral law against murder has to allow some exception. The Nazi tyranny, he reasoned, could only be stopped by the murder of Hitler. "The question of the good is posed and is decided in the midst of each definite, yet unconcluded, unique and transient situation of our lives, in the midst of our living relationships with men, things, institutions, and

powers—in other words, in the midst of our historical existence."
Given the infinite variety of life, persons, and situations, Bonhoeffer became convinced that ethics must be "situational":
considered and decided in the unique *context* of life situations.

Other leading advocates of "situation ethics" include the
great German New Testament scholar Rudolph Bultmann
and Paul Lehmann, professor of Christian Ethics at Union Theological Seminary in New York City, who speaks of "boundary
situations," human encounters which lie outside the domains
regulated by the rules of conventional morality. Lehmann argues
that the rules of conventional morality are useful as guides in
ordinary situations, but they cannot be absolutes suited to regu-
late all and every situation. Paul Tillich and Martin Buber both
accepted a form of situation ethics, as did, in a more remote
time, Augustine, Bishop of Hippo, and Martin Luther, though
these two moralists did not extend their principles to their
logical conclusions in ethics.

In the items of evidence offered above, Fletcher and
Wassmer openly take a situational approach to sexual morality.
The authors of the other items also adopt this approach, though
less explicitly.

No advocate of Christian situation ethics would justify bed
hopping, wife swapping, or the Playboy orgy. Even a sex pundit
as radical as Dr. Alex Comfort, who views sex as a playful game
and nothing more, sets out two "unbreakable rules": "Thou
shalt not exploit another person's feeling and wantonly expose
them to an experience of rejection," and "Thou shalt not
under any circumstances negligently risk producing an unwanted
child." Mere mutual attraction and/or erotic arousal would not
justify extramarital intercourse. While there is considerable disagreement on what unique situations would justify this relationship, there is a consensus that, whatever the situation, the
relationship must be based on and rooted in genuine Christian
love, an outgoing, sacrificial concern for the other party's welfare, an absence of selfish exploitation, and a cocreative mutual-

ity expressing the flesh—the union of two persons in the fullest sense.

Some biblical scholars have suggested that Christ's statement that "he who looks after a woman in lust has already committed adultery" has been misinterpreted by ignoring the key word: lust. They suggest the real meaning is that any man or woman who *uses and exploits* another person for his own sexual pleasure is *treating him as an object*, which is both inhumane and immoral.

But does this mean then that the exclusive possessiveness with which we have encircled the monogamous marriage may not really be in keeping with the spirit of Christ? Does the often jealous sexual exclusivity of the monogamous marriage accord with the risk in loving which the Christian commitment demands? "It is utterly ridiculous to say on the one hand, 'Greater love hath no man than this, that he lay down his life for his friends,' and to assert immediately that it is impossible and unnatural for a man (or a woman) to agree to share his (or her) spouse with another. We are claiming then," the authors of *Honest Sex* acknowledge, "that no black-and-white case can be made against sexual intimacies (including coitus) between persons not married to each other."

But let me carry this one step further and ask whether situations do indeed exist where Christian concern and need render "adultery" a Christian obligation. In his landmark exposition, *Situation Ethics*, Joseph Fletcher ventured a guarded "yes" to this radically new question: "Adultery, for instance, is ordinarily wrong, not in itself but because the emotional, legal, and spiritual entailments are such that the overall effects are evil and hurtful rather than helpful—at least in our present-day [1966] Western society. But there is always the outside case, the unusual situation, what Karl Barth calls the 'ultima ratio,' in which adultery could be the right and good thing." Fletcher then admitted that *he personally knew of such a situation.*

This is a crucial admission, for it seems that theologians and moralists are either unwilling or uninterested in exploring the possibility of exceptions to the traditional concept of marital exclusivity. This unwillingness and/or disinterestedness usually remains quite strong until the aloof theologian personally encounters some friends or close associates involved in such a situation. Then, as counselor, confidant, and friend, he is drawn into the relationship. The bonds of friendship make the abstract theoretical discussion impossible. The situation becomes too real for that. Likewise the human needs and ethical obligations become too clear and authentic to be dismissed by recourse to a legal proscription. I have noticed that many of the theologians who have written on this question have had their interest triggered by a very real situation into which they were drawn as confidant and adviser. The non-theologian—the housewife, the blue-collar worker, the college student—likewise seems to respond to the realities of life. As one priest told me after a lecture in the Midwest: "A year ago I would have been up on that stage and thrown you out of here personally. But then I ran into a situation a while back that made me think twice about this whole extramarital thing, and now I really wonder."

This priest went on to explain how as a young altar boy he had idolized an assistant in his parish. This inspiration led him into the seminary and the two men became close friends. After the young man was ordained he was assigned to his old friend's parish. Several years passed and the new assistant began to wonder about a marvelous relationship that existed between his pastor and a middle-aged couple in the parish. The couple were practically "assistant pastors"; they were leaders in almost every facet of the parish life and worked closely with the pastor and his assistant. Finally it dawned on the young priest that the couple and his old friend were involved in a triangular relationship. Greatly disturbed, almost shattered, he spoke with each of the three, and learned to his surprise that the relationship was far deeper and more Christian than he could possibly have suspected at first. The triangular relation had not only marvelously strengthened a very happy Christian marriage, it had also turned an average pastor into a dynamo of priestly dedication and concern.

Do you remember the outcry that greeted the movie *The Sandpiper?* The reviews of the movie were scathing in condemning the movie's theme: an unmarried woman, played by Elizabeth Taylor, is befriended by a minister, played by Richard Burton. Their friendship develops in a very credible way and eventually leads to sexual intimacy. As in the situation told to me by the Midwestern priest, the minister in *The Sandpiper* comes out of the relationship a much improved man of God. But, of course, this is *verboten* to our Victorian hypocrisy on double grounds: it suggests that ministers—priests and rabbis, too—are sexual persons with a sexual life and also that extramarital relations are not always destructive and patently sinful. What a change has occurred in the few years between *The Sandpiper* and the recent release of *The Priest's Wife*, which deals with a very similar theme in a more humorous vein!

In *Sex and the Christian Life*, Seward Hiltner asks about a slightly different situation with which he was familiar: two young couples are neighbors and very close friends for some years before one of the men is drafted. The husband left behind then plays the father role for his friend's children, helps the wife with her car, her income taxes, her leaky basement. Is it right only to help with physical needs but not the "widowed" wife's needs for companionship, friendship, love? Is it absolutely certain that extending the relationship beyond the bounds usually set by society and church would destroy the marriages?

The Roys have in a decade or so encountered a wide spectrum of triangular situations which have lent authenticity and realism to their discussion of comarital relations. Let me cite one situation from their book *Honest Sex:* "Of two families intimately known to each other, one wife dies in her forties; the other husband and wife are constant companions of the bereaved husband and children. They almost live together in those first months of adjustment. And, as the shock wears off, the solid friendship continues. The wife nurses her friend's children through sickness, often being over late at night. Sometimes her husband is away and she stays for coffee. The bonds of genuine friendship, affection, and Eros become stronger and stronger, yet no physical expression occurs. The husband and wife often allude to the anomalous situation, and joke about one woman being able to handle several men. The husband has conceptually confronted the possibility of physical intimacy between his wife and another man and not reacted violently. The widower discusses with the wife his deep attachment to her and in the conversation, it is he who finds it most difficult to justify the taking of another person's wife. Interestingly enough, this is the reaction which is most depersonalized, treating the wife as property belonging to another. [Many men believe they have "taken their wives out of circulation" in a sort of possessive propertied contract.] When physical sexual intimacy begins, it runs within a few weeks to coitus. When the husband is first told of the events, in spite of all his preparation, reactions of hurt and grief are present. (This emotional reaction we have found occurs in almost all cases despite any intellectual acceptance, but lasts for only a relatively short time, on the order of some weeks.) Months later, as he becomes assured of the continued stability of his marriage, he gradually accepts the existence of a long-term relation including complete sexual intimacy between his wife and his friend."

One characteristic of the 1970s is already emerging in the fact that many young people are not afraid of or averse to letting people know they are involved in an alternative pattern of marriage. For instance, in a special feature "The American Family: Future Uncertain," *Time* included a wedding picture and a brief account of one triangular marriage in La Jolla, California. "Michael, an oceanographer, and his artist wife, Karen, both 27, had been married for four years when Michael met Janis, who was studying at the Scripps

Institute of Oceanography. Janis often came to study at Michael and Karen's apartment, and a strong attachment developed. When Michael took off on a field trip to Antarctica, the two women became good friends and decided that because they both liked Michael, all three ought to live together. Last May [1969] the trio formalized it all with an improvised wedding ceremony attended, incidentally, by other trios. As the three were leaving for a summer session at the University of Oregon, they were delighted to learn that Karen was pregnant. 'We'll all take turns caring for it,' says Janis, 'just as we share all the household chores. That way each of us has time for things we like to do best.'"

Real life can be far stranger than fiction, yet, as the authors of the Quaker statement accurately observe, "The 'triangular situation' is too often thought of as a wholly destructive and irresponsible relationship, the third party being at the very best an intruder and at worst an unscrupulous thief. Its portrayal thus in fiction and drama no doubt contributes to the stereotype. . . . Not sufficient recognition is given to the fact that a triangular situation can and often does arise in which all three persons behave responsibly, are deeply conscious of the difficulties and equally anxious to avoid injury to the others. . . . It is worth noting that in the two-woman-one-man situation, the very happiness of the marriage may attract a young girl or a sensitive responsible woman. . . . By the same token, it would surely help a nervous youngster to fall in love with a happily married woman."

This positive and creative aspect of the triangular relation is the theme of the stage play and movie *Tea and Sympathy*, in which a college professor and his wife befriend a very gifted but shy student. The wife soon perceives that the lad's shyness and sensitivity will prevent his ever relating deeply to a woman, and that she can strengthen his shaky image of himself as a man by gradually making love with him. This she does with real Christian concern, only to be irately divorced by her husband.

Adultery, cheating, affair, extramarital—all the terms we have traditionally used as descriptive labels color the picture rather deliberately in shades of black. We do not have a single term to describe the triangular relation that is not in part pejorative. It is indicative that we have in fact moved into an entirely new world of human relations when we recognize the need for a new term to describe sexual relations beyond the married couple which are motivated by true Christian love, which express an awareness and concern for the needs of others, and this within the creative context of a happy marriage. Wassmer commented on this need for a new term, and apparently was not aware that in discussing this problem with the Roys some time ago, the Reverend William Genné, Director of Family Life Services for the National Council of Churches and a Methodist, coined the label "comarital." Genné suggested "comarital" to "describe without the pejorative connotation of the term *extramarital*, any man-woman relationship, and/or sexual expression thereof, which exists alongside of and in addition to a marriage relationship. Such relationships are basically not competitive with the marital relationship; they may have a neutral or even a positive effect on it. The term *extramarital* will still be used to describe situations which are not as clearly noncompetitive" (from *Honest Sex*).

The concept of "comarital" shatters the egotism à deux which has distinguished our image of monogamy. It introduces the sense of Christian community, not because it allows sexual relations outside the marital bond but because it allows between men and women not married to each other the opportunity to develop a deep, warmly human relationship which meets the needs of several people. The Roys are quite right in their claim that "the first essential step in the evolution of monogamy is the recovery of the role of community in our lives." Many of the insights in *Honest Sex* stem from the Roys' discussions, counseling, and experiences in the Sycamore Community, an ecumenical group located at State College, Pennsylvania, where the Roys teach the physical sciences at the university. The sense of community of which the Roys speak is a vital need today. "There is an inverse correlation between the complexity of a highly developed society and the strength of community channels and bonds." In our technological society, people have turned to the monogamous marriage and the nuclear family as the one personalized shelter against the depersonalized outside world. "But monogamous marriage is altogether too frail an institution to carry that load also."

For some time I have been uneasy with the term "comarital" because I have sensed that it does not quite express the nuances of these new relationships. Thus when I discussed the term with John and Barbara Williamson, founders of the Sandstone Community, and they suggested making a distinction between primary and secondary relationships, the terminology question became sharper in my mind. After some quiet germination, a new verbal symbol has turned up which I find very satisfying, certainly more satisfying than either "comarital" or "primary/secondary relationships." This is the conception of "satellite relations," in the sense that a married couple (twin stars or sun and moon) naturally experience a variety of satellite relationships of varying intensities and durations. A satellite relationship may orbit one or both of the couple at varying levels of intimacy, or flash in and out of their orbit also at different levels. There may even be an occasional rare collision. With these and other analogies possible for the satellite relationship, I find this expression more descriptive of what the Roys, Genné, Wassmer, Hobbs, and others are trying to say.

"Most of us," as the Roys observe, "are many-sided polyhedra needing several people to reflect back to ourselves the different portions of our personality."

The evolution of comarital relations to meet the multifaceted needs of real people is evident in some recent novels. Robert Rimmer makes an argument for bigamy in *The Rebellion of Yale Marratt*. The triangle formed by Yale Marratt,

Cynthia, and Anne is as realistic as one could want. Rimmer explores with his characters all the problems, tensions, joys, creativeness, and sorrows of a situation that builds into a life-long bigamous marriage in which each of the three members complements and meets the needs of the other two in truly human and Christian concern.

Henry Sackerman makes a similar attempt to deal with the triangular relationship of nineteen-year-old Connie Baxter, the sensitive, intellectual, poetic Arthur, and the sensual, rebellious, and athletic Brad. But *The Crowded Bed* is not nearly as successful as Rimmer's novel, perhaps because its potentially serious message is masked by a satirical, near farcical treatment.

The Vietnam war has added another very real dimension to these fictional accounts of bigamous relations. On April 30, 1971, the *New York Times* family page carried a story of the many problems created by the Vietnam conflict. One of these is the at least two hundred thousand children born to Vietnamese girls and their soldier boy friends. Many of these women know full well that the soldiers have wives back home, but they also know that in their culture it is traditional for men to take a concubine. "They expect the American to treat them as a second wife. They don't understand a system of morality that allows a man to have kids by two women but only one wife," reports Donald Luce, an authority on the Vietnam scene.

Della and Rustum Roy believe that legalizing bigamy would paradoxically strengthen contemporary-style monogamy and also provide the easiest next step toward a pluralizing of our male/ female relations in society. In the ordinary suburban subdivision the over-all structure and pattern of society would be unaffected if one woman in twenty had two husbands, or one man in ten had two wives. If every single female between thirty and sixty-five in America were attached to a married couple, only one married couple in ten would be affected. In many cases these plural spouses would be located in different cities or in different sections of the town.

Gerhard Neubeck, in fact, takes this approach in two fictional episodes designed to tax the reader's fantasy. In an essay, "Polyandry and Polygyny: Viable Today?" Neubeck offers two vignettes, one of Fran and her two husbands, Phil and Greg; the other of Jim and his two wives, Vicky and Ann. Within a few pages Neubeck makes it easy for his readers to imagine themselves in Jim's or Fran's kitchens, in their yards, in their beds and bathrooms—trying on their skins and experiencing what they might feel with an extra spouse.

Neubeck adopts several simplifications engineered to reduce tensions in a society that is making the transition, *as we seem to be doing,* from a strictly exclusive monogamy to a pluralism that accepts bigamy and polygamy. He alludes to basic problems that must be solved without offering definite solutions, such as the legitimacy and parenthood of the children, the emotional interplays between mothers who might be tempted to use their children as wedges with their joint husband, the pull of multiple in-laws, inheritance rights, and possible competitiveness—which Neubeck tries to reduce by placing the two wives or two husbands in separate households. (This is hardly a fair criticism, for Neubeck's prime purpose is to move his readers to think the unthinkable.)

Mobility might well pose the most serious complication for plural relations. The average American moves every five years, and to move two households simultaneously could be a real task. In "Is Monogamy Outdated?" the Roys "see the need for developing acceptable patterns for altering such relationships creatively after the two-to-five-year period which often brings about sufficient changes to suggest reappraisal in any case." This suggestion might apply to the long-term bigamous relation, but it is far more vital in considering the life of short-term multiple relationships, particularly those which arise when a single person is integrated into an already existing couple marriage in what is mutually accepted as a temporary community. "In the new dispensation, a much more active and aggressive policy should be encouraged to incorporate single persons within the total life of a family and a community. She or he should be a part of the family, always invited—but not always coming—to dinner, theaters, and vacations. The single person should feel free enough to make demands and accept responsibility as an additional family member would. The single woman, thus loved and accepted by two or three families, may find herself perhaps not sleeping with any of the husbands but vastly more fulfilled as a woman."

The Roys have encountered several such relationships—where single persons have been integrated into the couple structure—that have contributed much to the growth of the single persons. Many of these, but not all, have involved a complete sexual intimacy.

In 1965 two sociologists at Ohio State University, John F. Cuber and Peggy B. Harroff, did a study of the sexual behavior of affluent Americans. Finding that even then informal triangular "marriages" were not uncommon, they discussed these relationships with an attorney in order to secure information about their legal status. He admitted that he had several clients who have evolved patterns of this type. He also confirmed their findings that the "marriage" did not originate necessarily because of any manifest failure of the first marriage or necessarily from a refusal of the first spouse to agree to a divorce. The principals involved simply recognize either that certain personalities cannot be encompassed in any one relationship or that compelling relationships between adults can arise after marriage as well as before. They honor those arising after marriage just as they accept the moral validity of premarital relations. As a rule, the first wife publicly maintains the fiction that she does not know about the second "marriage," since she is likely to be, in Russell Lynes' sense, an "upper bohemian" rather than a true one. She finds it easier psychologically to live this fiction in homage to the publicly sanctioned system, rather than to fight it.

Cuber and Harroff also got an interesting response from a clergyman in a large, predominantly upper-middle-class congregation who told them that "he was aware of numerous such arrangements and had observed that '. . . these always seem to be extremely vital and energetic people—people who have the capacity and the desire to live unusually fully. They seem to want to live two lifetimes in one life span.' And it does seem as if a few of them are able to achieve such an ambition with more vigor than other people can muster for one mating."

Though there are many couples who have shared in a co-marital relationship involving a single man or woman, it is not easy to establish an over-all picture of the benefits and risks involved in such relations. Despite the lack of in-depth studies, the insights of observers like the Roys, Robert Rimmer, and others offer us some outlines, if not a paradigm, for the comarital triangle. (The paradigm for this relation is not around the corner; it is more likely that we will end up with a dozen or more models of comarital relations simply because each situation we learn of presents its own uniqueness although there may be similarities with other such relations.)

One general rule has emerged from observations and this has been concisely stated by the Roys in "Is Monogamy Outdated?" "No couple should enter such relationships unless the marriage is secure and the sexual monopoly not crucially important: yet all concerned couples should be caused to wonder about their values if their fear of sexual involvement keeps them from ministering to such obvious needs." Few marriages can handle the comarital relation in their first five or even ten years, probably because the couple must first adjust to each other and become certain of their own relationship before assuming the responsibilities of a third party. Yet the Roys have found that strong couples can handle the relationship even in their early years. After the age of thirty-five, despite their schooling in exclusivity and possessiveness, perhaps as many as one in ten middle-class American couples can handle the comarital relationship.

The real problems of comarital relations are fairly mundane. The emotional investment and cost is higher for the single person than for the couple involved. The greatest burden is in accepting the partial nature of the relationship, even when the "official wife" completely accepts the single person. "Secrecy," the Roys maintain in *Honest Sex*, and I would agree, "is becoming less important as, in our mobile society, meetings are much more easily arranged in cities, on business trips, in resorts, on vacations. In urbanized culture, the anonymity of cities allows such couples an existence of their own. In the post-feminine-mystique era, women do not have to seek their only fulfillment through their husbands. The cost to the wife (or husband) is highest in the early stages, even if communication has been clear and thorough. That this cost is not an impossible one is borne out on every level. In our view, acceptance by two or three of one's closest friends could radically change the picture of the present high emotional cost to the single person."

If all the many responsibilities of a comarital relationship, however short- or long-lived, are taken seriously, there is something to be said for the relative simplicity of monogamy. There are all kinds of complications, such as fiscal responsibilities and child support, which become quite complicated even in a monogamous marirage. Though seeming peripheral to the question, these are matters which must be seriously considered and maturely handled in a human relationship.

In *The Significant Americans*, Cuber and Harroff point out some of the advantages and disadvantages of maintaining two separate households for one's two spouses. Dilemmas abound on how to divide one's leisure time between two men or two women. The financial end is not insignificant, nor is the question of when and how to explain the situation to the children. The risk of public exposure, especially if the man is prominent, is still with us, but this is lessening with each passing year. These men, Cuber and Harroff note, "seem to move through life about as inconspicuously as anyone else—whether more totally fulfilled or not, one cannot objectively say."

As a result of their many travels cross country and informal discussions with many Americans experimenting with new life styles, Barabara and John Williamson suggest that a new development is occurring in middle-class-American triangle marriages. In the past year or two they have noticed a tendency for these to become more and more open as one-household families.

Informal bigamy not only frees the husband from the restrictions of monogamy; it also frees the wife who can then on occasion play the single-woman role, or have an affair of her own. But very often the wife finds no compulsion or interest in having a relation of her own. She is satisfied to share her husband with another woman because he is the man he is. As one wife candidly admitted to Cuber and Harroff, "Having half of my husband is worth more to me than having one hundred percent of any other man I have ever known." She said uncomplainingly and without pretense that she would not prefer it otherwise. In many such situations there is simply an acknowledgment and acceptance of a situation as it has developed and the recognition that life is not fashioned from textbook maxims and romantic fairy tales.

Another risk is the possibility of the single person falling into a second-class status, being accepted by the husband or wife, or by both, as a concubine rather than as a wife with equal status and dignity (whether this be on a temporary basis for a few years or for a lifetime). But perhaps for some a second-class status might prove more tolerable than no status at all. Can the single person retain his or her freedom? The freedom to change jobs? The freedom to move? The freedom to entertain other serious relations? The freedom to develop one's independence, even to the point of establishing another marriage? Some of these questions are dealt with by Calder Willingham in an absorbing, but at times tortuous and pedantic story, *Providence Island*, where a missionary's inhibited wife, an even more inhibited businesswoman, and her male business associate find themselves drawn into a temporary triangle that evolves into a more traditional marriage with the rescue and return of one "wife," who is now pregnant, to her missionary spouse.

The critical role of the triangular relationship in our transition to plural patterns of marriage and a more realistic, flexible understanding of fidelity turns up in a prediction offered by two New York sociologists, Myron Orleans and Florence Wolfson. In "The Future of the Family," they suggest that "more likely, we will witness the proliferation of triangular relationships which combine components of the monogamous family and the communal system without requiring any drastic change in living accommodations. While the composition of the triad will depend on the sexual preferences of the members, it appears that the two-female, one-male form will predominate. This can be attributed primarily to the deficit in eligible males. This kind of arrangement allows for a great deal of social and sexual variety, particularly if one of the partners is a revolving one. If nothing else, the general presence of the triangular relationship will condition society eventually to accept totally free sexual expression as legitimate, and lead people to think of communal-type family systems as socially viable and beneficial." My own strong conviction is that the flexible couple, with either comarital relations or a revolving third party, will provide the *most common adaptation in American family life in the decades ahead.*

As the seventies pass we should learn to distinguish and evaluate different types of extramarital and satellite relations. We should learn to distinguish healthy from neurotic reasons for adopting an alternative pattern to strict monogamy whether this be the traditional "affair" or the more open patterns of spouse exchange or satellite relations. Albert Ellis has listed some "healthy reasons" for entering a traditional extramarital relation based on his experiences in counseling: sexual varietism, love enhancement, experimental drives, adventure seeking, sexual curiosity, social and cultural inducements, a low frustration

tolerance, hostility to one's spouse, ego bolstering, self-depreca-
tion, escapism, marital escapism, sexual disturbances, and excitement needs. This "incomplete list" almost leaves one wondering what Ellis would consider a neurotic reason for an extramarital affair. Still the list is helpful if only because it can serve
as a base for sorting out what we find to be morally and humanly acceptable reasons. Some of these reasons might be acceptable as motives for a comarital relation also.

Ellis' list of characteristics for "the healthy adulterer" is far
more realistic and balanced, and while conceived within the
venerable tradition of the extramarital affair, it seems to me very
helpful in the context of comarital relations. The man or woman
who approaches an affair maturely, according to Ellis, should
not be demanding or compulsive. He or she should be able to
live without the extramarital relation and not be frustrated
when it is not available or feasible. Being able to live better
with the extramarital relation, he can seek it out, but not in a
frantic, compulsive way. He or she also manages the relationship
discreetly, realizing that this is a transitional society, and without unduly disturbing other obligations and relations. He is not
ridden with guilt and does not use the relationship to avoid any
serious problem in his life. He or she is realistic about a relationship that is developing in the wrong direction and takes steps
to terminate it. He is tolerant of himself, of the limitations of
others, and of the routine problems of everyday life. Finally he
or she does not let the relationship adversely affect his sexual
relations with his spouse.

Thus far the concept of comarital relations and flexible marriage partners has been dealt with within the rather strict con-
fines of deep personal relationships. But there are some other
modifications of marital fidelity which we must deal with. Following Rustum Roy's classification in "New Dilemmas in Sex,"
these can be divided into classifications of therapeutic, casual,
and recreational sex.

With the recognition that a healthy sexual behavior is a

learned art comes the possibility of treating frigidity and other inhibited behavior by exposure to satisfying staged situations using "surrogate partners." The apparently quite successful work of Masters and Johnson in St. Louis, widely proclaimed in popular and women's magazines, falls into this category, and raises the question whether the frigid wife of a Methodist minister should go to their clinic for treatment. Would this use of surrogate sex partners be adultery? Should her husband agree? Or as Rustum Roy starkly asked, "Would the Masters-Johnson treatment become right if a machine were used? Is a 'surrogate partner' an honorable profession for a Presbyterian seminary student working his way through college?"

The clinical use of therapeutic sex will undoubtedly remain very limited, but its popular use is already very extensive outside the clinics, in the "human potentials" and "sensitivity" movement. Weekend marathons create an intense if short-lived community and mutual personal responsibility. Until recently the advocates of this form of developing human potentiality focused on aggression, believing perhaps that Konrad Lorenz, Robert Ardrey and Desmond Morris have determined the essence of human behavior in our territorial imperative and unexpressed violence. More recently, the very obvious but heretofore disguised sexual aspects of sensitivity workshops, marathons, and weekends has been recognized more and more for what it is: a form of therapeutic sex. Warm communal baths amid candlelight and seductive music, a "blind walk" through the woods, lightly clad and led by a partner of the other sex, the sensualness of a massage, and the relaxed naturalness of communal nudity—not in some stylized ritual but during the everyday events of eating, recreating, walking around, working, and relaxing—all are forms of therapeutic sex, occasionally involving sexual intercourse. In the semi-impersonal, semi-clinical atmosphere of the sensitivity weekend, where mutual responsibility is limited to a few days' commitment, these new avenues of personal growth and maturity are likely to become even more popular for our puritan culture than they are now. In a modest but very real way a case can be made for the therapeutic character of all sexual behavior since its prime motive is to minister to the needs of people and to contribute to their growth as mature, loving persons.

The advocates of recreational sex abide by what Rabbi Eugene Borowitz calls an "ethics of healthy orgasm." Viewing sex as man's best game, it stems from a post-sensitivity experience and is very much focused on the individual. One has a responsibility to enjoy life as much as possible as a complete person. And since sexual activity and healthy orgasm are part of the pleasures of life, this fact alone justifies any sexual behavior, including extramarital relations of any kind that contribute to the fullness of one's enjoyment of life. Pleasurable sex, these advocates claim, is one of the most powerful forces for re-creating the whole human when it is engaged in with a responsive partner. Furthermore, participating in recreational sex helps to break the possessiveness syndrome of our Western culture. While recreational sex is still in its infancy, it may well become a major factor in molding our sexual ethics for tomorrow.

Sex admittedly does have its playful, festive, celebrational component, but is this sufficient to justify it ethically? Sexuality, Snoek maintains, "is a serious matter affecting the basic human situation, as an invitation offering the radical possibility of taking man outside himself, to live for another person, in the direction of liberation and self-realization, or, if he refuses the invitation, in the direction of self-enslavement, alienation and self-extermination." Snoek points out, however, that this serious side of sexuality should never exclude the playful element inherent in all healthy eroticism, whether this be sexual intercourse, dance, poetry, or song. "But one has to get away from a purely recreational and infra-ethical view of sexuality, which, like any other form of diversion, also requires a more serious engagement in the sense of encounter with a 'thou.' Sexuality,

in fact, has to do with life and death. Harvey Cox criticized
the *Playboy* outlook not on the grounds that it was excessively
sexual, but because it was antisexual (treating females as sex
objects rather than as persons). So true sexuality involves the
whole person. To reduce it to mere genitality is a new form of
dualism, more subtle (and no less dangerous) than the Mani-
cheism from which we have hardly yet freed ourselves."

Snoek has a good point, but so does Rustum Roy when, in
"New Dilemmas in Sex," he foresees a wholly new distinction
being possible beyond the present separation of sexual intercourse from procreation, the NEW distinction between *sensuality* and *sexuality*. Sensuality describes the individual's own
reaction to his non-personal physical and physiological environment. Sexuality, on the other hand, deals with interpersonal
reactions. A sexual ethics which places prime importance on
persons and their responsible interaction is surely capable of
dealing with sexuality as urged by Snoek. However, what happens when an individual approaches sexual intercourse *not in
the context of mutual personal growth, but purely and simply
as an individual-centered form of sensual enjoyment?* Dr. Roy
asks, "Can we, or dare we *not* affirm the beauty of feeling deeply
through all our senses? If so, what of bodily touch, massage,
stimulation—even sexual stimulation? Are they excluded?
Beyond some point?"

Perhaps while sexual intercourse as a sensual experience is
admittedly personal but not interpersonal, it may still help build
up the whole person. In moderation, could *sensual intercourse*
be just as moral as eating, drinking, watching a sunset, swimming, hiking along in a pine forest, or listening to a symphony?
Roy suggests that we might fittingly end a discussion of recreational sex "on this uncertain note in answer to such a question
which could not have been seriously asked five years ago—for
it is a measure of the rapidity of change—and the kinds of
questions which churchmen will surely debate in the eighties."

Rabbi Borowitz is purely negative in his critique of an

ethics of healthy orgasm, but if the fresh insight of Rustum Roy holds true to the mark of reality, then I see no reason not to apply the evaluation of theologian Michael Valente that the moral acceptability of something like recreational sex depends on "the extent to which love or concern is present or absent and on the basis of whether the presence or absence of this love or concern causes injury to oneself or one's neighbor or is essentially non-injurious." In dealing with recreational sex we must answer the question of whether there is anything immoral about two adults mutually agreeing to "exploit" each other in sensual intercourse for their individual pleasure. This type of recreational sex may appear to some as very limited in any mutuality or concern for the other person, but even this relationship may express some mutual concern and interpersonal responsibility, at least the intent not to injure the other. Each of the partners may well feel he or she is conferring on the other the opportunity for release of sexual tension, and thus be really altruistic rather than selfish and purely egotistic.

Over two million middle-class Americans are "swingers," according to a July, 1971 report in *Newsweek*. The spouse-swapping phenomenon today is promoted by more than fifty magazines, running from shoddy pornographic tabloids to very polished and discreet glossies. An increasing number of clubs, bars, and journals cater to the interests of Americans seeking sexual variety. This is not really a new phenomenon in a sense, for the aristocracy has for centuries engaged in various forms of spouse exchange. "What is new," according to California psychiatrist L. James Grold, "is that respectable middle-class people who a few years back would have been horrified by the thought are now indulging in activities historically coveted only by the wealthy leisure class."

Most swinging couples, according to anthropologist Gilbert Bartell, author of *Group Sex*, seem to enter into casual sex as an escape or to overcome sexual boredom while preserving their marriages. Swingers observe very rigid rules designed to reduce the emotional involvement to a minimum and yet maintain a maximum of variety in the search for the ideal sex partner. Many researchers have observed a compulsiveness among swingers that verges on addiction. Chicago psychoanalyst Ner Littner feels that swinging couples are incapable of intimate relationships even with their own spouses and use wife swapping "as a safety valve that keeps intimacy at a level each can tolerate." Bartell and others have found swingers almost devoid of outside interests other than sports, television, and group sex. As one San Francisco housewife conceded, "Swinging cemented my marriage because it gave me something to talk to my husband about again."

For most couples swinging breaks down sexual exclusiveness, but some swingers candidly admit that they never really overcome their fears and jealousy and only go along because of their spouse's insistence. Swinging, because of its tight restrictions on emotional involvement, has little if any effect in reducing emotional exclusivity and possessiveness. Bartell compares the suburban wasteland with the sterile arctic habitat of the Eskimoes, who share their wives with weary travelers. The sterile suburban environment, he concludes, may lead some people to try group sex out of sheer boredom.

"Swingers" is a very imprecise term which is often used without distinguishing just what is meant in terms of extent, motives, and goals. For instance, one type of swinger is looking only for variety and the perfect technique. These people are completely preoccupied with their own sexuality. They are addicted to the quest for the perfect high, the perfect orgasm. They might be even described as sex gluttons, rather than sex gourmets. A second type of swinger is not so preoccupied with sexual intimacy, because his occasional sexual experience outside marriage has developed within a group that already existed for other purposes. Sexual intimacy, in this case, does not replace the original purpose of that intimate group, but continues to complement it. A third type of swinger usually develops when two or three couples who have known each other intimately learn to exchange partners occasionally, particularly on a special occasion like a vacation together. In this type the pleasure and language of sexual intimacy is added to an already rich relationship, and occurs relatively rarely. Sex contributes to only a small fraction of their deep multifaceted relationship.

Some social scientists, and many swingers, see this form of casual sex as an attempt to redefine marriage and fidelity in radically new terms that would make sexual intercourse as casual and unemotional as a handshake or eating a steak. But sexual intercourse without some form of personal relationship is, to borrow Rustum Roy's definition, "Venus without Eros." Sex in this context becomes a joyless, mechanical, disassociative, endless pursuit of the perfect technique and the perfect partner. Sex manuals illustrating every possible position become indispensable in the pursuit of the perfect orgasm. It is almost as if some Americans have lunged out of Puritanism into promiscuity, jumping from the restriction of all sex to marriage to the other end of the rainbow, casual sex, without passing through or touching true sensuality. Venus without the courtship of Eros can be deadly dull.

Rustum Roy delightfully paraphrases the Frenchman's appraisal of the American swinger, wryly commenting that "in America they tend to eat the fruit of coital sex green." Which prompts me to recall Rollo May's portrait of the American sexual scene as "too much sex, too little joy."

The Frenchman, however, should be careful about casting stones, for his own reputation is changing quite drastically along similar lines. The illicit love affair has always been very close to the Frenchman's heart. He has always treasured the sentiment of Henri II's sumptuous gift of the Château de Chenonceaux to his mistress Diane de Poitiers, admired the artistic tributes of Zola and Bonnard to their mistresses, and gloried in Charles Boyer's dashingly romantic Casbah thief in the 1938 movie *Algiers*. *The Sexual Behavior of the Married*

Man in France, according to the author, Jacques Baroche, confirms this traditional wanderlust. Ninety percent of the married men interviewed by Baroche admitted to being unfaithful. But the pace of modern life has taken its toll, for many Frenchmen are apparently discarding the leisurely long-term affair with a mistress in favor of quickie sex.

Mistresses are obsolete, one interviewee suggested, because "only one thing counts in love—it is the brief encounter." In un-French tones, a financier added that "the principal quality of a woman is neither charm nor beauty nor intelligence, it is novelty." The Baroche study, limited as is its sample, reveals a disturbing fact: many Frenchmen are becoming completely bored with the courtship, the foreplay, and all the preliminaries they used to treasure. It seems almost as if the American is finding his way toward a more leisurely and diffused sexuality while the Frenchman is evolving in the opposite direction toward quickie, unvarnished sex. These two trends on the Continent and in America may well continue, particularly as Europe becomes more "Americanized" in its industry and the United States becomes more leisure-oriented, with four- and even three-day work weeks.

Having applied our rearview mirror to the monogamous marriage, two basic questions remain to be answered as we move ahead. First, with all that has changed in our reproductive technology, our marital and extramarital behavior, our theology of fidelity and sex, and our social mores, *what new and deeper meaning will we give to marital fidelity in the days ahead?* Will we return to the true meaning of *fides*, devotion to one's duties and responsibilities, personal loyalty? Will we scrap the narrow and unrealistic reduction of fidelity to sexual exclusivity? And second, will the younger generation be less possessive and exclusive-oriented in their personal and sexual relationships? Will we realize, as the Roys suggest in *Honest Sex*, that "men and women were not created to belong exclusively to each other in a marriage contract"? So often in condemning extramarital relations, theologians have resorted to the ploy that since sexual intercourse is the TOTAL gift of oneself to another, the lifelong marriage is the only proper place in which this TOTAL giving can be properly made. This assumes that a finite creature can give himself totally in any finite act. Men and women are oriented and created for union with God and mankind. As the Roys note, this belonging to God and mankind is made real for us partly in our concern for that handful of people we can know and love deeply and personally, a knowing—perhaps in the deep biblical sense of knowing—which enables us to serve the widest circle of people and their needs.

What kind of forecast does our rearview mirror suggest for the married couple and monogamy? With the Roys, "We believe that in the coming generation a spectrum of sexual expression with persons other than the spouse are certain to occur for at least the large majority, and possibly most persons." Marriage, I am convinced, will remain as one of the main patterns of human relations, but its traditional basis of sexual exclusivity will be modified—as it already is being modified—to allow for a variety of deep comarital and satellite relationships, lifelong or revolving triangles, and other less intimate relations.

SEVEN

Group Marriage and Christianity's Grand Apostasy

The common acceptance of the monogamous marriage as the Christian ideal is "the grand apostasy of Christendom." In fact, the exclusive, idolatrous bonds which bind the average married couple in cast-iron rules and selfish modes of behavior were for the members of the Oneida Community the most disastrous development in the history of Christianity.

Thumbing through the *Daily Journal* and *The Circular* published by John Humphrey Noyes and the Oneida Community is like tumbling into a kaleidoscopic other world.

The Perfectionists of the Oneida Community "hold that two distinct kinds of sexual intercourse ought to be recognized; one simply social, and the other propagative; and that the propagative should only be exercised when impregnation is intended and mutually agreed upon."

The First Annual Report of the Oneida Association, dated January 1, 1849, maintains that "dividing the sexual relation into two branches, the amative and propagative, the amative or love-relation is first in importance, as it is in the order of nature. God made woman because 'he saw it was *not good for man to be alone*' (Gen. 2:18), i.e., for social, not primarily for propagative purposes.

"The amative part of the sexual relation (separate from the propagative) is eminently favorable to life. It is not a source of life (as some would make it) but it is the first and best *distributive* of life.

"The propagative part of the sexual relation is in its nature the *expensive* department. While amativeness keeps the capital stock of life circulating between two, the propagation introduces a third partner" (from Robertson's *Oneida Community*).

The Oneida adventure spans the years between 1831 and 1881 with an incredible list of accomplishments. The saga began during the second Great Awakening of Protestant America when a disciple of the most powerful revivalist of the period, Charles G. Finney, held a "protracted meeting" at the home of John Humphrey Noyes in Putney, Vermont. Vowing fidelity to the "revival spirit and [to] be a young convert forever," the 20-year-old lad entered Andover Theological Seminary. After transferring to the Yale Theological School in New Haven, John received his license to preach in August of 1833. Soon an offshoot of Wesleyan Methodism, the Perfectionists, attracted John Noyes' logical mind. Perfectionism, which was popular with the revivalists of New England, New Jersey, and New York State, did not expect or require its members to be sinless, though they advocated the way of perfect holiness. This was a contradiction to John Noyes, and his claim that men must be perfect quickly led to the loss of his preaching license and his withdrawal from Yale.

In 1834 Noyes and a friend, James Boyle, began a paper which they daringly called *The Perfectionist*. In 1837, John sent a letter "in the nakedness of privacy" to a trusted friend and disciple, David Harrison, explaining his rapidly evolving views of marriage. The gist of the letter was that Noyes could accept neither monogamy nor polygamy, only a *nullity* of wives. "When the will of God is done on earth as it is in Heaven, there will be no marriage. Exclusiveness, jealousy, quarreling have no place in the marriage supper of the Lamb. God has placed a partition between man and woman during the apostasy for good reason: this partition will be broken down in the resurrection for equally good reasons. But woe to him who abolishes the law of the apostasy before he stands in the holiness of the resurrection! I call a certain woman my wife. She is yours, she is Christ's, and in Him she is the bride of all saints. She is now in the hands of a stranger, and according to my promise to her, I rejoice. My claim upon her cuts directly across the marriage covenant of this world and God knows the end."

In March of 1838, John wrote to his young female bene-factor, Miss Harriet Holton, one of the strangest proposals any woman has ever received: "We can enter into no engagement with each other which shall limit the range of our affections as they are limited in matrimonial engagements by the fashions of this world" (from Robertson's *Oneida Community*). The young couple were married in Chesterfield, New Hampshire, on June 28, 1838, and returned from an Albany honeymoon to create a commune of true believers in Putney. The commune was soon incorporated and by March, 1834 numbered thirty-five persons.

Despite his forthright statement on marriage and his rather unorthodox proposal of marriage to Harriet, John Noyes found two major obstacles to putting his theory into practice in the community. Theologically he had always insisted that the resur-rection of the body must precede the advent of "complex marriage" in which everyone is "married" to all the saints. After ten years of pondering, however, he began to think that, because of the close interaction between social changes and the lives of individual people, perhaps the practice of complex marriage could help introduce the resurrection power of Christ into this world now. Biologically, the problem was his agree-ment with Malthus on the absolute need for control over propagation. The solution to the apparent incompatibility between complex marriage and control of reproduction came with his discovery of male continence. This form of contracep-tion, used in the Orient for centuries, involves prolonged inter-course but without the male reaching orgasm.

Having finally overcome these basic obstacles to introduction of complex marriage into the life of the community, four couples, led by John and Harriet Noyes, signed a "Statement of Principles" on the first of November, 1846.

"In the kingdom of heaven, the institution of marriage which assigns the exclusive possession of one woman to one man, does not exist (Matt. 22:23–30). In the kingdom of heaven, the intimate union of life and interests, which in the world is limited to pairs, extends through the whole body of believers; i.e., complex marriage takes the place of simple (John 17:21). The abolishment of sexual exclusiveness is involved in the love-relation required between all believers by the express injunction of Christ and the apostles and by the whole tenor of the New Testament. 'The new commandment is that we love one another,' and that not by pairs, as in the world, but *en masse*. The restoration of true relations between the sexes is a matter second in importance only to the reconciliation of man to God" (from Robertson's *Oneida Community*).

The Oneida Community, as it was known after moving to Jonathan Burt's sawmill property near Oneida, New York, in 1847, had set its goals: developing the religion of the New Covenant through communal living and "laying the foundation for a new state of society by developing the true theory of sexual morality."

A January, 1853 issue of *The Circular* explained in more detail the Oneida theology (from Robertson's *Oneida Community*): "The doctrine that *death* is the legitimate end of the contract of marriage is distinctly conceded by all. Paul and Christ found a way to introduce what may be called a posthumous state into the world, by the application of the death of Christ. Their doctrine was that, by believing in Christ, we are crucified with him. If one died for all, then all died. This doctrine of the believer's death and resurrection by union with Christ was, with the primitive Church, the very core of the Gospel. They realized that they were past death and so were delivered from sin and legality." The Oneida

Community would not follow "the grand apostasy of Christendom" and forget the radical implications of this sharing in Christ's death by adopting the monogamous custom of the world. Christ's death and resurrection did away with marriage; what remained for the believers was only the openness of pantogamy, or complex marriage.

In a community of several hundred adults the male/female relations could become quite sticky unless some sort of order was maintained. It could easily become a chaotic community of "free love" and license, a possibility the Oneida people were determined to avoid. In his biography of John Noyes, *A Yankee Saint*, Robert Allerton Parker describes some of the structures devised by the Community to maintain order and reduce tensions: "Exclusive, idolatrous bonds between two members, attachments 'unhealthy and pernicious to the whole system of complex marriage, must never gain foothold in the Community. Hearts must be free to love all of the true and worthy.' This precaution suggested the intervention of a third party—so that all attachments might be brought under the inspection of the Community; so also that women members might, without embarrassment or restraints, decline proposals that did not appeal to them. No member should be obliged to receive—to this they pledged themselves—at any time, under any circumstances, the attention of those they had not learned to love. The Community promised to protect its members from social approaches that might, for one reason or another, either temporarily or permanently, be deemed unattractive. Every woman was free to refuse any, or every, man's attention. When two members aspired to closer relations, an intimation to that effect was given by the man, but always through the medium of an older woman who represented the Community and was authorized to control such negotiations. This was for the double purpose of overseeing and advising the young people, and of allowing the woman so approached to be perfectly free to decline without embarrassment."

The Oneida Community met many challenges and pioneered a number of social developments during its existence of nearly half a century. Industrious and inventive, the Community held an impressive and varied list of patents, including carpet travelling bags and lunch pails, innovations in the casting of steel traps, sash weights, window caps, architectural columns, wagon fixtures, sleigh shoes, machine for silk works, and the famous Oneida Community Silverware. When they had to turn to outside labor in their industries, they pioneered wages based on piece work and the eight-hour workday.

Oneida also pioneered in granting full equality to their women. They anticipated the unisex fashions of today. According to *The Circular*, "Woman's dress is a standing lie. It proclaims that she is not a two-legged animal, but something like a churn, standing on castors! When the distinction of the sexes is reduced to the bounds of nature and decency, a dress will be adopted that will be at the same time the most simple and the most beautiful; and it will be the same, or nearly the same, for both sexes." By midsummer of their first year at Oneida, Harriet Noyes, Harriet Skinner, and Mary Cragin had discarded ankle-length skirts in favor of pantalets and knee-length skirts. And in a really shocking innovation for the time, the women gave up their routine of devoting an hour each morning to combing their waist-length hair in favor of shoulder-length styling. Two women ran the local Express Agency. Exciting weeks were spent in 1868 discussing the impossible styling of women's shoes, the fashionable high-heeled Balmoral and Gaiter boots which proved very impractical in the farm work of the women. They decided to design and make their own ankle-high shoe with a low, flat heel. Their rubber-lined shoes were comfortable and could be slipped on in a minute. "The children's feet were [also] to be treated scientifically—never deformed by misshapen clumsy boots."

Education was a prime concern of the Community. Everyone studied English grammar, German, French, Greek, mathematics, and writing. Play and sports, including swimming, were on a coed basis. A Community university was planned but unfortunately did not get off the ground. Malthus, Plato, Greek history and literature, the classics, as well as a variety of fiction and current periodicals, lined the many shelves of the Mansion library where men and women gathered frequently to read and discuss intellectual issues.

At its peak the Community at Oneida had over 350 members. A branch in Brooklyn had twenty-five members and the Newark Commune, fifteen members. The Wallingford Community had eighteen members and smaller associations existed in Putney and Cambridge, Vermont.

On March 9, 1876, *The Circular* announced that John Humphrey Noyes was retiring as leader of Oneida to devote his full time to editing a new paper, *The American Socialist*, leaving his son Theodore Richards Noyes as new president of the Community. On August 28, 1879, the Community announced its intention of giving up the practice of complex marriage and of returning to the common social custom of monogamy. Communal life continued, however, along with the common ownership of their businesses and other properties, and with the communal care of the children. Then on January 1, 1881, the Oneida Community dissolved with each member receiving a proportionate share of stocks in the assets.

My reason for detailing the fortunes of the fantastic and not commonly known Oneida Community should already be evident in the context of our discussion earlier of monogamy and its alternatives. Oneida in many ways was a world of its own, but it was also one of the few successful attempts at communal living and group marriage in the American tradition. More important for our purposes, I find in the success of Oneida cause for serious skepticism about the possible success of today's group marriages and communes as an alternative to monogamy viable in our American culture. An expert on family patterns around the world, sociologist William Goode, echoes this pes-

simism (in Packard's *Sexual Wilderness*): "No communal family
pattern in the modern world has ever evolved naturally, without
political force and revolutionary fervor, and both Russia and
Israel have already retreated toward the conjugal family after considerable communal experience." It may well be that communal
marriages are viable only in an agrarian and non-technological
society. But there are other factors, for Oneida certainly was
technologically and industrially oriented for its day.

In commenting on the still unexplained death of the Oneida
Community, Constance Noyes Robertson, John Noyes' grand-
daughter, suggests that "the chief general cause of the fatal
change was a gradual loss of the religious faith which was their
reason for being, the cement which held them together through
so many vicissitudes. When they lost this, they began to lose
everything—their security, their agreement, their selflessness,
their happiness. What brought about this irreplaceable loss may
be a point of debate. It may be as simple a fact as that faith
cannot be inherited or is not transmissible from one generation
to another. Or possibly the most important cause was the
ageing and then the retirement of their leader, John Humphrey
Noyes.

"His intelligence, his wonderfully magnetic personality, his
strong influence and control, his extraordinarily intuitive dealing with the human problems involved, or perhaps most of all
his absolutely unflagging faith could not be reproduced, even
with all the good will in the world, by his successor."

Today's commune movement is inspired, like all its utopian
predecessors, by a quest for community, unselfish love, and an
expanded family relation. Having studied the movement in
depth for a number of years during which he convened national
gatherings and met with participants in dozens of communes,
Rustum Roy, in "The Obsolescence of Marriage, American-
Style," comes to the very pessimistic conclusion "that while
some sort of joint living arrangements will continue on a
fairly widespread scale within the college population, the com-

mune as a pattern of life and interpersonal relations is not a live option on the U.S scene. This conclusion is based on two very simple facts of life: First, that life in a commune demands the mutual commitment to a substantial degree of some ten or more persons. This is a statistically unlikely event. Second, life in a commune demands much more structure and discipline (about authority, economics and sex) than an ordinary marriage; and young Americans today are especially short on discipline. Many communes fail because members cannot agree on who should do the dishes or carry out the garbage!"

Even the staunch advocate of sexual liberalism Albert Ellis agrees, in Otto's *The Family in Search of a Future*, that "it is highly unlikely that group marriage will ever fully replace monogamic mating, or even that the majority of Westerners will voluntarily choose it instead of our present marital system." But even when practiced by a relatively small number of very dedicated and serious people, Ellis finds that "many serious difficulties and disadvantages" plague the best of group marriages: the difficulty of finding four or more adults of both sexes who can truly live together harmoniously in scheduling the daily chores, in mutual creative interests, in balancing the inevitable tensions of sexual and emotional involvements, and in balancing the sex ratio since many more men than women seem interested in group marriages. The advantages, however, are also present and include a considerable amount of sexual variety, a widening and enhancing of love relations for many individuals, an intensified family life, a sharing of social and economic responsibilities which makes living easier, and a heightened sense of brotherhood.

Yet, with all these advantages, Ellis and others have observed that inevitably these group marriages "last from about several months to a few years and then seem to break up for one reason or another, particularly for nonsexual reasons." Nevertheless, in December, 1970 the *New York Times* conservatively estimated the number of communes in the U.S. to be well over two thousand scattered through at least thirty-four states.

In Denmark the idea of a modified megafamily has gained considerable popularity and social acceptability. In the late sixties one group of thirty-three families jointly planned a megafamily unit just outside Copenhagen in which each family has its own split-level house with the children downstairs, separated from the parents upstairs by a middle span of family rooms. These individul homes are then clustered around shared gardens, outdoor kitchens and workshops, a swimming pool, playground, a kindergarten, a teen club complete with discothèque and greenhouse, and even a small zoo. A short distance away, in another Copenhagen suburb, a second group has ventured into building a "megahouse" large enough for at least 100 people, its two-and-a-half stories covering two acres. The interior of the megahouse has been described by Jan Gudman-Hoyer, its architect, as "something like a monastery. The private sleeping rooms for parents and children are narrow —rather small. Each room has its own 'minikitchen,' but the size of these rooms will encourage families to share the larger common rooms."

One form of large group marriage or commune that seems to have the best viability potential on the American scene is a modified version of the religious community seen in Oneida. In Chicago, 250 adults and children have adopted a "family-style monasticism" under the auspices of a new ecumenical organization. Members of the Ecumenical Institute share the same quarters, cook and eat their meals together, worship together, share their responsibilities for child raising, and pool their financial resources. But like other modern successes in communal living, they have reduced a prime source of tension by remaining monogamously coupled. Alvin Toffler reports that by mid-1970 at least sixty thousand people had passed through the Ecumenical courses and spread out to establish similar communes in Atlanta, Boston, Los Angeles, and other cities. The Society of Brothers, Bruderhof, in Rifton, New York, is a similar religious group testing the family-style monastic life in common.

Israel's kibbutzim are the prime example of family life modified along communal lines. The kibbutz, Ferdynand Zweig reports (*Israel: The Sword and the Harp*), "is a multi-functional institution with many contradictory features. It is a cross between a large estate and a village; it has traits of both a large family and a monastery; it has the air of a labour camp as well as a holiday resort. It displays also characteristics of a training camp, a summer school and a first-class educational establishment. It has something of the utopian-like communistic early settlements in the United States but it also has some features of a military camp of the Teutonic Knights fighting on the border against the Slavs. It has something of the character of a permanent discussion group and a Jewish Congress, a first-class political unit. For all its features as an integral collective, it lays stress on the free development of personality, encouraging all sorts of artistic and cultural activities. In the Kibbutz the full personality can grow and reach its full stature, and the potential artist can express himself and directly reach his audience. For all its egalitarian ideology, the Kibbutz members acquire something of the status of the landed nobility, staffing the highest positions in government, Histadrut and officer corps. For all its modernity, the Kibbutz is part of the larger process of archaization of Israeli society, of the archaic turned modern."

The first two modern kibbutzim were founded in 1908 and 1909, as an attempt to link a highly developed technological economy with a traditional form of village life. This was done by forming a work-together/live-together community bonded by common ownership, common production, and a communal spirit of comradeship, mutual help, and understanding. Since members of the kibbutz must not only work together but also live together, a great number of potential candidates and interested parties are eliminated because they cannot adapt to life in common. A one-year probation is a minimum requirement before full admission to the kibbutz. The exercise of authority in the kibbutz differs quite a bit from that in the Oneida Community and relies on a rotating leadership and the self-discipline of its members rather than on a charismatic leader.

Sixty years is a long life span for a communal venture, and observers like Zweig report that a "certain erosion of the original spirit and enthusiasm has taken place. Both the institution and the pioneers have aged. . . . Disenchantment, routinization, formalization, friction and strain follow the realization of an idea. The revolutionaries of yesterday became the Establishment of today and the imaginative and the inspiring of yesterday became routine and boring. The pioneers became disillusioned and somehow they were unable to impart their original enthusiasm to their sons. When one asked a veteran kibbutznik whether the new generation has the same enthusiasm, he answered, 'They take it for granted, it all fell into their lap ready made.'"

Zweig attributes the decline of the kibbutzim to several factors: the new ease of affluence, an enormous demand for professional, technical, and scientific workers which the kibbutzim schools cannot meet, depoliticalizing of the movement, the decline of agriculture, and an increased immigration of oriental Jews who have not been influenced by Western socialism and the co-operative movements.

The future of the kibbutz as a modified form of family life is still problematic in Israel. Whether it can be adapted to life in the United States or anywhere outside Israel is another question. In the many writings about the kibbutz, one small observation might be recalled here before we pass on to other random mixes. In the early days of the kibbutzim, marriage was relatively informal: two adults simply asked the community for double living quarters. They moved in but kept their original names. If later they had a child, they were officially declared married. As their children matured, each was given a room of his own, a mark of some independence. Premarital sex was taken for granted, and if a young couple decided to marry, it was taken for granted that they would follow the same informal pattern as their parents had. But the younger generation is reverting to the ostentatious, formal engagements, showers, and full-blown wedding celebrations of other Western cultures.

However unstable the large communal "marriage" might prove when it is not religiously oriented and sexually monogamous, a different situation arises when we try to evaluate the much less visible and far more extensive small group marriages involving two or three couples. Could Bob and Carol, Ted and Alice have made it as a group marriage? There are many similarities between their situation and that of the two respectable middle-class couples in Robert Rimmer's novel-essay *Proposition Thirty-one*. Unlike their cinematic quadruplets, Nancy and David Herndon face their involvements with Tanya and Horace Shea without the safety valve of a Hollywood cop-out. After many conflicts and tensions, and a near-perfect weekend together with their children at a ski cabin in New Hampshire, the two couples decide they cannot continue as sexually exclusive couples. They must share their future as a plural marriage.

Today's multilateral marriages, Larry and Joan Constantine have observed in their studies, appear to be a *substantially new development which must be viewed in a new perspective.* Unlike multilateral and communal marriages of the past the contemporary plural marriage is not based on male or female dominance, or on implied possession of the spouse as in polygamous marriages of past generations. Furthermore, today's multilateral marriage does not find communal living under one roof a necessity. It can and often does thrive with separate households.

Models of today's multilateral marriages are as varied as the individual experiences. Paradigms are impossible to set up, for the groups may vary in the number of participants, the sex ratio, the types and strengths of heterosexual and homosexual affections, their structure (ranging from patriarchal to amorphous), and their underlying basis (love, the charisma of one individual, the mutual convictions of politics, a common vocational interest, or deep psychological dependencies).

Some broad generalizations, however, are possible, and Larry and Joan Constantine, directors of the Multilateral Relations Study Project, have sketched these in an article for *The Futurist* in a way that offers some insights into what we can expect to see in multilateral relations in the years ahead. They note, for instance, that participation in multilateral marriages is not experimental. "Virtually all of our respondents intend their multilateral relationship to be permanent or long-lived. Many of these people are in their thirties and forties and regard a multilateral marriage as a major step in 'settling down' after a prolonged period of experimentation. In the near term, at least, many groups are stable; some of our respondents have several continuous years of successful joint residence and interaction behind them."

Children, the Constantines point out, "are major beneficiaries. To our initial surprise, children seem to respond exceptionally positively to a multilateral marriage by their parents. They thrive on the extra affection and attention, the multiplied security, the more relaxed, less-harried parents. The multiplicity of adult models enables a wider expression of their own selves, avoiding the stereotypification engendered by a single pair of parents. Though a major longitudinal study is clearly called for, at present it appears that the laterally expanded family is a much improved child-rearing environment.

"Integration is a difficult and complex process. We cite this most important limitation for its implications for society. Finding reasonably compatible couples or individuals and integrating them into an emotionally positive, functioning multi-person family unit may be orders of magnitude harder than forming a productive dyadic marriage." In a traditional marriage there is one basic two-person relationship to cope with; in a triangular marriage, three basic relations exist; in a four-party marriage, there are six relations; and a group marriage of 15 people has to deal with 105 distinct relationships!

The dynamics and stability potential of the multilateral marriages pose a perplexing task for the analyst. Models which in theory appear to have a very high stability potential may in practice prove very unstable because of the individuals involved, their lack of commitment, their naïveté about the complexities of the relationship, or their immaturity in a variety of ways. Still the threesome, or triangular marriage, discussed in the previous chapters appears by far to be the most stable paradigm. After discussing the relative stability of three-, four-, and six-party marriages with Robert Rimmer, I chanced on an article about Buckminster Fuller and the many problems to which his principle of geometric stability in the triangle and geodesic dome has been applied, even in the study of human relations. This coincidence led me to wonder about a possible connection between the relative stability of geometric and human triangles in contrast with squares and four-party marriages, which frequently evolve into a triangle, with one of the four persons being shoved onto the sidelines.

Six-party marriages have a definite advantage over both triangles and quadrangles because they provide a situation that is less sensitive to the moods of any one individual. A marriage of six can probably tolerate some relatively permanent competition, indifference, or even antagonism that smaller groups cannot cope with.

Carefully planned experiments in multilateral relationships and communal experience are rare today, but one strikes me as being particularly viable and important. This is the Sandstone Retreat, or more formally, the Sandstone Foundation for Community Systems Research. Founded four years ago by Barbara and John Williamson, this experiment nestles on the crest of the magnificent, wild Topanga Canyon, just north of Los Angeles. The panorama sweeps from the austere but rich Malibu Mountains down over the Santa Monica Bay to the offshore island of Santa Catalina, perfect for the relaxing experience and sensual atmosphere Sandstone tries to offer its members.

"The strength and lasting significance of the Sandstone experience lies in human contact divorced from the cocktail party context with all its games and dodges and places to hide." The founders of Sandstone refer to its setting as a "retreat from artificiality," an environment deliberately and carefully designed to promote human relations on all levels, "a new kind of community where a person's mind, body and being are no longer strangers to each other."

The physical facilities of this intentional community offer a variety of moods and environments: a 100-foot-long plushly carpeted main living room with its mammoth fireplace, a large buffet dining room, the comfortable kitchen usually populated with more men than women—all this plus a bedroom or two on the upper level; on the first floor of the U-shaped ranch set in the hillside, a large paneled lounge sensually lighted with strobes and colored lights, a pool table and bar, several water beds, another stone fireplace, and a cozy room off the end replete with wall-to-wall mattresses; in a nearby building an indoor swimming pool, sensually warmed to body temperature; and clustered around the main buildings, several cottages.

In this unusual environment the varied members of Sandstone are free to relax and do whatever they wish in a spirit of natural community and mutuality. Members come from a functional cross section of the Los Angeles area and include doctors, factory workers, actresses, accountants, nurses, students, business executives, lawyers, artists, explorers, teachers. Their individual reasons for coming to Sandstone are as varied as their backgrounds. Their unity lies in a deep-seated need for honesty, sharing, and freedom from the artificial. In this atmosphere open sexuality and physical nakedness is relaxed, low-keyed, and fully human without pressure or fear or compulsion.

One of the many fascinating aspects of Sandstone is the open acceptance of pluralisms within its structure. There are many levels, from the intimacy of the basic core group flowing around Barbara and John Williamson, Marty and Tom and Sondra on a more permanent level, to what I might term a secondary plane of secure, relaxed couples who find in Sandstone a retreat from city noise, tension, uptightness, and compartmentalization by dropping by during the day or on quiet evenings. A third, much more peripherally involved group of "swinging" couples attend the twice-weekly parties.

It is impossible to verbalize the realities of the diffused, low-keyed, "McLuhanesque cool" sensuality-sexuality which permeates the Sandstone community. But the steady reliance on feedback and constant re-evaluation within a basic but flexible process philosophy makes me think that such intentional communities, combining a variety of levels of intimacy, sensuality, and life styles, might prove very valuable in our age of transition.

Actually, Sandstone should not be described as an "intentional" community. A more accurate description would place it in the area of an intentional or engineered environment that facilitates the formation and evolution of *various types of communities* among its members. Sandstone simply tries to *facilitate human relations and intimacies of all types and intensities* within an atmosphere that respects human dignity and individualities. It is a search for the *possibilities of what communities might be.*

Like the Roys and other observers, Larry and Joan Constantine view the multilateral marriage as a "promising growth-oriented form of marriage," but a venture "limited to a relative few." However, they are quick to emphasize that "the fact that a form so far removed from the norm of American marriage is attempted at all, is encouraging."

In "How to Make a Group Marriage," Larry and Joan Constantine touch on many practical points which might be of interest recalling here. They suggest that each participant in a multilateral marriage must examine and know his or her own motives. Real difficulties in an existing marriage are not going to be solved in a group marriage. Then each participant must be willing to accept an evolution in his or her implied structures of interpersonal relations. There has to be a real commitment to genuine, substantial, and unrelenting personal growth. Dragging a reluctant spouse into a multilateral relationship is sheer disaster, though married couples can make the transition more easily than a single person, perhaps, because of their experience in adapting to a two-party marriage. People are far more important in a plural marriage than the idea which brings them together, with the ability to have fun and relax together being vital to their survival as a group. In building a plural marriage, the Constantines suggest a real advantage in an initial commitment for a specified period of time to avoid constant and corrosive re-evaluations. Everyone in the group must become aware of and build on the strengths and assets of all the members and of the group as a whole, avoiding group pressures on any one person and also the subtle pressure that all relationships within the group should develop at the same pace.

The sexual relations of a group marriage often bring to the surface hidden jealousies, possessiveness, exclusiveness, and competition. Group sexual experience in particular brings these tendencies into the open. Men become competitive. They wonder how they compare with other men and how the women rate them as lovers. Winners and losers appear in the group. Homosexual hangups also can surface. All of these must be dealt with openly and frankly by the group. Some observers suggest "swinging" as a good treatment for jealousy and exclusivity, but as we pointed out in the previous chapter, this generally does not solve the real problem of human possessiveness.

Finally, the Constantines are very strong in urging the necessity of privacy for all parties in a multilateral relation. A "private turf" is an important stabilizer which the women (and men) who stay at home with the children lack far more often than the men and women working outside the home. Rules and regulations are very helpful but there is always the danger of over-ritualizing an exploratory, dynamic, and ever-changing relationship.

All this reveals some of the complexities of multilateral relationships and why they are not likely to outnumber the more easily attained benefits of flexible monogamy and the triangular marriage.

Having worked our way back to three-party marriages, let us take off on a slightly different tack and explore two modifications in parenthood: the possibility of our increasing reliance on professional parents and the possibility of postponing parenthood to an early retirement age.

EIGHT

Professional and Retired Parents

No GENERATION of humans has ever devoted as much time or effort to the all-important task of child raising. Yet no generation of humans has wasted more time or effort on the non-essentials and ignored more completely the essence of proper child raising. We devote millions of dollars each year to educating our young people for the professions in which they will be earning their livelihood. Yet our only formal investment in preparing our young people for responsible parenthood comes in the form of lavish weddings, showers, and the inevitable white-leather copy of Dr. Spock's classic. Parenthood is the only profession for which our modern society offers no formal training or preparation. We assume that every young person is endowed by nature with all the instinct, ability, and skill necessary to be a good parent when he or she says "I do" and receives a social license to procreate at will.

This problem was faced with considerable courage by the members of the Oneida Community in their boldest undertaking, the Stirpiculture project. "Stirpiculture" is a term John Noyes derived from the Latin word for stock, *stirpes*, and the English word for cultivating, with a view to improvement. The new term was deliberately chosen to express the belief of the Oneida Community that the *art* of reproduction and raising children is the highest and most sacred art human beings can undertake. It requires tremendous skill, patience, and talent to be a good parent. But the Oneida people also undoubtedly chose this sedate term to offset some of the sharp denunciations of licentiousness, adultery, "free love," and debauchery heaped on them by outside critics. An experiment in marriage and parenthood as radical as Oneida could not escape public criticism, even though two grand-jury investigations found nothing to condemn in their customs and even though the Governor of New York and other prominent men who received copies of the Oneida Annual Reports likewise found nothing to object to in the detailed accounts of complex marriage and Stirpiculture.

For twenty-one years, from 1848 to 1869, the Community struggled to achieve the financial security that they felt was necessary for a successful outcome of their eugenic project. During these years only thirty-five children were born, less than two a year in a population of more than three hundred. Male continence was rigorously practiced in the Community and with great success. Those children that were born were permitted as a concession to the women who would likely be beyond child bearing by the time the Stirpiculture program could go into effect.

Finally, early in 1869, the whole Community gathered to vote on the new project. The original documents are no longer available, but we do have a report from Robert Parker, author of *A Yankee Saint*, who examined the original records thoroughly before they were unfortunately burned after the death of John Noyes' brother, George. Parker reports that the discussion resulted in a unanimous vote by the members to launch the program.

A statement was then signed by the fifty-three women who testified to their willingness to serve this novel project. The statement is both humorous and fascinating for its insights into the psychology of the Community and its female members. The young ladies affirmed:

"1. That we do not belong to ourselves in any respect, but that we belong first to God, and second to Mr. Noyes as God's true representative.

"2. That we should have no rights or personal feelings in regard to childbearing which shall in the least degree oppose or embarrass him in his choice of scientific combinations.

"3. That we put aside all envy, childishness, and self-seeking, and rejoice with those who are chosen candidates; that we will, if necessary, become martyrs to science, and cheerfully renounce all desire to become mothers, if for any reason Mr. Noyes deem us unfit material for propagation. Above all, we offer ourselves 'living sacrifices' to God and true Communism."

The young men signed a similar but briefer statement: "The undersigned desire you may feel that we most heartily sympathize with your purpose in regard to scientific propagation, and offer ourselves to be used in forming any combinations that may seem to you desirable. We claim no rights. We ask no privileges. We desire to be servants of the truth. With a prayer that the grace of God will help us in this resolution, we are your true soldiers."

Eventually, according to *The Circular*, one hundred men and women shared in the Stirpiculture experiment, and eighty-one of these became parents. "Fifty-eight live children were brought into the world; there were four still-births. During the earlier years couples desiring to undertake a Stirpicultural experiment applied to the cabinet of central members to decide on their fitness. This meant that in reality John Noyes directed the mating (for procreation), and in certain cases strictly forbade it. On January 25, 1875, a formal Stirpicultural Committee was appointed by the Community. This committee was composed of six men and six women. Two of its members were graduates of the Yale medical school and the rest were chosen for their exceptional experience and sagacity. However, this committee functioned during a period of only fifteen months. After April 20, 1876, direction of the Stirpicultural policy again passed into the hands of the central members of the Community. These changes of policy seem to indicate some inner disagreement.

"Records of the Stirpicultural Committee indicate the general method of selection. In the majority of cases, application to the Committee was made by couples desiring to become parents. After due consideration, the Committee either approved or vetoed the selection. If an application was disapproved, the Committee would always undertake to find other combinations satisfactory to all concerned, which it could approve. Occasionally the Committee itself took the initiative in bringing about combinations which, in its opinion, were specially 'indicated.'"

Fathers of the Stirpiculdts, as the offspring were called, were on an average twelve years older than the mothers. This age difference could be traced in large part to the fact that leaders in the Community were fathers more frequently than younger males. John Noyes fathered at least nine of the fifty-eight children born during the experiment. The central committee was much more concerned about the selection of fathers than it was of the mothers, perhaps reflecting the common belief of the day that the male seed is far more important than the female incubator.

Of fifty-one applications from prospective parents, nine were vetoed and forty-two approved. The Stirpiculdts were treated no differently from the other children in the Community. During early infancy they remained in the care of their mothers and were admitted to the day nursery in the Children's House only when they could walk. During this period the mother took care of the child at night. From the beginning of the play stage until adolescence the Children's House had complete charge though the parents dropped by to visit their children regularly and the children visited the parents at home. In the Children's House much attention was devoted to diet, clothing, sanitation, and "profitable activity." Epidemics that were common in the outside society did not appear in the Community, while sickness in the Children's House was rare. In case of sickness, the children had immediate medical care and nursing. There were facilities for quarantine, night nurses, and appliances for comfort and convenience that few private families could afford.

The seriousness of this experiment is indicated in a discussion from the April 3, 1865 issue of *The Circular:* "Assuming then that we have to deal with a science of breeding that gives definite results, we refer again to our question, what is the point to be first aimed at in the improvement of the human stock? Shall it be physical perfection, beauty of form, strength, complexion, health? Shall it be sagacity, acuteness of mind? Shall it be amiability of disposition? These are questions for consideration. Again, shall we adopt some fixed type, as the Anglo-Saxon man, or the classical Greek type, and selecting the most beautiful examples of one of these classes, breed to them as a standard? Or shall we recognize the variety of nature as the rule, and seek only to perfect the multifarious types that are now extant, each according to its own peculiarities of style and constitution? These are to be resolved by careful thought. The subject is new, and will have to be approached by degrees, until practical experiment shall have thrown its light upon the broad pathway that, through truthful, scientific propagation, must lead the race up to its ideal and destiny."

Oneida's Stirpiculture project began a hundred years ago. In an age when unlimited reproduction was taken for granted and women had as many children as they could bear, the members of Oneida were very selective about how many children they had and who had them. In a child-centered culture, they boldly proclaimed that "the love and care of children in parents should not supplant or interfere with their love as man and woman." Long before the advent of today's nuclear family, while children were still basking in the relatively broad environment of the nineteenth-century extended family, they argued that "the child is best brought up in an open Community element, and not in a closed circle of family relatives." The members of Oneida took parenthood and child raising so seriously that they were not willing to leave it to just anyone who decided to sleep with someone and have a child. The Children's House at Oneida was staffed by what sociologists today would call "professional parents," the same kind of gifted, trained adults that some educators and psychologists maintain we desperately need today.

In seventeenth-century France, one quarter of all children born died in their first year and only half of all the children born lived to see their fourth birthday. Women spent practically all their adult lives giving birth and caring for their children, though as psychologist and historian David Hunt points out in his *Parent and Child in Seventeenth-Century France*, any mother who could afford a full- or part-time nurse was more than happy to be rid of the burden of child raising, simple as it was in those days and limited to a short seven years. Today, a mother of two usually plans on spending about 12 percent of her adult years caring for her offspring full time and then sharing her responsibility with professional educators, summer-camp directors, day-care and nursery staffs, Boy and Girl Scout leaders, and other parental substitutes for another 30 percent of her adult life. In many respects we already have an extensive staff of professional "parents" at work in our society.

The American family has not yet formally opted for "professional parents," but we are certainly well on our way to this custom. Gene Weltfish, an anthropologist at Fairleigh Dickinson University, often speaks of the "loyal person" whose services parents can contract for in helping them to meet the complexities of child raising in today's society. Some sociologists have, for instance, found very close similarities between the American suburban and inner-city families and the modern version of Oneida's "professional parents," labeling our present custom of child raising, with summer camps, day-care centers, nursery schools, and extracurricular school activities, a "modified American kibbutz."

In drafting plans for a model society most utopian thinkers, both contemporary and past, set a primacy on professional child care by the whole community and a trained staff. These planners are also quite concerned about liberating married men and women from their routine homemaking tasks. This is obvious in the workings of both Oneida and the modern kibbutz, which offer some interesting comparisons with our more moderate institutionalized communal child care in America. In the kibbutzim, the newborn child spends most of his first year with his mother, often being breast-fed; but nurseries are available. In some settlements, a mother can keep an eye on the nursery flagpole from the fields, knowing that when her baby needs her her flag will be flown and she can hasten back to the compound. After the first year communal nursery schools take over complete care of the child during the day and the parents see their offspring only during the evening hours and on holidays. A similar pattern held in Oneida.

But how do the real mothers, with their "maternal instinct," react to what appears to us as a very unnatural arrangement? A hundred years ago one new mother from Oneida described her feelings in *The Circular*: "Corinna has now been in the nursery two weeks, and as my room is nearby I've had a chance to observe the working of the new plan and am convinced that she is happier and has as good if not better care than when I had entire charge of her myself; and when I go every evening at six to get her she is always delighted to see me and I, feeling rested and fresh instead of tired and impatient, take more real comfort than before. The love I've had for my baby has never given me the happiness that I expected to realize, for with it has been a feeling of anxiety and worry lest she should be sick, and perhaps taken from me, or that some accident or other might come to her; but since I gave her up that trouble has been taken from me, and in its place I have a feeling of rest and thankful-

ness. I now realize as I did not before, that the old way of each
mother caring exclusively for her own child, begets selfishness
and idolatry; and in many ways tends to degrade woman. The
new system works well in every respect, but particularly do I
appreciate the opportunity it affords me of not only joining in
public work but of self-improvement and 'going home' to God
every day."

Oneida's professional parents were just as enthusiastic. As
one substitute mother explained: "The feeling that the mothers
are in full sympathy with us gives us good heart, and the babies
do not suffer from the separation as they would if their mothers'
hearts were bleeding. I have never felt so interested and given
up to any work that I have ever been in as this, and it was
never so easy for me to ask God for help in any work as this.
The babies are all well. We spread an old quilt on the carpet
and they sit on it with their play things a good share of the time,
and seem to think it is the nicest place in the house. Their
fathers come in often and give them a tossing, and baby-lovers
all through the Community find a new source of enjoyment.
The four are getting into the habit of taking their naps at about
the same time, which gives us a chance to rest."

But what about the effect on the children? Would this
"abnormal situation" create confusion in their minds? Parents
in communes have always been aware of this danger. But it
seems that the children are able to accept as "natural" whatever
the community and their "parents" treat as natural, much the
same way an adopted or artificially inseminated child accepts his
condition as normal and natural provided the parents treat it
that way.

In Oneida the children ended up with several parents, starting with their biological father and mother and the "third
parents" in the Children's House. Since the mothers also sometimes exchanged children or temporarily adopted those not
their own, more parents were involved. To complicate the matter further, when a child went to Wallingford or one of the

other communes, it might pick up still another set of parents. The result was a unique set of relations that puzzled inquisitive strangers, as one story in *The Circular* recalls: "Yesterday a carriage containing some fashionably dressed ladies drove round the buildings and passed in front of the Children's House. Conspicuous among a group of children at play was Temple (four years old), first on an inverted wheelbarrow. The carriage stopped.

" 'Where are your parents, little boy?'

" 'My Papa Noyes and Mama Miller are at Wallingford.'

"Now the ladies evidently felt themselves on the right track. Another charge as successful as this might result in storming the fortification.

" 'Miller! That's a nice name; and what is your own name besides Miller?'

"The reply has such amplitude, such rolling fullness, such *naïveté* and simplicity, that we record it: 'My name is Temple Noyes Dunn Burt Ackley!'

"We scarcely need add that the enemy was astounded, repulsed, utterly discomfited, and sped away."

Is this an "unnatural" reaction, for the strangers, or for Temple?

Many social scientists and educators have been deeply interested in the impact of the kibbutzim system on today's children. Bruno Bettelheim, a leading expert and advocate of the communal raising of children, argues that the bad name associated with communal child raising can be traced to situations where a large number of children were placed under the care of poorly trained and indifferent adults. In the typical kibbutz, where small groups and skilled, devoted staff are the rule, Bettelheim concludes that the "children turn into exceptionally courageous, self-reliant, secure, un-neurotic and deeply committed adults who find their self-realization in work and in marriage. Though most have some previous sexual experience, they marry in their early twenties and soon have children who in turn are brought up in the communal nursery schools. There are almost no divorces . . . and adultery is rare and severely punished" (in *The Children of the Dream*).

Albert Rabin, a child specialist at Michigan State University, has compared kibbutzim children with children of the same age from regular families and found those raised in communes unusually frank, friendly, generous, and willing to share. They were also more trusting and less reserved, and generally had a higher intellectual development and emotional maturity. As for their sexual code, it was much stricter than that of non-kibbutzim children.

What happens, though, to the parent/child interaction in this situation? What happens to the emotional and personal growth of the parents when they are relieved of most of the woes, tensions and exasperations, disciplining, and opposition that parents usually encounter? They enjoy, as New York psychologist Howard Halpern notes, all the fun and none of the anguish of parenthood. An answer to this question will require observations over several generations, which we do not have at the moment. However, as Bettelheim has already observed, the relations between parents and their children in the kibbutzim lack a certain intensity and resemble more the relationships that ordinarily exist between children and their grandparents. "Kibbutz children," Bettelheim suggests, "were not beset by parents' typical anxieties—the hopes and fears we harbor about children who are ours." Halpern, however, is more pessimistic about the impact on the parents, wondering whether the kibbutz situation can really satisfy their desire to create, guide, and shape a new individual. He contends that the trials of parenthood may play a major role in developing an adult's capacity for giving, sacrificing, protecting, and loving. In short, he is convinced that full parenthood and its trials are a powerful influence in the maturing of people, in shedding their tendencies to narcissism and self-involvement, and that the kibbutzim arrangement works against this maturing challenge.

The Soviet family relies very heavily on industry-sponsored day-care centers. After breakfast, David Mace reports, the typical Russian mother leaves her baby or toddler at the nursery attached to her place of employment. Well-trained doctors, nurses, and other attendants then care for the child, with the mother dropping by for a half hour every three or four hours to nurse her child. This absence from work is allowed for by the company and the mother is not docked for her time off. She is also allowed four months' paid vacation when her child is born. For older children, the schools provide a whole range of classes, study periods, and school activities to occupy the children till their mothers are home from work.

The very emotional controversy over working mothers and their neglected and emotionally deprived offspring that racked American families during the Second World War has not faded completely from our consciousness, and many Western observers read about the Soviet working mother with great skepticism. But Mace contends that Soviet children as a whole had a high emotional security, and Bettelheim notes that Russian children are very well behaved and relate well with their parents.

On the American scene some interesting trends toward an American-styled kibbutzim society appear in the increased demand for day-care centers and nurseries both in the inner city and in the suburbs. But New York psychologist Carl Levett carries this one step further, and suggests the emergence and acceptance of professional "third parents" in the American family. "Future family configurations will need to form and meander freely," Levett argues, "rather than to be adjusted to a fixed and preconceived traditional formulation. If this concept can be accepted, then so can a changing family model whose paternal figure no longer serves the classical father-son child-rearing role....

"The evolution of a third-parent model is likely to begin in family establishments whose fathers function in a free-form manner. These men, highly respected and successful in their own fields of endeavor and heavily committed to extra-marital responsibilities, are people-oriented as well as performance-oriented; they retain a sincere concern and devotion for their children's welfare, but because of limitations of time and energy are unable to provide a personal and responsive flow of contactual experience with their sons."

Levett believes that with paternal figures in diminishing supply, greater use will have to be made of supplementary masculine figures to maintain a proper father-son relationship. This masculine figure does not need to be the blood-kin father, and often in situations of single mothers, the blood-kin father is unavailable for this purpose. "The trend toward specialization of skills and talents will make possible the emergence of a 'third parent,' a male figure educated, trained, and equipped to serve the socializing needs of male children. Substitutive forms of help from paternal figures (such as camp counselors, pediatricians, school psychologists, and scoutmasters) are being offered to young males in increasing degrees. Such efforts are essentially piecemeal and lack the continuity of the breadth-and-depth involvement of a third-parent relationship aimed at serving the whole child in terms of potentiality release, parental and family integration, peer participation, and development of sound personal values."

Obviously, the role and function of a masculine "third parent" should not be limited to young boys. Single mothers, whether divorced, widowed, or merely unwed, surely could make valued use of a "surrogate father," specially trained, dedicated, and skilled. Likewise, many single fathers could use a feminine "third parent."

My good friend and futurist colleague Irving Buchen told me recently of his experience in addressing a convention of summer-camp directors and counselors on the future of the family. Several of the directors approached him afterward to discuss their new and frightening role as "third parents." One director recalled a very explosive situation in which without warning a divorced father presented his three teen-age daughters with his prospective bride, a swinging lass only a few years older than his daughters, scantily clad in hot pants and the briefest halter. The confrontation occurred at camp and the mother was extremely grateful that the camp counselors could work with her daughters individually to help them overcome this emotional shock. We are likely to see much more of the third parent in various guises in the last third of this century.

In 1971 a new social phenomenon clearly moved us further along the line toward "professional parents" when the news media suddenly discovered a rather widespread suburban custom: child swapping. Quietly and without publicity, it appears suburban parents across the country had become aware that the occasional "difficult periods" of child raising when parent and child lose the ability to communicate might be solved quite easily by allowing the child to move in with another sympathetic family. The authority challenges of a growing child, it seems, can be facilitated if instead of confronting his threatened parents head on he can learn to express his individuality under the guidance of a sympathetic and impartial outside authority in whose house he has freely chosen to live for a time. This is just another variation on the theme of the "professional parent" on a part-time basis, but it too is indicative of the future.

The Industrial Revolution has had its definite impact on family life in the past two centuries, with the evolution of child-labor laws, the need for increased education and training, and an expanded social adolescence. But it is already impacting on family life from a totally new angle. More and more industries and service vocations, such as police, firemen, and sanitation men, are accepting union contracts which allow retirement at full or partial pay after twenty or thirty years' employment. This means that a man can retire in his forties, financially secure, with considerable leisure, and the stability of a paid-for home. In his younger days, he and his wife may travel and enjoy their togetherness as a couple without the worry of children. Then, with retirement, the couple can take advantage of their security and leisure to raise a family. Several possible avenues would be open to raising a family at this age: ordinary conception, artificial insemination with the husband's or a donor's frozen semen, test-tube fertilization of the wife's egg with her husband's semen followed by embryo transplant to a surrogate mother.

The possibility of retirement parenthood contains many very positive advantages, one of which was pointed out to me by an Irish friend. The Irish have practiced retirement parenthood for centuries in a modified form, but for entirely different reasons than it is being advocated today. In 1970, only 30 percent of the Irish men between twenty-five and thirty-four were married. My friend's father, for instance, was in his forties when my friend was born. The relationship that then developed between them was more like that between a grandfather and grandson. Gary told me that as a result of this age disparity many Irish fathers are far more tolerant and understanding, and much less inclined to be impatient with a son who does not do things their way because they realize from experience that there are many ways of doing something, not just one way. They are also more inclined to consult and guide indirectly rather than by issuing orders.'

But again, past experiences are helpful only to a point. What we are facing today with the possibility of "third parents" and retirement parenthood is something essentially new in many respects. It would be very dangerous to fall into the trap of saying that we have had this or that option before and handled it this or that way, so all we have to do is look to history for the answer. We are creating new options which have at best a superficial if instructive resemblance to past customs.

NINE

Polygamy for Senior Citizens; Contract, Unisex, and Celibate Marriages

POLYGAMY as an alternative to monogamous marriage in our culture today? "Not likely. . . . It might be all right for the Mormons in frontier days, but we are too sophisticated today to accept a man having several wives." Most people today dismiss polygamy in terms as offhanded as these.

Yet writer Ben Merson recently visited several polygamous families in Utah where certain fundamentalist Mormons still regard polygamy as essential to their religion. His estimate is that some thirty thousand Americans are living today in underground polygamous marriages. In *Future Shock*, Alvin Toffler offers a serious projection that "as sexual attitudes loosen up, as property rights become less important because of rising affluence—and I would add here, as women become more financially independent—the social repression of polygamy may come to be regarded as irrational. This shift may be facilitated by the very mobility that compels men to spend considerable time away from their present homes."

Admittedly, polygamy as practiced by Mormons and Africans has certain disadvantages—but every form of human relation has both advantages and disadvantages. In the Mormon tradition, a woman could not reach heaven unless she was married to a Mormon male. In the Mormon tradition and also in African cultures women were tied into a system of male dominance and often treated as the implied or open possession of the man. On the other hand, Dr. Seth Cudjoe, chief Ghanaian delegate to the thirty-nation Pan-African Cultural Congress held in Algiers in July, 1970, had a valid point when he remarked that "clearly the hypocrisy of secretive extramarital relations on which monogamy survives precariously in Europe cannot be maintained in African societies, which from the very beginning have never had any real quarrel with plural relationships." The intrusion of European monogamy into African colonies has brought a painful increase in illegitimate children sired by men "whose current marital status legally restricts them to one woman only, irrespective of whether or not she is capable of bearing children." And when one realizes that a childless marriage is not considered a valid marriage by the African cultures, the problem is further complicated.

The African view of polygamy is far from being primitive, though Christian missionaries and colonial administrators commonly painted it that way. In a colloquium on sexuality at Louvain University in Belgium, anthropologist Eugeen Roosens emphasized the sophisticated character of African polygamy. First of all, the right to take a second or third wife is carefully regulated by the tribe. A man cannot obtain permission until he has reached a mature age of thirty-five to forty. The polygamous state is considered a privileged one, reserved to the elders, those who by their wisdom are thought to be closer to the source of all life. But another characteristic advantage of African polygamy lies in the multiplication of matrimonial lines. The polygamist binds his family to several other families. He thus multiplies the representatives of his clan and lineage. He transmits life in abundance, which is a privilege reserved to persons with superior knowledge and social maturity. The polygamist also strengthens the economic position of his family, for in most African societies manual labor, the key to subsistence, is allotted to the women and children. The more women, the more children, the greater wealth. And this wealth in turn raises one's prestige in the community and serves the interests of the familial community, the clan, and the lineage. The polygamous husband also creates a large progeny to continue on earth the community of the elders and ancestors.

Small wonder, then, that as colonialism wanes, the Africans are reaffirming their original traditions, including polygamy. In July, 1969 the Parliament of Tanzania gave tentative approval to a new marriage code legalizing polygamy for Christians. Ir a population that is 25 percent Christian and 31 percent Mos lem, marriage practices are so fragmented and divergent among Moslem, Christian, and tribal codes that the government de cided some national structure had to be adopted. The result is that any husband may now take a second wife if his first wife "voluntarily and freely" gives her consent. For Christians, big amy would be permitted only if the husband had married the first time in a civil ceremony. A form of tribal marriage was also approved by a statement that if an unwed man and woman live together for two years, they are considered legally married. Naturally, some women objected and opened a campaign for the right to have more than one husband, while the Moslems objected to the voluntary-consent provision.

A serious question remains, considering the origins of po lygamy, whether it can survive in a capitalistic culture such as we have in Europe and America. Sociologist Alain Aymard has asked some cutting questions along this line: "For example— and this is only one among many other examples—if we study sexuality in our own society, we can pose such questions as this: how is it that in a society as monogamous as America it is so dangerous to take the [New York City] subway after nine o'clock at night because of the great risk of crime or rape? What form of sexuality is revealed in a society, however monogamous, which makes such use of sex in advertising? There is no end to the coarse and illogical absurdities: 'Use shampoo X and your wife will love you more'; 'Buy this product and your personality will blossom.' A serious study of this genre of advertising will uncover something of which advertisers are well aware and which they call 'conditioning': it is a matter of utilizing frustrations, to supply substitutes for them, to canalize them and exploit them for commercial ends. For example: What does it mean that an effective sales appeal, for whatsoever object, is conveyed by a semi-nude woman? What are the implications as to the attitude to sexuality at play? The feminine press is another point: as everyone knows, in France it is in the hands of men. An analysis of the content of such journals as Nous Deux and the like would result in any number of astonishing—I would even say, infantile—images and arguments which are the product of a monogamous society. . . . It can be asked whether monogamy does not accord particularly well with capitalistic society."

This last question-statement of Aymard deserves some serious consideration. It is very evident that sexually exclusive monogamy has succeeded in dominating *only in capitalistic industrial cultures*. In tribal cultures, polygamy and flexible forms of monogamy have endured and dominated because they serve the psychological, emotional, economic, and social conditions much better than strict monogamy would. But it is also evident that even as our culture is becoming more industrial and more technologically oriented, mass communications and travel are shifting us into a type of tribal culture: Marshall McLuhan's basic insight into the modern "global tribe." The concept of individuality in our culture is rapidly yielding, however slowly and painfully, to the concept of the collective communal person. Thus, if we are indeed moving toward a type of tribal consciousness on a global scale, perhaps polygamy can be modified and adapted to serve the new demands of a new social environment.

Another factor we might consider in this context involves work and leisure ratios. In a pure capitalistic society, most of one's energies must be spent on surviving, leaving little time or energy for anything beyond the minimum of sexual activity. But in a welfare socialistic society, the type of society we seem to be already pursuing, the basic needs are provided for by the community, and some of the energies previously devoted to surviving can now be turned to more leisurely living. What happens as more and more industries move toward a forty-hour, four-day workweek, or even a three-day workweek? Will polygamy gain new popularity as we become a leisure-oriented culture?

One modified, non-patriarchal form of polygamy which appears definitely in the winds of change is the very practical application and option of polygamy for senior citizens.

The Presbyterian statement is quite forthright in its approach to this option, noting that "the number of single persons is growing in our society, primarily as a reflection of the higher survival rate among women past sixty-five years of age. Present demographic projections suggest that the ratio of women over sixty-five to men of comparable age may be as high as 1,403 to 1,000 by the year 1980. Current medical research has produced readily accessible forms of hormone therapy which are designed to offset some of the disabilities and discomforts of the aging process, and which have the effect as well of preserving the capacity for full sexual functioning by men and women well into the sixties and seventies." The Presbyterian statement then goes on to ask a straightforward question, *either, or*: "Is abstinence or sublimation the only advice the church will have to give to single persons? Or, will it be able to explore new forms of male-female relationships and, while affirming the primacy of [monogamous] marriage and the nuclear family as the [ideal] pattern for heterosexual relationship, be able to condone a plurality of patterns which will make a better place for the unmarried?" This is a clear invitation for the churches *to recognize polygamy for senior citizens as a morally acceptable pattern.*

Dr. Victor Kassel has specialized in the problems of the aging since 1951. He is a Fellow of the Gerontological Society and of the American Geriatrics Society, former Chief of the Geriatric Unit of the Salt Lake City Veterans Administration Hospital, Board Member of the Utah Council on Aging, and served as a delegate to the White House Conference on Aging in 1961. He is also the originator of a plan for and staunch advocate of polygamy for senior citizens, which he first proposed in detail in an article for the professional journal *Geriatrics* in April, 1966.

The needs of the aging today fall into three categories according to Kassel: medical, psychological, and social. Yet practically all our attention is focused on the first two, perhaps because they are easier to deal with technologically.

Offering the legal option of a limited polygamy for senior citizens might solve many serious social problems for the aging. Among these Kassel lists the opportunity to re-establish a meaningful family group for many widows who could not otherwise hope to remarry in a monogamous culture where men are at a premium. A single person has little inclination to cook balanced meals, whereas the social atmosphere of several adults eating together would stimulate an interest in food. A limited income, inadequate retirement and social-security benefits in an inflationary economy make sharing of income far more attractive and practical. Many of our aging do not require the intensive care of a nursing home but could benefit from the concern and interest of companions in the informal setting of a shared apartment or small home. Housework would be much easier for the aging when shared. A small community of men and women would encourage better grooming, which the aging person living alone often tends to neglect. Group living would certainly reduce depression and loneliness. And finally, an advantage the Presbyterian statement meets head on, despite the very common inclination to ignore it: polygamy would allow the senior citizen a normal and sanctioned avenue for sexual expression. It is very unrealistic and impractical, as well as inhumane, to deny any interest in sexual activity to people over fifty, however embarrassing we might find this thought.

In an essay for Otto's *The Family in Search of a Future*, Case Western Reserve sociologist George Rosenberg argues that two major obstacles stand in the way of introducing this form of polygamy: the firmly implanted monogamous values of most older females today and the disruption this relationship would bring into our traditional kinship systems because of inheritance outside the original family lines.

After the Second World War the Lutheran Church in Finland considered the imbalance of the nation's sex ratio so serious that it moved to the brink of legalizing bigamy. But in a few years the proportion of males born rose considerably— the high frequency of sexual intercourse by returning soldiers favors conception of males—and the question was eased to the side. But given the rising imbalance in our own population and an increasing capacity for social change in America, the Roys suggest, in "Is Monogamy Outdated?" that "perhaps bigamy will have to be legalized first under Medicare . . . once the doctrinal smokescreen [prohibiting it] were to be exposed for what it is."

One totally new option to our traditional monogamy came close to becoming a legal possibility in the spring of 1971. Some sociologist had in the 1960s half-jokingly suggested that a contractual marriage, renewable at specified intervals, might offer a practical way to avoid the many disadvantages and problems of present-day divorces. Then, in March, 1971, two Maryland state legislators introduced a bill for consideration in the House of Representatives. The bill would allow a young Maryland couple to choose between a traditional "until-death-do-us-part" marriage license and a three-year renewable contract which could be canceled by either party on expiration. The bill's sponsors were Mrs. Lena K. Lee, fifty-eight, a widowed lawyer who was happily married for twenty-two years, and Mrs. Hildagardeis Boswell, a thirty-seven-year-old divorced law student. Both women are black, Baltimore Democrats, and deny any connection with the women's liberation movement.

Despite their lack of optimism about the bill passing into law the first time around, both legislators feel such a modification and option is necessary. "We have to offer something more than the same archaic marriage pattern, the same mind-draining guilt," is Mrs. Boswell's argument. Mrs. Lee adds that their bill "is particularly aimed at helping youth. Across the country today, young people are living together, 'shacking up,' as they call it, and disregarding old-style marriage vows. We're also hearing from older people who were victimized by the present divorce setup. Personally, I'm for marriage—mine was a success —but marriage is under threat. Let's find out what it takes to adapt or modify it to a new generation's needs."

It is an interesting coincidence that the one case I know of, of a couple actually working out a contractual marriage, occurred in the Baltimore area. The situation involved a man who had been previously married and divorced with tremendous emotional and financial costs only to find himself deeply in love a few years later with another woman. The specter of his previous experience left him with an almost paralyzing fear that a second marriage might bring the same traumatic end. His fiancée, very much aware of his concern and fear, fortunately was a very mature woman and also a lawyer. With his consent, she drew up a legal contract to accompany their marriage license and ceremony, allowing for an amiable termination of the marriage by either party after five years. All the financial details, child support, and custody were spelled out in the contract, very much relieving the gentleman's fears. The marriage, however, was a success, and after five years the couple happily renewed their contract for another five years under the same terms. This is a rather unique case, but it illustrates the possible usefulness of contractual marriages as one option among others. I wonder whether the renewable contract marriage may not cause more psychological problems and tensions than it would solve in the ordinary situation. To make a really happy marriage requires tremendous commitment and effort. Would the open end of a contractual marriage provide an escape door that many young and old people might use rather than putting forth the effort necessary to make a marriage succeed?

This brings me to another new development which most people find equally disturbing and even more embarrassing.

In 1968 the Reverend Troy Perry, a Baptist minister, placed a small announcement in a newspaper called *The Advocate*, which circulates primarily in the homosexual community around Los Angeles. It was an invitation for the readers to share in Christian worship at Sunday services offered by the Reverend Mr. Perry. Only nine friends and three strangers showed up the first Sunday, but by the fall of 1970 the Metropolitan Community Church was holding regular Sunday services for its 420 homosexual members in an old theater in Hollywood.

In the past few years a major revolution has shaken the average person, who previously spoke of homosexuals and lesbians only in the dark. Then came the Gay Liberation Movement, Radical Lesbians, and other groups seeking to break down public prejudice and discrimination by holding marches up New York City's Fifth Avenue and public meetings with various official church groups. The Presbyterian statement on human sexuality called for Christian understanding of the homosexual. So also do the Quaker and British Council of Churches statements. Even the very conservative Lutheran Church in America, the largest Lutheran denomination in the States, pointed out that "persons who engage in homosexual behavior are sinners only as are all other persons—alienated from God. However, they are often the special and undeserving victims of prejudice and discrimination in law, law enforcement, cultural mores, and congregational life." About the same time a group of leading American Episcopal clergymen publicly stated that, under certain circumstances, homosexuality might be judged morally good. Some of these circumstances were spelled out in the Presbyterian paper where it is noted that St. Paul's condemnation of homosexual acts

182 Eve's New Rib

focused on the "antisocial and personally destructive" forms of homosexual conduct such as pederasty, homosexual prostitution, and similar "neighbor-disregarding actions."

Michael Valente challenges the lack of consistence we now find ourselves in with regard to homosexuality and other types of sexual activity traditionally condemned as "unnatural." It seems obvious that in the past, homosexuality, oral intercourse, sodomy, and bestiality were repeatedly condemned as unnatural because they violated the natural law that all sexual activity was designed by the Creator solely for the purpose of procreation; hence any use of sexuality in a non-creative context was and always is immoral. We no longer accept this unilateral approach to human sexuality. We very much accept the social function of sex and the fact that a loving, mutually creative personal relationship can justify sexual intercourse that eliminates the possibility of conception. But do we then carry this distinction to its logical conclusion and ask whether we can continue to condemn oral intercourse, sodomy—which is still grounds for divorce in New Jersey's statutes, which were revised in 1971— and homosexual acts between consenting adults?

A few years ago such questions would have been totally unthinkable in the Christian churches. Yet in Holland a Catholic priest witnessed the marriage of two homosexuals and drew only a mild rebuke from the Vatican. His response was that the couple "are among the faithful to be helped." An October 12, 1970, article in Newsweek reported that the Reverend Mr. Perry had witnessed thirty-six homosexual marriages, eight of them among lesbians. The California law, like that of several other states, recognizes all marriages between partners who can show a certificate from an ordained minister proving that their marriage has been solemnized by a church ceremony. The law does not spell out that the partners must be biological male and female, only that they be "husband" and "spouse." However, in his marriage ceremonies, the Reverend Mr. Perry substitutes the word "spouse" for both "husband" and "wife." In a tele-

vision special in June, 1971 on *Marriage—Who Needs It?* another homosexual minister was shown witnessing the marriage
of two lesbians. In Washington, D.C., nine lesbians in a group
marriage are seeking court permission to adopt a child, while
New York State officials have ruled that there is no legal bar to
a homosexual adopting a child.

In July, 1971 the six-hundred-member parish of the Beloved Disciple held its first anniversary service in New York
City and laid plans for expansion as the nation's second homosexual denomination. One highlight of the service was the
installation of the first three members of the homosexual
church's own religious order, the Oblate Companions of St.
John. The guest preacher was the Reverend Troy Perry. Also
marking the anniversary was a "Service of Holy Union" for
Father Robert Clement, pastor of the Beloved Disciple parish,
and his "lover" of twelve years. During the observance, Father
Clement announced that steps were being taken to link his
parish with the Ethiopian Orthodox Church, thus permitting
the organization of a diocese, election of a bishop, and formation
of other congregations.

These developments very clearly point to another option
in marriage and family structures: the homosexual or unisex
marriage.

Jessie Bernard, the astute author of *The Sex Game* and
more recently *The Future of Marriage*, has provided a very
appropriate introduction for our exploration of the final option
in our list. In a lead article for *The Futurist*'s special report on
the future of women and marriage, Dr. Bernard claimed that
"the next step is even more revolutionary. It is the statement
that marriage is not the *summum bonum* of life, that celibacy
is not a fate worse than death, but an honorable status. The
radical women say that we must come to realize that celibacy
is a state that could be desirable in many ways, in many cases
preferable. To quote a radical woman, 'How repugnant it
really is, after all, to make love to a man who despises you, who

fears you and wants to hold you down. Doesn't screwing in an atmosphere devoid of respect get pretty grim? Why bother? You don't need it.' "

This, Dr. Bernard admits, "is not a call for celibacy per se, but for an acceptance of celibacy as an honorable alternative, one preferable to many male-female relationships. 'Only when we accept the idea of celibacy completely will we ever be able to liberate ourselves. Until we accept this completely—until I say I can control my own body and I don't need any insolent male with an overbearing manner to come and gratify my needs—they will always have over us the devastating threat of withdrawing their sexual attentions and, worse, the threat of our ceasing to be even sexually attractive.' In an era in which reproduction was, in the last analysis, the *raison d'être* for relations between the sexes, other kinds of relations, no matter how much desired, had to take second place. But radical women, who already sense that reproduction will be a minor part of life in the future, want something other than primary sexuality to become the basis of relationship."

To this comment of Jessie Bernard and her radical woman, we might add a note from the Presbyterian statement that "indeed, many marriages survive with either minimal or no coital relations," as a prelude to our discussion of the "celibate" or "celebrational marriage" advocated by two Catholic philosophers, Robert and Mary Joyce, the authors of *New Dynamics in Sexual Love: A Revolutionary Approach to Marriage and Celibacy*.

The Joyces offer an interpretation of certain biblical passages which is totally the opposite to that taken by the Oneida Community. Whereas the Oneida Community accepted the fullness of marriage in the life hereafter as including all the blessed in an openness to sexual intercourse, the Joyces argue from the same texts for the continuance of marriage and human sexuality but in an angelic condition that excludes sexual intercourse as unnecessary. And since we let the members of Oneida speak for themselves earlier, we might call on the Joyces to present their position in their own words.

"Though there will be no husbands and wives in the new creation, there will be men and women. Likeness to the angels does not mean the passing away of human sexuality. The bodies of the resurrected persons will have all the organs of sexuality, manifestations of deeper sexual differences originating in the very being of man and woman. The organs of sexuality, as well as other bodily organs, will have surpassed their ministerial meaning, both in the generation of new life and in the expression and strengthening of love between husband and wife. But these sexual manifestations in the glorified body will exist wholly as celebrations of the being of man and woman. Even in this life sexual organs exist in persons primarily, though not entirely, as celebrations of being. It is good for man's sexuality just to be, without any goal-directed functioning. This is part of the meaning of celibacy as the power of true sexual freedom, both for the fullest life on earth and its continuation in the resurrection.

"In the context of marriage, the power of true sexual freedom includes the ability of husband and wife to engage in meaningful coital union. Their acts of making love in this manner are experienced as celebrations of their being love with each other and of their desire for children. But these acts are not regarded by them as an absolute necessity for the survival of their marriage. This insistence that genitality should result from the true sexual freedom increases, rather than decreases, the value of the coital act. When coital union is thought to result from an appetite like the appetite for food, this union of love is reduced to the level of involuntary needs or impulses and is thereby devaluated.

"When contemplative and loving coition occurs in marriage, it is also a celebration and a fine art to a great extent. In his book *Nature, Man, and Woman,* Alan Watts portrays this love-making with freshness, originality, and some measure of trans cultural perception. But in the world of the resurrected, sexuality will be wholly non-functional celebration, and celibacy will be the manner of this celebration—not the old celibacy of sexual renunciation, nor even the provisional celibacy of sexual affirmation in this life, but the completed celibacy of being. In the powerful act of being love, the sons and daughters of the resurrection will be completed in their likeness to God who *is* love."

Bringing their proposal to a conclusion, the Joyces suggest that "in view of the 'marriage of the Lamb' and the glorified state of human sexuality in resurrected men and women, only a certain kind of marriage will be surpassed with the fullness of time and the new creation. Another kind of marriage, the celebrational and celibate union of all, will emerge. But there is a real continuity in this process. One stage of life passes away and another emerges from within it, because the new existed already in the old. Every good union of husband and wife involves some participation in the marriage of the new creation. There is no separation between living in this world here and now and living in the world of the resurrected, just as there is no separation between living as a child and living as an adult."

The celebrational marriage, then, is a celibate union of husband and wife in which *being love* becomes a "sustained non-genital fulfillment" without the necessity of *making love* in sexual intercourse. Such was the marriage practiced by George Rapp's Harmony Community in the Midwest during the last century and by the Shakers. It is certainly a projection that would be most agreeable to St. Augustine and many of the early church fathers. But it is only fair to point out that the biblical texts used by the Joyces, and earlier by Teilhard de Chardin, in extrapolating to a virginal afterlife can be given a quite different interpretation. Thus, "In the Kingdom, there will be neither giving nor taking in marriage" can be interpreted in terms of the Jewish concern for progeny to mean that in the life hereafter there will be no procreation or inheritance of property, but sexual intercourse may well remain as one of the deepest modes of human interpersonal knowing in the biblical sense. The Jesuit Joseph Donceel, a long-time defender and exponent of Teilhard de Chardin's evolutionary synthesis, once suggested at a Teilhard symposium that man's life hereafter can *transcend total dependence and enslavement to eating, breathing, feeling, touching, seeing, and sexual communion without thereby abrogating all functioning of these sense activities and bodily activities.* Personally, I prefer Donceel's interpretation, and that of the rather unorthodox Oneida theology, and, as I have pointed out elsewhere in a discussion of Teilhard's celibate marriage in this and the afterlife, I am convinced this extrapolation stems more from the unconscious myopia of a French clerical, truly celibate biologist than from a valid interpretation of the evolution of human sexuality in the past and present.

However, there is no question that some married couples may happily choose the celibate or celebrational marriage as their way of life. It certainly has a valid place among the options open to us today. And I might add that the celebrational marriage probably finds much more extensive acceptance as a *partial option*, a pattern of male/female relations which many married couples move in and out of for varying periods during their years of living together.

We are faced, then, with at least twenty basic options for men and women in the days ahead, and with the perplexing question of how we are going to cope with this revolutionary pluralism.

TEN

Coping with Present Shock—Education
for a Pluralistic Society

SEX EDUCATION in the American family and school is a Total Disaster! At its very rare best it deals with only a few basic elements in the sexual lives of young people today. At its very rare best it amounts to a mere token gesture in the direction of what should be done.

As a result, *at least one half of all the girls and one third of all the boys entering college in 1972 will not be aware of the most basic facts of human reproduction. One half of the freshmen women and one third of the male freshmen.* Consider that *two million* young Americans will enter college in 1972.

This fall parents around the country will pack their young naïve offspring off to college with a kiss on the cheek, an encouraging handshake from Dad, a comfortable wallet with a charge plate or two, and a checkbook. But then comes the emotional shock that their parents told them nothing about. A coed dorm suite shared with three or four other girls, one of whom likes to invite her boy friend to stay overnight, a suite mate who needs an abortion for his girl friend, a quiet but panicked rumor of rampant venereal diseases, a cover-up for a close new friend who wants to move off-campus with her boy friend, the peer group pressures to lay a girl or share in some group sex.

I know from past experience that many readers of this book

will object vehemently to my percentages: "In this day of sophistication, sexual intercourse in the movies and pornography, your percentages are incredible, impossible!" But I stand by them. If anything, my estimates are *conservative*. At least that is what I am repeatedly told by campus nurses, student counselors, deans, dormitory directors, and students working in contraception- and abortion-information centers. And it does not matter much whether we are talking about students at a state university, large public college, small private college, a Protestant or a Catholic school.

Let me turn this around into a constructive approach. Let us take a look at an outline for a course that would prepare the student in junior or senior high school for *the realities of human sexuality as he and she are meeting them in today's world*. For this course outline I will draw on a basic sketch by Robert Rimmer, who was challenged by the many readers of *The Harrad Experiment*, *Proposition Thirty-one*, and *The Rebellion of Yale Marratt* to come up with a concrete program for the Human Values course mentioned in the Harrad curriculum. This Rimmer does briefly in about six pages of *You and I . . . Searching for Tomorrow*. Using Rimmer's outline as a springboard, I have expanded the course here to what I feel is a fairly complete program.

Let me first state the purpose behind a course dealing with the human values involved in interpersonal and intersexual relations. I have almost given away the purpose by extending Rimmer's terse title, a "Human Values" course, but let me expand my meaning a bit further. This course, as I see it, would build on the biological facts of human reproduction that would be taught at appropriate depth and times throughout the elementary- and junior-high-school education. We would presume on that basic information and go far beyond it, preparing the high-school student to deal with his own sexuality in terms of the many avenues of development open to him. It would prepare him or her to enter and live in the adult world of interpersonal and intersexual relations where pluralism reigns. To achieve this the "Human Values" course must be oriented to a historical perspective, however much young people today rebel against history and reject the relevance of anything that happened more than five years ago.

As for the mechanics of the course, I agree with Rimmer that a year-long series of weekly two-hour evening sessions, each followed by an open dialogue for another hour or so, would be ideal. Rimmer suggests a class of about fifty high-school juniors, equally divided as to sex, and *their parents*, or a total class size of approximately 150. However, from my own experience in dealing with the social implications of new trends in human reproduction on the college level, I think a class size above thirty prevents real dialogue and allows some more reserved students to sit in the background and shut off the input completely.

As for the parents, whose role can be crucial to the success of the course, their attendance would be optional, with a strong encouragement for at least one of the parents to attend regularly. A joint exploration might help break down part of the generation gap that is likely to expand if the young people move more openly into pluralism without a corresponding education of their parents.

In the ordinary senior high school, students and their parents may range all the way from ultra-conservative advocates of no sex education outside the family—such as the members of the John Birch Society and groups like Holy Innocents Safeguarded and CUFF (Catholics United for the Faith)—to the staunch and often uncritical advocates of complete sex education in the schools. How can you get such a diverse group of children and parents into a "Human Values" course? To accomplish this obviously will require a superhuman skill in public relations. Rimmer suggests that a husband-and-wife teacher team be used and that they "make every effort to involve every student and parent" in each session.

I would go beyond this to recommend an approach I have used on the college level. This is to admit frankly that many of the topics we deal with are controversial and even morally repugnant to some students. But we are simply reporting objectively what is happening to the family and human reproduction in today's world. Beyond this, my task as teacher is to catalyze serious discussion and an open exchange of views among the students. We want the students to express their own views as clearly and as logically as they can, to share their convictions and appraisals of a particular situation or custom with the rest of the class. We would also ask everyone in the group to leave the discussion open-ended and without a value judgment. My experience with this objective-reporting, open-ended-discussion approach has been the complete absence of objections or protests and a very favorable response from students and parents of all persuasions despite the sensitive issues we deal with.

While the most traditional and conservative parent might vehemently object to his child being exposed to these plural patterns and options, a teacher can point out that by letting the student discuss these possibilities openly he will be less likely to marry someone without making sure beforehand that his intended spouse agrees with and sincerely holds the same traditional views as he does. Without this open education, the student might find out after marrying someone that his spouse expects to have comarital relations, perhaps believes in contraception, abortion, comarital relations, and/or group marriages. I might add that if these parents and students are so convinced of the validity of their beliefs, they should also feel a responsibility to share this truth with others.

Agreement with the content of the course is not necessary: we are reporting various ways men over the centuries have viewed their sexual nature and various ways they have solved the tensions of family life and marriage. The class will discuss the facts and perhaps even reach some sort of consensus now and then. Yet even in a case where we reach a consensus, individuals may continue to disagree and hold their own views. We are simply trying to make the students aware of the problems of today's marriage, family, and male/female relationships and offer some insights from mankind's past experiences. This orientation may have to be brought back into focus many times during the course.

So much for the organization of the course. What about its content? The early sessions of the course would deal with man's first attempts to depict his sexuality and cope with it in the context of a pastoral culture. Color reproductions of early cave paintings, phallic statues, and fertility sculptures such as the famous Venus of Willendorf would be shown. Reproductions of some of those early sculptures could be obtained on loan or purchased from museum art shops. More contemporary and very similar representations by modern African and Polynesian artists could be shown. Ancient religious myths dealing with man's earliest attempts to understand his "split nature"— the androgynous myths of Greece, for instance, which portray the human as a bisexual who is split into two sexes by the fates or gods—would be explained and discussed as a natural reaction to man's early discovery of the "not me," the other, the uncontrollable, unpredictable world outside. We would touch on the axial role played by concern over the fertility of the crops, the birth and survival of children, and the fertility and abundance of the hunted animals, in understanding early man's image of human sexuality.

Contemporary traces of this mysterious and joyous image of human sexuality would be touched on in recalling a variety of European and American customs: the May pole, the corn goddess who moves through the fields of western Europe each spring, and other examples. Movies of sexual rites of puberty, marriage, and birth among the Polynesians, Africans, and inhabitants of Borneo could be very helpful. I recall some episodes from the marvelous documentary *The Sky Above, the Mud Below* which record the puberty and birth rites of natives in

Borneo with a sensitive and lucid commentary by the explorers who first saw and observed these ancient rites.

Rimmer suggests that this might be an appropriate place to compare and contrast the spontaneous, non-pornographic, celebrational joy in one's sexuality so evident in these early images with two modern images. The natural exuberance and ease of some poems from college publications, excerpts from *Woodstock* or other underground movies that treat human sexuality, love-making, and the human body in a joyful, playful way, could be contrasted with the joyless, posed, clinical sterility of *Playboy*'s air-brushed bunnies and the less sophisticated, crass images of today's pornography. This juxtaposition could easily lead the group into a lively and instructive discussion of the dehumanizing and depersonalizing aspects of much of today's pornography and film arts.

To add to this contrast we would show some slides of the very early Hindu *maithuna* sculpture from the temples. In Taoism and Tantric Buddhism the artists had a venerable and beautiful custom of portraying on the porticoes and façades of their temples that which Westerners commonly view as pornography. In actual fact, these bas reliefs, which seem to show nothing more than a wild variety of sexual techniques and practices, are far from pornographic. In *Nature, Man, and Woman*, Alan Watts explains that these sculptures "are, like sacraments, the 'outward and visible signs of an inward and spiritual grace.' . . . The general idea of Tantric *maithuna*, as of its Taoist counterpart, is that sexual love may be transformed into a type of worship in which the partners are, for each other, incarnations of the divine." We would try to explain the spiritual orientation behind this erotic art as a contemplation of nature and, rather than a sex manual in our modern terms, actually a portrayal of an inner spiritual consciousness that allows a man and woman to approach each other naturally and contemplatively.

The next few weeks could be spent on early civilizations,

beginning, since we have just touched on it, with the Hindu and working our way west through the Chinese, Persian, Greek, Egyptian, and Roman developments and the variety of attitudes toward marriage, family structure, the position of woman, the position and treatment of children, premarital and extramarital relations, homosexuality (particularly in Greece, where it was viewed as the true and highest form of human love), and other expressions of human sexual behavior. We could also touch on the simple sexual taboos which characterize the patriarchal society, even into the Middle Ages, when the invention of printing permitted extensive codification and dissemination of sexual laws and restrictions. We would touch on the position and role of woman as they emerged early in the Western patriarchal culture, which conditioned the domination and social control of female behavior even until recent decades.

To counter the shock of seeing the Hindu and other portrayals of sexual intercourse and at the same time create an interested observer's attitude, Rimmer suggests that from the very beginning of the course we keep the reactions of parents and students constantly in the foreground in easygoing verbal exchanges. I would hope that hot and argumentative reactions, which would detour the whole course, could be deflected by asking the group to withhold judgment on the course until the end. This would be difficult, but essential to the success of the course.

Another very difficult task in the early sessions would be to create an atmosphere of equality and free exchange so that both parents and youngsters would be completely frank, so that both would dare to verbalize their emotional reactions to their own sexual experiences. The parents would be encouraged to discuss the constricted environment of sex they experienced as young people: the lack of sex education in schools and at home.

One or two sessions would deal with the Hebrew tradition, both ancient and present, drawing out the major shift in the position of women that occurred in this culture. We could touch on points raised earlier in our sketch of the history of sexuality, in Chapter Two, and of the extramarital affair, in Chapter Five; on the Jewish view of the physical universe as inherently good, contrasting this with the Orphic idea of the world as evil; on the image of adultery as an infringement of property rights; and on the Jewish idea that social conventions are in a way the laws of God. We would discuss the evolution of monogamy from the time of the patriarchs, through the kings and prophets, keeping in mind the traditions of polygamy and concubinage, the dangers of sacred prostitution, and the celibate tradition of the Essenes, whose rich history we are just beginning to appreciate in the story of the Dead Sea Scrolls. An appropriate conclusion to this section would be a dramatic reading from the Song of Songs of Solomon.

We might then move into the early Christian era, discussing the conflicts and tensions that existed in the early church. We could use passages from the writings of the Apostles and the church fathers, especially Jerome and Augustine, to show how the expectation of the imminent coming of the end of the world and the return of Christ led Christians into a particular uneasiness with respect to marriage and sexuality. The influence of Persian and Platonic dualism, Neoplatonism, and Plotinus would enter the discussion, but only enough to give an insight without getting bogged down in comparative philosophies. We might also indicate something of the complex history of Manichean/Albigensian/Jansenist/Puritan/Victorian traditions in anticipation of later discussion.

A small note might be entered here contrasting the relaxed and joyful sensual sexuality of the earlier Greek (and biblical) writers such as Aristophanes with the tense, often licentious approach of Roman paintings at the time of Christ and the satirical approach to sex evident in Ovid, Catullus, and the Roman playwrights. We might also touch on the idealized female forms of earlier Greek sculpture, recalling, perhaps, the story of Praxiteles and his mistress, who modeled for the famed statue of Aphrodite of Cnidus about to enter her bath, and contrast this naturalness with the licentious, often lascivious rendering of later Roman works.

Then, in an aside suggested by Rimmer in *You and I . . . Searching for Tomorrow*, we should probably remind the class that "other than through the medium of painting—of which there was very little—sculpture and the verbal communication of plays, the average man could not be conditioned or influenced in his basic attitudes. There was no printing. [And no mass communications.] We are at a time in human history where the concepts of love and romanticism as we understand them today did not exist. Sadly, because even today we don't understand how fully the medium is the massage, most of our formulations of our sexual heritage are based on Charlton Heston movies and Hollywood spectaculars which simply superimpose our current sexual mores, or the script-writer's view of the past."

Reality is quite different from this distorted image, and our major task throughout this course will be to present a view of history as undistorted as possible.

This will be very difficult because the male, until very recently, has completely dominated history and culture. We have little if any idea of what the female of past ages felt or thought about man's world. Which means that we will have a wholly male view, even when we are dealing with obvious distortions such as the double standard of morality that is evident in most areas of life, present and past. Illustrations of the double standard abound in both religious and civil codes of law. As a first illustration we might recall the plight of Jacob Minline and Sarah Tuttle, the shameless Puritan couple we mention in Chapter Four. We could illustrate this double standard with some insights into the evolution of a special class of females whose sole function was in the beginning to provide both intellectual and extracurricular sexual enjoyment for upper-class males and whose role has gradually been reduced to providing unadulterated sex for the paying male.

Nor would we avoid that area of church history which practically every course in history avoids: the centuries-long dispute about whether marriage could really be a sacrament since it involved such uncontrollable emotion and passion, and the erratic, often (for us) scandalous history of clerical celibacy in the Western church. Here, Henry Charles Lea's *History of Sacerdotal Celibacy*, despite its bias, would provide a wealth of detail on daily customs and the sexual behavior of the early church. These two facets seldom turn up except in the quite prejudiced and tendentious comments of authors who have an ax to grind against religion or the Roman church. But if we refuse to impose our ethics and values on past cultures and accept the customs of the past as an expression of a particular stage of human history (just as primitive to us as our customs will appear to the people five thousand years from now), then we may learn from rather than be shocked by the fact that in medieval Spain and Switzerland, some parishes insisted that every priest have a concubine—clerical marriages being forbidden by papal edict—and the parishioners were human enough to want to protect their wives and daughters against priestly visitations; or by the fact that in Germany the number of offspring begotten by priests often outnumbered those born in wedlock; or that seven hundred prostitutes reportedly gathered around the bishops when they convened for the Council of Constance in 1414.

The theological arguments for the superiority of virginity, coming out of the Essene tradition, and Thomas Aquinas' terse comment that "beasts are without reason. In this way man becomes, as it were, like them in intercourse, because he cannot moderate the delight of intercourse and the heat of concupiscence by reason" could be explored, along with the suppression of normal marital sexuality. We might also ask why the artists of the early Christians, even through the Middle Ages, never painted or sculpted the naked male or female, why Christ was always depicted fully clothed on the cross.

Even though the patriarchal tradition was far from being threatened by the few rumblings of rebellion among women, we might set the stage for a later discussion of this phase in the history of human relations by recalling the humorous treatment of rebellious women given by Aristophanes in his *Lysistrata*. Or by Euripides' play *The Bacchae*, in which a repressive law-and-order mentality is compared with the freedom of the natural world and how this freedom is triggered to excess and bestiality by oppressive authoritarian measures. The emergence of women could then be traced, however faintly, in the unexpurgated writings of Boccaccio and Chaucer. The humor of the male's preoccupation with the fear of being cuckolded by finding that his wife is bearing another man's child could be delightfully compared with the fear and resistance of even liberal college males today to the thought of their future wives working and thereby enjoying the same freedom and sexual contact they have always enjoyed.

At least one, but perhaps two, of our thirty-six sessions would have to be devoted to the history of courtly love that we touched on earlier. We could explore briefly the Catharist world, so often misunderstood and condemned by the church, whose teachings placed women on a pedestal and prompted the troubadours to song. We could play some recordings of madrigals and troubadour songs for the class and perhaps read some excerpts from Joseph Bedier's *The Romance of Tristan and Iseult*, a modernization of the classic tale, to make the courtly-love tradition more understandable to the class.

The sudden emergence of a new image of sexuality in courtly love flowing into the Renaissance would have to be viewed with careful attention to the actual facts and without the distortion so common in popular accounts of this revolution. The appearance of a Marian cult in the great cathedral of

Chartres in the twelfth century or earlier in Notre Dame of Paris, the idealization of pure sexuality in the Immaculate Conception, the fact that no one dared portray the Holy Mother any way but fully clothed, and then the gradual emergence of the nude male and female, modeled first on the Greek and Roman mythologies, in the Renaissance, need to be stressed. Some of the bolder and lesser-known Renaissance paintings of Our Lady nursing the Christ Child or Christ and John the Baptist cavorting naked in a pastoral setting could be shown to the class.

Rimmer's sketch has a vitality about it and a spontaneity that sometimes skips over transitions and jumps into new topics without warning or preparation. While this makes for interesting reading, I think it weakens the educational impact of his outline, particularly, for instance, where he has an important point to make but where the reader is lost in shock without the proper transition or setting. Nowhere is this more evident than in a brief paragraph on slang. "By this time in the course, since we would have read Chaucer (unexpurgated) and balanced him with *Heloise and Abelard*, the four-letter words such as cunt, prick, fuck, shit, piss will be spoken easily by the instructors, and at first gingerly and then with some confidence by the parents and students. The long history of the word *fuck*, and its equivalent in other languages of the world would be a way of approaching words and meanings and how we perceive meanings." Rimmer has a valid educational end in mind, but it does not come through in the brief shock of a single paragraph totally disconnected from what goes before and after in his sketch.

The point, as I see it, is to show the class how a very realistic, rich, and natural vocabulary has been totally subverted by our Victorian prudery, how a meaningless collection of euphemisms has replaced expressions that are real, and how the real expressions have been distorted and twisted into the "dirty" or "vulgar" category. Let me illustrate.

Skeat's classic *Etymological Dictionary* suggests that the word "fuck" is an exclamation derived originally from a variety of roots in several European languages. The origins of the word "fuck," Skeat claims, can be found in other early words meaning fruit, fruition, function, felicity or happiness, and even fetus. These were the sources for the German verb for intercourse *verkehr*—just change the *v* to an *f*. The basic meaning of this classic exclamation, according to Skeat, implies *the joy of growing, of becoming, the joy of being, of dwelling and of building.* This early derivation we could then compare with the more recent interpretation of Eric Partridge, who suggests, in typical Victorian prudery, a dirty, vulgar origin of the term. In his book, *A Dictionary of Slang and Unconventional English,* Partridge traces "fuck" to the verb for "beat," and probably also to terms like "bash" and "bang," all three of which are commonly used today as synonyms for "fuck," but in the depersonalized and exploitative connotation of the word "screw," rather than as a joyous affirmation of being and growing.

Other examples of our selling out to the dirty-minded and dirty-mouthed can be found in the political satire of Jonathan Swift, for Swift despised the phony pretensions of England in his day. In *Gulliver's Travels* he often points out that the common slang of the day was much more psychologically sound than the phony euphemisms of society. In one marvelous scene he tells how Gulliver breaks into the Queen's chambers to put out a fire by pissing on it. Those who know that Swift was exiled from England by the Queen will catch the irony as well as the sarcasm of this item. Similarly, we might read and discuss with the class examples of forthright slang in Chaucer; for instance, his humorous vignette of the boy and girl making love in a pear tree with its use of the word "cunt."

This frank approach will likely bring to the surface the one continual threat to the success of our "Human Values" course: the antagonism of some parents, and probably also of some students, to what we are trying to accomplish, to the course's content, or to our approach, which is nothing more than an open exploration of mankind's historical wrestling with human sexuality. Rimmer warns that the instructors should be "more than willing to turn off the main road and pursue any byways." Still, some discipline will be required lest the main thread be lost as the group explores together the meanings of the past and present. There is a lot of material to cover in thirty-six sessions.

Creating a mutuality and openness to exploration of sensitive areas in human behavior, which many parents and students find embarrassing, even unmentionable, will require continual effort and consummate skill in handling people and controversial issues. Rimmer suggests that one possible way of defusing this tension, especially toward the end of the course, would be for the instructors "to move in and out of the chronological history, picking a war or a political overthrow, or a human catastrophe and trying to get behind the surface facts of history and speculate on the sexual lives of the protagonists as a conditioning factor. We will crawl into the brains of men like Julius Caesar, Mark Antony, Napoleon, Hitler, Henry VIII, Casanova, Don Juan, George III, George Washington, Robert Lee, Abraham Lincoln and be them or any other person in history, or *presently alive*, showing them as sexual human beings."

Mention of the sexual behavior of leaders of the American Revolution—of Benjamin Franklin's well-known philandering at the court of France and his return to his Philadelphian wife with an offspring, of George Washington's propensity for sleeping—in the slang sense—almost everywhere, and of Jefferson's relationship with his black servants—has led to the occasional dismissal of a high-school history teacher. Yet frankly facing the human behavior and customs in vogue at the time of our American origins might help us focus the issues and bring antagonisms to the surface where they can best be dealt with.

Then, as Rimmer suggests, "to show different attitudes to-

ward sex compared with our current values we would compare
the meanings of Rabelaisian and Chaucerian sexual humor with
the sickness and decadence of Marquis de Sade. We would compare the laughter and joyous copulation in the drawings of
Thomas Rowlandson with the sick sexual expressions of Marquis de Bayros and Aubrey Beardsley. We would ask if a newspaper like *Screw* was in the same genre as Chaucer, or if it
could be, and if not, why not?

"When we came to the repression of Victorian days some of
the male parents would read aloud from *My Secret Life* and
The Autobiography of Frank Harris and compare the attitudes
of these two men toward the female not only with each other,
but with the dreamy evocations of Robert and Elizabeth Brown-
ing, and Edward Fitzgerald's translation of Omar Khayyám with
current attitudes toward the females as expressed in John
O'Hara and Philip Roth or Mary McCarthy's novels."

Then as a transition to the present, we would discuss with
the class some recent best-selling novels such as *Portnoy's Complaint*, "the story of a man in love with his penis," as Rimmer so
aptly sums up this best seller.

I do not know that I would go along with the educative
value Rimmer believes could be achieved by taking the class
to see the stage production of *Che*, if this is still around, or its
sequel, whatever that might be. Though I must admit that the
possibility of following up this viewing with a dialogue with
the author, Leon Raphael, the director, Ed Wode, and the cast
might be of some interest and value. Rimmer suggests this
dialogue might focus on one key question: "Is this play an
honest expression of man's sexuality or man vis-à-vis man in any
aspect of his life?" Similarly we might ask whether the less
radical production of *Hair* makes a valid statement for today's
youth or whether it is more, as Rimmer suggests, a "slick, for-
mula musical which in and of itself may be fun, but having
nothing valid to say about life, love or human beings today."

The class might also find it interesting to discuss the many ambiguities and failures of modern censorship in dealing with all types of pornography. We might try to define our precise understanding the pornography. We might try to dissect and understand the fascination modern society finds in the pseudo-sophisticated hard-cover pornography of *Candy* and *The Valley of the Dolls*, which Irving Buchen aptly describes as "gross and vulgar not because they deal with sexuality or even perversions but because they are cheats—they pass off gilt for gold, technique for emotion." In *The Perverse Imagination* Buchen suggests that a very real difference exists between *Portnoy's Complaint* and *Candy*. In *Candy* the authors are safely removed from their characters, totally uninvolved, and manipulated mechanically through clicking typewriter keys. Roth, on the other hand, is deeply, ferociously within the skin of his creation, Portnoy. Obviously, the prime element of pornography is to treat the characters as robots, and this distinguishes true pornography from an artistic creation that may involve similar language and sexual behavior.

If I may borrow a phrase of Rimmer's slightly out of context, true pornography has "subtle overtones of hatred, a nuts-and-bolts [approach] signifying robots clanking penises and vaginas together." Or, as Buchen suggests, "to treat a man or a woman solely as a series of anal, oral and genital orifices which are to be filled, exhausted, emptied or violated is to practice the true pornographer's reduction: to cut the parts off from the whole." Yet America is experiencing an obsession with novels, movies, and stage plays that exploit and depersonalize the human male and female, that reduce human sexuality to the perfect technique with the perfect partner—read: with the perfect vagina or penis.

One wonders whether in trying to cast off their Victorian prudery Americans are not plunging into another equally deep pit, that of the adolescent male enraptured with sex and love, but not knowing what either of these mean in terms of human relations and people. But perhaps we have to pass through this adolescent fascination with all its distortions and depersonalized sexual intercourse to reach a more balanced, mature, and real image of male/female relationships.

Our exploration of human values must somewhere deal with three important and very dangerous myths rampant in our culture. The first is the *orgasm myth*, the belief that there is, if only one can find it, a perfect technique for "making love." If the right position, foreplay, etc., are once learned with the perfect partner, it will mean sexual ecstasy, mutual orgasm, bells ringing, and cosmic rainbows *every time*. How many newlyweds plunge into frantic self-recrimination and accusation if they do not achieve mutual and simultaneous orgasm every time? The husband feels inadequate as a male, the wife unresponsive or frigid. Yet neither stop to think that the sexual communion is more than mutual orgasm—indeed, more than orgasm—and cannot be a gourmet's delight every time. If it were, it would lose its richness, which comes mainly from contrast with more ordinary and less ecstatic unions. Our class will have to discuss this compulsive mechanization of sexual relations.

We will also have to deal with two myths of marriage, which are perhaps only two different faces of the same millstone, the *Love Story myth* and the *monogamy myth*. The immense popularity of Erich Segal's *Love Story*, both as a novel and as a movie, cannot be ignored. It reveals something very real about the mentality of Americans, young and old. *Love Story*, and before it *Romeo and Juliet*, harbors a deceptive myth. It is a story of beautiful people who never lived, and never could have lived. As such, its fascination and popularity are extremely dangerous because it is so misleading. It becomes an ideal toward which young people, husbands and wives, orient their lives. Jennifer and Oliver were the mythic ideal married couple in the minds of many Americans long before they appeared in print. Harvey Cox described their mythic state of marital bliss acidly: "This dynamic duo, they [sic] never argue (after a brief Cambridge tussle about phoning daddy), never get bored with each other, never wonder if the life they have chosen is really human, never doubt they should have been married, never exchange a word about the outside universe. You might almost hear them humming, '. . . and let the rest of the world go by.' "

Many readers and viewers pooh-pooh the impact and influence of *Love Story* and its many kindred tales, but its myth of monogamy and marital bliss remains. Most Americans still expect their spouses to supply all their varied needs—sexual, intellectual, emotional, psychological, recreational—*ad infinitum*. Despite the rosy gloss of *Love Story*, it remains to be seen how unrealistic this myth is in fact.

The *monogamy myth* is perhaps only the other side of the coin, for while we extol the glories of the ideal couple, we refuse to admit the reality of a dozen other options in male/female relations that we all know to exist around us but which we refuse to acknowledge. We might on occasion admit they do exist, but certainly not in our social class or circle of friends. Despite the strident insistence of many social observers and of the man in the street, Americans have never been able to come even close to a truly monogamous culture. I doubt whether even 50 percent of the population has approximated this mythic state. Pluralism has always been with us, albeit frantically swept under the carpet or around the corner into someone else's scandalous bedroom.

Yet, the orgasm, *Love Story*, and monogamy myths are in fact *pseudomyths*. Reinhold Niebuhr once said that "great myths have actually been born out of human experience and are constantly subject to verification by experience." I propose that not one of these three pseudomyths comes close to being born out of human experience, and certainly none of them can be verified in human situations. There is then only one way to cope with them—debunk them for what they are: impossible to achieve, hence inhuman as ideals. Demythologizing can best be accomplished by frank discussion of the facts.

At this point we might make valuable use of some current

films to illustrate the modern American experience of sexual awakening. The films will change with passing years, but let me illustrate with three films popular in 1970 and 1971. As an opener to this trilogy we might use *Suddenly Last Summer*, the story of four young people at a oceanside resort. One of the two girls has everything going for her: looks, money, personality, popularity, intelligence. And she uses all to her advantage, offering constant come-ons to the two fellows, one a very earthy, often gross person obviously out for all the kicks he can get, and the other sensitive, innocent, well intentioned. The second girl, freckled, a wallflower, is mostly ignored as she tags along after the two boys pursuing the blonde. The two boys, who have never had intercourse, often talk about the possibilities of getting the blonde to go all the way with them, but there is a decided difference in the way each talks and thinks about girls. Finally they decide she has done too much teasing. One lad, the instigator, obviously treats girls as sex objects, while the more sensitive lad is reluctantly enticed into this game of exploitation, as they decide to push all the way. In the end, the calculating female neatly diverts the boys onto her "friend," who is raped by the two as she watches. Four young people, each wrestling with his or her emerging sexuality, and two at least struggling to treat others as sexual persons rather than as sex objects, provide genuine educational and ethical insights, without moralizing, into problems of sexual awakening.

Carnal Knowledge is a very depressing, if similarly instructive, film. It traces the lives of two college chums through into their forties. Again the contrasts are well drawn: a young puzzled college lad, Jonathan, who tries to treat his dates as persons, versus the crude, vulgar, sex-obsessed Oscar. Jonathan marries a typical good housewife-mother, and though a bit bored, he might be content, except for the constant needling of Oscar, who sees women as objects to be screwed. After marrying Ann-Margret, an airline hostess with a perfect body, Oscar keeps Jonathan in jealous turmoil with his vivid details of her abilities

in bed. Both marriages end in divorce. There is some small hope
for the searching Jonathan, who seems to be learning something
of the meaning of life and love from a girl half his age. He has
hope in people. But Oscar closes the movie in a highly depersonalized and pessimistic scene, nearly impotent, obviously all
wrapped up in himself, as a prostitute mechanically tries to
arouse him not for intercourse but for a narcissistic erection.

In contrast, *The Summer of '42* is a beautiful film, warm
and human. Oscie, whose counterparts in the other films appear to win out, here takes a back seat. His exploitative approach
to sex and girls and his obsession with the mechanics of seduction are handled with a fine humorous touch that brings out
the ridiculous and pathetic nature of his growth. Hermie comes
through as a lovable and warm fellow, a very nice lad who constantly rejects the temptations offered by his friend. Hermie's
relationship with a young war bride at the shore is real, sensitive,
and well played. When he stops by one evening to talk with
the young woman he idolizes, and finds a telegram from the
War Department with news of her husband's death, his reaction
is touching. In her despair and torment Dotty turns to Hermie
for comfort. That night, she makes love with Hermie in a con-
vincingly human relation that is handled cinematically with unusual delicacy and beauty. When Hermie returns to her cottage
in the morning, he finds only a poignant note tacked to the
cottage door. That note expresses very well the whole intent,
tone, and purpose of this course in "Human Values."

As a conclusion to our course I suggest an extension of the
pioneering work of Deryck Calderwood with Guidance Associates, of Pleasantville, New York. In a too brief twenty-one-minute
audio-visual program on *What Is Marriage?* for senior-high-school
students, Calderwood has a couple from a group marriage, two
males in a gay marriage, a single man and a single woman, a
couple informally living together, and a traditionally married
couple discuss the pros and cons of their options in an open-
ended dialogue. The filmstrips are too brief and only touch

the surface, but in conjunction with a series of other filmstrips, this program could trigger lively and educationally sound discussion of the alternative patterns now being tried in America, their advantages and disadvantages. As supplementary material, a taped interview with Robert Rimmer offering his insights into alternative patterns is available. I was fortunate to be invited to share in another filmstrip in this series, *The Future of the Family*, dealing with alternative forms of parenthood and new modes of human reproduction. Too brief as these programs are, they are the kind of approach to pluralism we need. They should be developed and expanded. A course in "Human Values" that does not deal in depth with the pluralism of our society today is unrealistic and amputated. Movies illustrating the variety of male/female patterns evident in other cultures as documented by Margaret Mead in the South Pacific and by Beach and Ford would be well worth incorporating into the course. Such films, if available, could do much to destroy the *Love Story*, monogamy, and orgasm myths along with demolishing our chauvinistic American belief that our way is the only right way to handle human relations.

This is a heavy meal to digest, I admit. The course will undoubtedly shock some. And perhaps many readers will shake their heads and say it is an impossible dream, sheer visionary stuff, especially since a study of the problems and personalities in American sex education by Mary Breasted has confirmed what most people already know: that sex education in the American schools is "very bad overall." Textbooks are out of date, the approach is more often than not prudish, moralistic in the worst sense, frequently preachy, and generally defensive in dealing with anything that deviates from society's mythic images. This defensiveness, which is hardly conducive to motivating and influencing young people today, Breasted found very common in the treatment of premarital sex, even in the public statements of Dr. Mary Calderone of SIECUS, the Sex Information and Education Council of the United States; in discussions of masturbation; in the almost absent mention of different positions for intercourse; and in discussions of contraception. In this atmosphere my proposal sounds like an idle pipe dream. But I wonder.

I am not underestimating the problems involved in improving our sex education, either in the schools or at home. Perhaps the course I have proposed might be more practical if it were made available to parents as teachers, with all the source material, so that it could be used in the informality of the family. After some initial reactions from church leaders and parish educators, I suspect the program wouldn't be too difficult to introduce into the Sunday-school and Confraternity of Christian Doctrine courses, where parents and teachers usually work in collaboration. If the course proves successful there, it might then be possible to introduce it in a formal school situation.

Dr. William Cole, author of *Sex and Love in the Bible*, has drawn an informative comparison that applies to our education situation, noting that even in the New Testament there is a dialectic tension between the moralism of Jewish legalism and the libertinism of Greco-Roman paganism. The former thought the Gospel a scandal; the latter viewed it as foolishness. Today's Pharisees and Judaizers, Cole maintains, continue to "set up their standard of law, strictly forbidding any and all sexual relations outside of marriage." The Greeks have their descendants in the apostles of carte-blanche sex and total license (provided there is no violence, seduction, or perversion of the young).

Whatever their secular or religious persuasion today, the heirs of the Torah, the defenders of black-and-white morality, are naturally frightened that Christian freedom in sexual matters will lead inexperienced innocent young people astray, that premarital and extramarital relations will erupt everywhere in a nationwide orgy. The only answer they can see is a clear, unequivocal "Thou shalt not." They are convinced that anything less forceful would open the doors to complete moral disintegration.

But legal, dogmatic prohibitions are ineffective today for three reasons. First, they do not communicate their message to today's youth because they run completely counter to the anti-authoritarian and antiestablishment psychology of youth. More important, they appear as laws for law's sake with no relevance to the prime concern of today's youth: their personal growth as loving persons in a community of loving, concerned persons. Finally, such prohibitions cannot possibly encompass all the radically new situations young people are placed in today by our social, technological, and biological revolutions.

Dr. Cole has suggested an alternative to the dilemma posed by the lethal letter of traditional Christian legalistic ethics and the open license of a depersonalized Playboy ethic. "The gospel of Christian liberty offers escape from a rigid legalism which says implicitly, if not explicitly, what the young know to be false—that sex is shameful. Biblical faith proclaims the good-ness of all the created world, including sexuality. It also declares, however, that man is more than an animal, that he is his brother's keeper, that he has a responsibility for his neighbor. He who loves the God revealed in Jesus Christ also loves all those in whose midst God has set him down. In every human encounter he meets God, who demands of him a response. Each encounter is absolutely unique, defying calculation or prescrip-tion by Law."

That last sentence is critical, for the whole context of Cole's conclusion is very much in line with Michael Valente's state-ment that "sexual activity is tied to one's total development as a . . . person." Radically this personal development is other-oriented, involving dialogue, which means that while laws may be ineffective, we can certainly make use of guidelines drawn from three sources. Dr. Kenneth Vaux, of the Institute of Reli-gion and Human Development, in Houston, speaks of retrospec-tive, introspective, and prospective sources for our ethical judg-ments and guidelines today. I interpret this to mean that our guidelines must be devised from the richness of mankind's past *and* present experience coupled with insights from our reasonable projection and anticipation of the outcome of contemplated action or behavior. The prime concern of these guidelines would be to protect the integrity and foster the growth of the individual person by shedding light on his responsibilities to those he relates to in loving concern.

What some of these moral guidelines are should already be evident in the statements from theologians and church groups we cited earlier. At this point, however, it would be helpful, I think, to tie these principles together in a sort of *charter of human sexual behavior.*

Let me begin with a foundation drawn from the Presbyterian document and then get down to particulars: "We regard as contrary to the covenant all those actions which destroy community and cause persons to lose hope, to erode their practical confidence in the providence of God, and to lose respect for their own integrity as persons. Clearly, such actions are not susceptible of being catalogued, for sexual gestures which may in one instance cause deep guilt and shame, whether warranted or not, may in another context be vehicles of celebrating a joyous and creative communion between persons.

"By the same token, those sexual expressions which build up communion between persons, establish a hopeful outlook on the future, minister in a healing way to the fears, hurts and anxieties of persons and confirm to them the fact that they are truly loved, are actions which can confirm the covenant Jesus announced."

The Presbyterian statement stresses the relational and celebrational character of sexual activity at least as much as and often more than its procreative function. In this it highlights the "Christian calling to glorify God by the joyful celebration of and delight in our sexuality." And while admitting that the relational and celebrational function of human sexuality cannot be adequately or exhaustively described, there are some goals we should consider in appraising each of our unique human relations, whether or not they involve full sexual communion.

"Interpersonal relationships should enhance rather than limit the spiritual freedom of the individuals involved. They should be vehicles of expressing that love which is commended in the New Testament—a compassionate and consistent concern for the well-being of the other. They should provide for the upbuilding of the creative potential of persons who are called to the task of stewardship of God's world. They should occasion that joy in his situation which is one of man's chief means of glorifying his Creator. They should open to persons that flow of grace which will enable them to bear their burdens without despair."

"A moral judgment," Catholic moralist Cornelius van der Poel tells us, "is made not so much about a human act in itself as a separate entity, but rather the individual human act should be evaluated insofar as it contributes to or destroys the building of this society." This does not mean that the end justifies the means, but rather that the end determines the human meaning of the means. Persons, human needs, and their unique situations "matter more than principles, infinitely more," as the Roys maintain in *Honest Sex*.

Some readers, I know, will immediately see in this situational approach to human values a hedonistic license to indulge any and all sexual impulses. But recall the two inviolable guidelines set forth by one of the most liberal advocates of sex as a game, Dr. Alex Comfort: "Thou shalt not exploit another person's feelings and wantonly expose them to an experience of rejection. Thou shalt not under any circumstances negligently risk producing an unwanted child."

When Jesuit moralist Thomas Wassmer speaks of "loving concern" as being essential to any moral human relationship, marital or otherwise, he is arguing for the most authentically Christian and humanly moral guideline we can imagine. Far from being license, this guideline is *much more demanding of the individual* than the simple invocation of some traditional law.

For instance, a married woman might find herself deeply involved with a young man and his growth as a person. She might, as the college professor's wife in *Tea and Sympathy*, face a situation where Christian love and concern for a fellow human seems to urge a relationship the law would term "adultery," totally immoral. An advocate of legal morality would ignore the whole situation and simply state that regardless of human needs no one can morally enter into an adulterous relation. An advocate of situation ethics would consider all the facets and circumstances as objectively as possible, weigh them, and then make the best decision he could in terms of loving concern and Christian responsibility for all involved. The wife in *Tea and Sympathy* took this last approach. She did not just meet a young fellow, feel an animal attraction, and tumble into bed with him. The same was true of the widow in *The Summer of '42*. There was an obvious step-by-step escalation in these relationships, centered on the very deep human needs of another person approached with some openness. The decision in both cases, though more reasoned out in *Tea and Sympathy*, was far more humane, Christian, and demanding than if the parties had simply applied the law, and disregarded the needs of a fellow creature.

Some of the guidelines implicit in *Tea and Sympathy* have been expanded by the Roys in "Is Monogamy Outdated?":

"OPENNESS: Contrary to folklore, frank and honest discussions at every stage of a developing relationship between all parties is the best guarantee against trouble. We know of husbands who have discussed with their wives possible coitus with a third person, some to conclude it would be wrong, others, unwise; others to drop earlier objections, and still others to say it was necessary and beautiful. We know of wives who have said a reasoned 'no' to such possibilities for their husbands and kept their love and respect; and many who have said 'yes' in uncertainty and have found the pain subside. Openness is not impossible.

"OTHER-CENTEREDNESS: Concern for *all* the others—the other woman or man, the other husband or wife, the children—must be front and center in reaching decisions on any such matters.

"PROPORTIONALITY: Sexual expressions should be proportional to the depth of a relationship. This leads, of course, to the conclusion that most coitus and other intimate expressions should only occur with very close friends: a conclusion questioned by many, but essential for our theory.

"GRADUALISM: Only a stepwise escalation of intimacy allows for the open discussion referred to above. Otherwise such openness becomes a series of confessions."

These guidelines proposed by Roy deal with comarital relations but they are easily adapted to all the other situations we have discussed here.

"The new patterns of sexual behavior that are still to be worked out should be," as Snoek argues, "at the service of true, personalizing communication." Complete openness and honesty from the very beginning of all relationships and open, honest discussion among all parties concerned are ideals that are feasible only when young people know before they get married the many paths their relationship might take. Unless there is frank and complete discussion of pluralism and alternative relationships *before marriage* and a parallel realization by the couple *before they marry* that their relationship might flow into one of these alternative patterns, the couple will most likely find themselves suddenly confronted with a very deep and demanding relationship. Not having faced or admitted the possibilities beforehand,

married couples often find that a relationship has reached a
critical point without their being aware of its seriousness. It is
far easier for all concerned when they have mutually discussed
a deepening relation as it evolves over some time, gradually adding new dimensions to which each party can adjust.

However, *this is a transitional generation*. We do not have
anything near the openness and completeness of the sex-educa-
tion program just outlined. Most couples in their thirties and
forties have married with the monogamy myth unquestioned.
Then suddenly they confront reality: an alternative relationship
is right in front of them without warning. "My spouse wants to
sleep with someone else!"—the end of a world, the harsh end
of a myth; an illusion has been shattered with apocalyptic swift-
ness. And how do you cope with this? The gradualism, openness, proportionality, urged by Roy is impossible. Perhaps at
best one can hope for a gradual retroactive openness that starts
with the *de facto*, fully developed relation and travels back in
time psychologically to expose the roots of the relation. This
inevitably means much tension and frustration, and requires a
lot of sensitive intuition that will permit tacit and fearful acceptance without pressing immediately for completely open and
unreserved assent.

The education of today's youth and adults must be designed
to communicate the realities of our pluralistic culture, its various
pros and cons; and guidelines must be drawn from past, present,
and future riches of our heritage. This is the only way our
loving concern for others can be responsible and creative of
human dignity. We all share a tremendous responsibility as
co-creators of our fellow man, as co-creators of other sexual
persons with whom we enter into dialogue on a variety of levels.
This responsibility as co-creators of our fellow men I have
detailed in my book *Evolving World, Converging Man*.

Our education must also be *designed not to communicate
set and unchanging mystiques for either male or female*. It must
be designed to mature each person's self-identity, each one's

sureness of himself in a world of change. It must prepare one to make decisions independent of peer-group pressures.

Our education has to be designed also to communicate a real sense of religious responsibility or humanistic morality.

In some European countries where an extramarital relationship is more openly accepted by society, the serious responsibilities of all parties are clearly spelled out by custom. A Frenchman of Voltaire's day was allowed any number of mistresses *provided* he could care for them properly. A woman was likewise allowed any number of lovers, but only one at a time. If a woman's husband left town for any length of time her lover was obligated to provide for all her financial needs, her housing, and upkeep. She might even move in with him until her husband returned. If her honor was impugned, her lover was expected to fill in for the husband, even if this meant a duel. More recently there is a tendency in some countries to spell out these obligations in law. For instance, a Swedish government commission is considering a law which "will expect partners to honor certain obligations to each other, but not to practice absolute loyalty." In the future, a married Swede, male or female, will have a legal right to take an outside partner. Here, of course, it is much easier to spell out obligations.

The major problem with our American hypocrisy is that by ignoring the realities of premarital and extramarital behavior, we have allowed these to become common practices *without the slightest sense of responsibility.*

The American college couple living together with the silent non-objection of their parents, dorm directors, church officials, and school administrators are left without any guidelines about their responsibilities by the very guides who should provide these. The parent with his head in the sand is not likely to utter helpful advice on a situation that he is not even willing to admit exists, either emotionally or intellectually. The married person furtively engaged in an affair is also without any guidance to his responsibilities to anything except his own instinct for self-survival, self-indulgence, and a fallible, fragile sense of personal integrity which secrecy often undermines.

When society does not openly face the realities of premarital intercourse and offer responsible guidelines, it is inevitable that unthinking young people will often live together without the slightest thought given to contraceptives, or to the emotional and financial risks and obligations. The same holds true when society does not face up to the realities of comarital relations, except that most of the burden and shortchanging then falls on the third party, with the married person often able to avoid all obligations. Without open discussion it is very easy for anyone to slip into an "illegal" relationship under the veil of secrecy and without considering the outcomes possible. What if after sleeping with her for months, he announces he can marry only a virgin? What if after living together one or the other decides he does not want to marry?

This ambivalent, irresponsible, and reluctantly pluralistic situation can mean only one thing for the decades ahead: *an era of increasing tensions and conflicts for all,* but especially for two groups: for married couples caught in this age of transition without preparation, and for young single men who must accept the demolition of the male mystique just as they are trying to find the meaning of their own masculinity, just as they struggle to adjust to the liberated young women who refuse to be squeezed into the kitchen and nursery. I hope, however, that open discussion on all levels will soften the tension and smooth the conflicts somewhat.

Margaret Mead argues that we are in a prefigurative society, a transitional culture without models. One of our main problems then becomes the task of adapting psychologically to the fact that never again will men and women be able to look for comfort to neat pigeonhole models according to which they can mold their lives.

Our *present* age is, as the mystic William Blake suggested, the time of infinity. You can dial almost any conceivable human relationship on our present time machine, from past or future, and find it being lived in our society. There are no models, no paradigms, only individuals creating an endless series of unique variations on some twenty basic themes.

Thus each one of us creates and evolves our own models and paradigms for the male/female relation, for marriage, and for family. These cannot be the fixed metaphysical archetypes common in past cultures to which one simply molded his personality and behavior. They have to be, in the words of Ludwig von Bertalanffy, "flexible and dynamic working models," unique for each individual.

In this creation of new models, open discussion and exchange of experiences among pioneering persons can lead to a shared wisdom that learns more rapidly from failure and painful explorations. Gradually, out of such sharing of insights, will come basic skeletons, flexible and dynamic working models that can serve as guides for those to follow without inhibiting the initiative of these second-generation pioneers in adapting the valuable insights of the model to their own unique situations.

Peter Berger has suggested that the churches' traditional role has been to *legitimize the present*. I believe that if the churches are to have any influence at all on human relations in the decades ahead, if they are to cope with present shock, their leaders must do much more than merely legitimate the present institutions—especially when these are based on myths. The churches will have to make a contribution to working out a new sexual ethos and boldly apply the wisdom of the past to testing *new* models. The churches must then share in the creation of prophetic models, *anticipating human needs* in new situations rather than sitting back to pontificate on the legality of behavioral models proposed by the grass roots. This requires a colossal aboutface, and perhaps it is not psychologically possible for many church leaders. But it must happen if the churches are to have any impact. Yet I am not pessimistic. I find some real encouragement in the statements of the Presbyterians, the

British Council of Churches, and the Quakers, whatever might be their semi-official status. I also find hope in the statements and views of the dozen or more theologians we have quoted. Small as these may be as a first step, tentative and hedging, they remain a creative step toward the future.

We desperately need the historical perspective and the rich insights that remain hidden in our Judeo-Christian and Western history. We need this wisdom, for we are grappling with revolutionary options in human relations. We are exploring human life, and the more information we have at hand, the better off we will be.

Without doubt some of these experiments will end up as evolutionary dead ends. This has happened countless times in past evolutionary gropings, cultural as well as biological, and the dead ends will continue to appear here and there. Some of our new models will abort, exploding under the pressure of external forces of technology and economics, or from the internal pressure of unchanneled, undisciplined, or unmanageable human emotions. Some of them will remain as nothing more than a minor species.

One essential trait of all pioneering elements at any critical threshold in evolution is a certain creative instability expressed by unspecialized individuals who are unhappy with and ill-adapted to their environment. These men and women today who are exploring and creating new structures of sex, marriage, and family are just such unspecialized individuals. They are unhappy with their environment. They are socially and psychologically ill-adapted to cope with it. They are unstable, unspecialized, unhappy with and disturbed by certain aspects of the traditional monogamous culture in which we are born and raised.

In rejecting the traditional values and structures, these people naturally encounter considerable psychological pressure from the more conservative and traditional elements in the society they hope to change. Emotional conflicts are inevitable in their own painful personal gropings, and bring even more hurt and risk when they try to work out new solutions with others. Exploration and growth cannot exist without some pain, some risk, some danger. Painless growth does not exist. The question is how to reduce it to a minimum and eliminate the needless, senseless pain.

Despite the pain, however, the end result of these explorations may well be the richness of a pluralistic world in which each sexual person is free to develop and expand his potential to the fullest as the spirit moves him within a community of free and lovingly concerned human beings. This may sound utopian, but there is no unrealism in the expectation that an openly pluralistic society will contain more opportunity for men and women to develop their personalities, more opportunity for a fuller expansion of the unexplored richness of male and female. An openly pluralistic society is more human than today's hypocritical, mythic monogamous culture. Certainly an openly pluralistic society would eliminate the necessity of each one of us squeezing into some predetermined role. We would then have a free, human choice among many options, or even the option of creating our own totally new niche in society as a sexual person.

EPILOGUE

Eve's New Rib: Twenty Faces of
Sex, Marriage, and Family

THE BOOK of Genesis recalls the beautiful and perennial myth of the first human "mother," Adam. From Adam's rib came the first "baby." And men kept her a social infant even when they left their fathers' house to cleave to her as two in one flesh. The child bride remained the emotional, half-human, imperfectly formed, miscarried male whose world revolved around the men to whom she was meant to cater.

Within the last century, however, women have begun to view their delegated task of motherhood in a new light. As a result of reproductive and contraceptive technology, developed by males who wanted to reduce their burden as parents while increasing their pleasures, women are now emerging as persons in their own right. In this maturing, women have decided to create the male and female of tomorrow in some new images. In many ways women are pioneering the creation of new faces for sex, marriage, and family.

As we explored the changing male/female relations of today's society and tried to calculate the impact of social trends and of sophisticated reproductive/contraceptive technology, a list of options began to emerge. The list is far from complete, for we are still exploring, still changing. Still, I think the list below is fairly complete as a base on which one can build an unlimited variety of unique combinations during a lifetime. Here, then, are the twenty faces of sex, marriage, and family as I see them today:

1. The traditional monogamous, sexually exclusive marriage will remain for many, but certainly not the majority of people, a desirable and viable pattern despite the increasing tensions of leisure, mobility, women's liberation, our contraceptive technology, negativism of the nuclear family, and an ever-increasing life expectancy.

2. An increasing number of men and women will find an alternative mode of coping with these tensions in a more flexible monogamy allowing for comarital experiences by mutual consent of both parties. This modified marriage, I suspect, will become the most common form of male/female relationship, since it accommodates the new tensions noted above without demolishing a structure which has become almost instinctual for Western man and woman. The third parties in these comarital relationships would change periodically, few lasting more than two to five years.

3. Serial monogamy or consecutive polygamy, which is already commonplace in our patterns of divorce and remarriage, will in the future resolve the patriarchal inequities of alimony, child support, and custody in favor of a "no-fault" dissolution of the marriage. With a more realistic image of the problems of marriage today and a social acceptance of comarital relations, serial polygamy will be less popular than it is today, though it will still remain a human necessity for those couples who find after some years that they have grown in totally different directions or at such different paces that communication and communion are psychologically impossible.

4. Trial, or two-step, marriages will be socially accepted, to allow a young couple to live together and share mutual personal growth and adjustment before they decide to accept the responsibility of producing and raising a family.

5. Polygamy for senior citizens will be accepted after a humane consideration of a variety of social and moral factors, the

economic limitations of single people on social security or retirement benefits, the increasing isolation of the aged from their children's families, the increasing disproportion between men and women in this age group, the need for mutual assistance in health care, food preparation, simple nursing, and friendship within their own group, and the extension of sexual activity into old age by chemotherapy.

6. Reversal of the traditional family roles will occur, with the husband staying home to care for the children and keep house while the wife works. This might be a long-term arrangement or, more likely, a rotating situation in which one party works one year and the other the next year.

7. Unisex marriages of two or more males or females will be accepted. Since we can no longer restrict sexual relations to a procreative function, homosexuality can no longer be condemned as immoral or unnatural merely because it is noncreative.

8. There will be an increased number of single parents, male or female, as the result of adoption, artificial insemination, or traditional conception: those who are anxious and willing to accept the responsibilities of child raising but cannot or do not relate this to the responsibility of living with another adult.

9. Group marriages will be more common for those who cannot tolerate the divisiveness and isolation of the nuclear family and seek the support of a tribal group.

10. Retirement parenthood will be chosen by those who want to achieve financial security and fulfill themselves first as individuals and as a couple before settling down to raise a family.

11. Contractual marriages will be arranged by couples who find the lifelong commitment of the traditional marriage unacceptable.

12. Couples disillusioned with the institution of marriage may choose unstructured but stable cohabitation.

13. As a result of our growing concern with the population problem and the increasing complexities of raising a child, parenthood may be limited to professionally trained couples.

14. A new group of professionals will emerge: third parents, trained personnel, single and married, who enjoy working with parents and their children.

15. Polygamy and polyandry, bigamy, or triangular marriages will be legalized for those who find more than one spouse a desirable and feasible way of life.

16. Multilateral or plural marriages involving both heterosexual and homosexual relationships will be accepted.

17. Some will choose the single life, which may or may not involve lifelong celibacy. This life might well involve some religious or social dedication in a formal way.

18. There will be single couples, two or more single people of the same sex living together without sexual relations but sharing or dividing the normal household tasks, one girl perhaps working to support the household, another doing most of the housework because she prefers this. Television's *Odd Couple* provides a good example of this.

19. The celibate, or celebrational, marriage will be chosen by couples not compelled to procreate and who find the co-creativeness of their relationship in other fields more than adequate compensation for the lack of physical expression in sexual intercourse.

20. Our list is incomplete without your own unique experience. You may want to add another possibility to complete the list, and this is your privilege, since you are just as much involved in this exploration of human society as anyone else.

These, then, are some of the progeny of Eve's New Rib, some of the faces of sex, marriage, and family we are already witnessing as we move into the pluralistic culture of the global tribe.

Acknowledgments

Eve's New Rib owes its genesis and growth to the generosity of many friends, colleagues, and chance encounters over the past five or six years.

Some key insights, suggestions, and correctives have come from my prime commentator and critic, my wife, Anna; from Ruth Elsasser, a dear colleague at Fairleigh Dickinson; from Dr. Nell Morton, professor emeritus at the Theological School of Drew University; from the Reverend Charles Moore, pastor of St. Giles Episcopal Church, Northbrook, Illinois; from Clayton Carlson, of Harper & Row; from Dr. Jean Houston Masters; and from my old friends Linda Burnett, Ann Lyons, and Richard Bibeau.

Special gratitude is due my friends at Friendship Library of Fairleigh Dickinson: to its director, James Fraser, and to the staff, especially Dorothea Creamer, Helen Ross, Robert Milford, and Joel Beane.

My students at Fairleigh Dickinson have contributed many candid and frank insights during our discussions, both in class and informally, of the new trends in human reproduction and their possible impact on marriage, family, and male/female relations. Various pieces of this book, insights, new relations, and examples from real life are due to unnamed benefactors in the audiences at my lectures at over fifty colleges and universities

My readers will quickly recognize two central influences around the country.

underlying this book. The first is the courageous and, I believe, prophetic utopian novel-essays of Robert H. Rimmer, author of *The Harrad Experiment, Proposition Thirty-one,* and *The Rebellion of Yale Marratt.* These novels have influenced my thinking very much in terms of the psychological and social problems to be encountered by individuals and by society as we begin to accept alternative male/female relations besides the traditional monogamy. The second support is more theological, though it also owes much to practical encounters with alternative life styles, especially the comarital relationship. The influence of Rustum and Della Roy's experiences and insights, first expressed in *Honest Sex: A Revolutionary Sex Ethic by and for Concerned Christians,* has been central to the development of this book. In a more personal way, the Roys and Rimmer helped resolve some key questions remaining in my mind as the task of writing approached completion, and without this personal sharing of views, *Eve's New Rib* might not have come into being.

Finally, I must thank two colleagues who read the rough draft of *Eve's New Rib* with a critical and creative scrutiny which enriched it considerably: Dr. Irving Buchen, professor of English and director of Fairleigh Dickinson's College of the Future; and Dr. Christopher Fullman, professor of English at Upsala College, whose friendship dates back to his essay on medieval love which appeared in my first book.

Selected Bibliography

"Adopting a Lover." *Time*, September 6, 1971, p. 50.
Report of two homosexuals solving the inheritance question by adoption.

Alpenfels, Ethel. "Progressive Monogamy: An Alternate Pattern."
In Herbert A. Otto, Ed., *The Family in Search of a Future*.

"Americana: The Whispered Faith." *Time*, October 11, 1971,
p. 25.
A report on the present practice of polygamy among the Mormons
and its return to popularity.

"American Family, The." *Look*, January 26, 1971, pp. 21–40+.
An outstanding issue. Especially good are dialogues with Alvin Toffler,
Shirley MacLaine, Erich Segal, Margaret Mead, and Betty Friedan;
also articles by Dr. Spock, stories on homosexual couples, radical families, executive mothers, and parents.

"American Family, The: Future Uncertain." *Time*, December 28,
1970, pp. 34–39.
A broad, balanced, detailed survey of the family crisis in the United
States and alternative patterns now being tried.

Aymard, Alain. "Louvain Colloquium on Sexuality: Sociological Approach." *IDOC-International* (North American Edition), October 31, 1970, pp. 65–68.

Bartell, Gilbert. *Group Sex*. New York: Peter H. Wyden, 1971.
An excellent anthropological study of "swingers." Detailed and balanced.

Benjamin, Harry. *The Transsexual Phenomenon*. New York: Julian
Press, 1966.
Still a basic source

Bernard, Jessie. *The Future of Marriage*. New York: The Macmillan Company, 1971.

———. *The Sex Game*. Englewood Cliffs, New Jersey: Prentice-Hall, 1968.
Absorbing, illuminating reflections of a leading sociologist.

———. "Women, Marriage and the Future." *The Futurist*, April, 1970, pp. 41–43.

Bertalanffy, Ludwig von. *Robots, Men and Minds*. New York: George Braziller, 1967.
Very useful insight into the nature of models and paradigms in sociology and psychology.

Bettelhein, Bruno. *The Children of the Dream: Communal Child-Raising and American Education*. New York: The Macmillan Company, 1969.

———. "Does Communal Education Work? The Case for the Kibbutz." In Edwin Schur, Ed., *The Family and the Sexual Revolution*.

Boalt, Gunnar. *Family and Marriage*. New York: David McKay Co., 1965.

Böckle, Franz, Ed. *The Future of Marriage as Institution*. New York: Herder and Herder, 1970.

Borowitz, Eugene B. *Choosing a Sex Ethic: A Jewish Inquiry*. New York: Schocken Books, 1969.

Boylan, Brian Richard. *Infidelity*. Englewood Cliffs, New Jersey: Prentice-Hall, 1971.
Superficial but some worth-while insights.

Breasted, Mary. *Oh! Sex Education*. New York: Praeger Publishers, 1970.
Very balanced and comprehensive survey of sex education in the United States.

British Council of Churches. *Sex and Morality*. Philadelphia: Fortress Press, 1967.
Still an exploratory, open, worth-while study.

Buchen, Irving. *The Perverse Imagination*. New York: New York University Press, 1970.
Collection of essays on pornographic literature, scholarly and heavy, but Buchen's preface is worth looking at for the average reader.

Calderwood, Deryck. *What Is Marriage?* Part 1. Expectations and Realities. Part 2. Possibilities for the Future. Pleasantville, New York: Guidance Associates, 1971.

Callahan, Sidney. "Fidelity: Bone-power." *National Catholic Reporter*, December 11, 1970, p. 13.
A reasoned defense of the traditional concept of fidelity.

Carter, Hugh, and Glick, Paul. *Marriage and Divorce: A Social and Economic Study*. Cambridge, Massachusetts: Harvard University Press, 1970.

"Changing Identities." *Newsweek*, September 6, 1971, pp. 44–45.
A brief report of comparative studies of male-female reactions to the Rorschach ink-blot test indicating some shift to unisex reactions.

Christensen, Harold. "A Cross-Cultural Comparison of Attitudes Toward Marital Infidelity." *International Journal of Comparative Sociology*, September, 1962, p. 7.

Cole, William Graham. "Religious Attitudes Toward Extramarital Intercourse." In Gerhard Neubeck, Ed., *Extramarital Relations*.
An important complement to *Sex and Love in the Bible*.

——. *Sex and Love in the Bible*. New York: Association Press, 1959.
A very useful introduction and survey of the biblical tradition on sex, marriage, and love.

Comfort, Alexander. *The Nature of Human Nature*. New York: Harper & Row, Publishers, 1965.
Excellent perspective on man and human nature. Chapter 2, on sexuality and social behavior, is very good.

——. *Sex in Society*. Rev. ed. New York: Citadel Press, 1966.
An excellent study of changing patterns of sexual conduct and attitudes, with some fine insights into monogamy.

"Connubial Utopias of Robert Rimmer, The." *The Futurist*, October, 1968, pp. 99–100.

230   *Selected Bibliography*

Constantine, Larry and Joan. "Counseling Implications of Comarital and Multilateral Relations." Obtainable from the Multilateral Relations Study Project, 23 Monegan Road, Acton, Massachusetts 01720. (Also next and fifth entries below.)
Key problems in group and open-ended dyadic marriages from the perspective of interacting professional observers and participants.

——. "Dissolution of Marriage in a Non-Conventional Context." An address for the American Association of Marriage and Family Counselors Conference on Divorce.
A case study of dissolution patterns in group marriages that have broken up.

——. "How to Make a Group Marriage." *The Modern Utopian,* Summer-Fall, 1970, pp. 3–4.

——. "Multilateral Marriage: Alternate Family Structure in Practice." In Robert H. Rimmer, *You and I . . . Searching for Tomorrow,* pp. 157–175.

——. "Personal Growth in Multiperson Marriages." *The Radical Therapist,* Vol. 2, 1971, pp. 18–20.
Explores the relationship between growth in self-actualization and group marriage, possessiveness, the effect of previous dyadic marriage, and jealousy.

——. "Sexual Aspects of Multilateral Relations." An address for the Society for the Scientific Study of Sex.
Sex as a motivation for participating in group marriages: sex and sexual problems in these relations.

——. "Where Is Marriage Going?" *The Futurist,* April, 1970, pp. 44–46.

Cooper, David. *The Death of the Family.* New York: Pantheon Books, 1971.
A very negative appraisal of the family as the worst enemy of personal growth and identity.

Cuber, John F. "Adultery: Reality Versus Stereotype." In Gerhard Neubeck, Ed., *Extramarital Relations.*

——. "Alternate Models from the Perspective of Sociology." In Herbert A. Otto, Ed., *The Family in Search of a Future.*

———. "How New Ideas About Sex Are Changing Our Lives." *Redbook*, March, 1971, pp. 85, 173–177.
Brief and not as explicit, but closely paralleling this author's projects. Worth-while.

Cuber, John F., and Harroff, Peggy B. *The Significant Americans: A Study of Sexual Behavior among the Affluent*. New York: Appleton-Century-Crofts, 1965.
Informative and important study of sexual behavior and infidelity patterns of upper-middle-class Americans.

Davids, Leo. "North American Marriage: 1990." *The Futurist*, October, 1971, pp. 190–194.
An excellent projection dealing with the future of the "parenthood myth," communal control of reproduction, courtship and new forms of marriage, and professional parents.

Dearborn, Lester. "Extramarital Relations." In Morris Fishbein and Ernest Burgess, *Successful Marriage*.

Dopson, Laurence. "Hope for the Childless?" *Illustrated London News*, March 7, 1970, p. 18.
Reactions and comments on embryo transplants.

Edwards, Robert G., and Sharpe, David J. "Social Values and Research in Human Embryology." *Nature* (London), May 14, 1971, pp. 87–91.
A perceptive discussion by a lawyer and by an embryologist involved in embryo transplants.

Elliott, Janice. *The Buttercup Chain*. New York: Pyramid Publications, 1970.
An early novel on group marriage and swingers.

Ellis, Albert. "Group Marriage: A Possible Alternative?" In Herbert A. Otto, Ed., *The Family in Search of a Future*.

———. "Healthy and Disturbed Reasons for Having Extramarital Relations." In Gerhard Neubeck, Ed., *Extramarital Relations*.

Farber, Seymour, Ed. *Teilhard de Chardin: In Quest of the Perfection of Man*. Berkeley: University of California Press, 1972.

Ferm, Deane William. *Responsible Sexuality Now*. New York: The Seabury Press, 1971.
A fine Protestant study, with good historical background of changes in

Christian, Western, and American thought on sex, marriage, and love. Thoughtful insights into the Swedish experience. Well written.

Firestone, Shulamith. *The Dialectic of Sex: The Case for Feminist Revolution*. New York: William Morrow & Co., 1970.
Heavy plowing, and not really that good.

Fishbein, Morris, and Burgess, Ernest. *Successful Marriage*. Garden City, New York: Doubleday & Company, 1947.

Fleming, Thomas and Alice. "What Kids Still Don't Know about Sex." *Look*, July 28, 1970, pp. 59–62.
Underscores the fact that the younger generation, who are supposedly leading a revolution in sexual behavior, are most often woefully ignorant of the basic elementary facts of reproduction.

Fletcher, Joseph. *Situation Ethics*. Philadelphia: The Westminster Press, 1966.
A landmark in Christian ethics and "must" reading.

Fletcher, Joseph, and Wassmer, Thomas A. *Hello, Lovers: An Invitation to Situation Ethics*. Washington/Cleveland: Corpus Books, World Publishing Company, 1970.
Broad discussion of ethics, with some occasional sharp insights into situation ethics applied to sexuality and adultery.

Ford, Clellan, and Beach, Frank. *Patterns of Sexual Behavior*. New York: Harper & Row, Publishers, 1951.
Essential reading for comparison of our American behavior and beliefs with those of other societies. American monogamy and premarital patterns are shown to be in the small minority.

Francoeur, Robert T. "And Baby Makes One: The New Embryology." *The Critic*, November–December, 1969, pp. 34–41.
A basic survey of new possibilities in reproduction. Reprinted in the *Sunday Independent* (Dublin), March, 1970, and in several Australian and New Zealand newspapers.

——. "The Christian Challenge of Utopian Motherhood." *The Methodist Woman*, June, 1968, pp. 437–440.
Some early comments on the new reproductive technology; dated.

——. "Conflict, Cooperation and the Collectivisation of Man." In Seymour Farber, Ed., *Teilhard de Chardin: In Quest of the Perfection of Man*.
An analysis and critique of Teilhard's extrapolation of a virginal universe and human relations.

——. *Evolving World, Converging Man.* New York: Holt, Rinehart & Winston, 1970.
An integration of the latest scientific views of human evolution, with changes in world images and theological questions of man's origins and future.

——. "Morality and the New Embryology." *IDOC-International* (North American Edition), August 15, 1970, pp. 81–96.
Still a valuable survey, with brief summary of social impact.

——. "Utopian Motherhood and the Control of Population." *Catalyst for Environmental Quality,* Winter, 1970, pp. 6–10.
Concentrates on the interrelationship of reproductive technology and population control.

——. *Utopian Motherhood: New Trends in Human Reproduction.* Garden City, New York: Doubleday & Company, 1970.
The most comprehensive survey of new possibilities in human reproduction, with a popular, non-technical background and projections for the future. The last chapter deals with some social and moral issues.

——. "Utopian Motherhood—Window of the Future." *Marriage,* April, 1969, pp. 4–9, 63–68.
An early summary of the biological revolution, with comments by Ashley Montagu.

Garrigan, Owen. *Man's Intervention in Nature.* New York: Hawthorn Books, 1967.
Early study of the biological revolution, but comments on nature of man and what is "natural" are still useful.

Gay, William. "An Analysis of the Dual Family." *The Futurist,* April, 1969, p. 52.
A perceptive review of *Proposition Thirty-one.*

"Gay Church, The." *Time,* August 23, 1971, pp. 38–39.
Three columns reporting the vigorous growth of homosexual churches, including the first induction of novices into the homosexual religious order of the Companions of St. John.

Genné, Elizabeth and William. *Foundations for Christian Family Policy.* New York: National Council of Churches of Christ in the United States, 1961.

Gill, James J. "Coed Dorms." *Medical Insight,* December, 1970.
A balanced and favorable impression of the growth potential of today's coed dorms by a Jesuit psychiatrist.

Gilman, Richard. "Where Did It All Go Wrong?" *Life*, August 13, 1971, pp. 48–55.
A brief but excellent survey of man's downgrading of women over the centuries. Not a rehash of commonly known and often repeated material.

Goldstein, Martin, and Haeberle, Erwin J. *The Sex Book: A Modern Pictorial Encyclopedia*. New York: Herder and Herder, 1970.
Ballyhooed as a major step in a new approach to sex education, but quite pedantic. The photographs are often confusing, with no labels. Published originally by a German Lutheran group.

Goode, William. "The Theoretical Importance of Love." *American Sociological Review*, February, 1959.

———. *World Revolution and Family Patterns*. New York: The Free Press of Glencoe, 1963.

Greenwald, Harold. "Marriage as a Non-legal Voluntary Association." In Herbert A. Otto, Ed., *The Family in Search of a Future*.

Greer, Germaine. *The Female Eunuch*. New York: McGraw-Hill Book Company, 1971.
One of the finest studies of women's liberation.

Grossman, Edward. "The Obsolescent Mother." *The Atlantic*, May, 1971, pp. 39–50.

Halpern, Howard. "Alienation from Parenthood in the Kibbutz and America." *Marriage and Family Living*, February, 1962.

Heinlein, Robert A. *Stranger in a Strange Land*. New York: Berkley Publishing Corporation, 1961.
A popular campus novel; science fiction with some influential conceptions of sexual behavior advocated.

Hill, Norman, Ed. *Free Sex: A Delusion*. New York: Popular Library, 1971.
A collection of essays dealing with a variety of aspects in the sexual revolution; a study of how mass media may be creating this and enticing people by brainwashing. Good reading.

Hiltner, Seward. *Sex and the Christian Life*. New York: Association Press, 1957.
A broad-scope treatment of sexual ethics with good biblical and his-

torical perspective but too early for concrete applications to present alternatives. Still basic reading.

Hobbs, Edward. "An Alternate Model from a Theological Perspective." In Herbert A. Otto, Ed., *The Family in Search of a Future.*
A Methodist theologian argues for the family as the center of child raising, but in a sexually open relationship.

"Homosexual Church, The." *Newsweek*, October 12, 1970, p. 107.

Hunt, David. *Parent and Child in Seventeenth-Century France.* New York: Basic Books, 1970.
A startling, informative study of parent-child relations and the position of the infant and child.

Hunt, Morton. *The Affair: A Portrait of Extramarital Love in Contemporary America.* New York: The New American Library, A Signet Book, 1969.
In-depth interviews with eighty unfaithful husbands and wives from which emerges a good over-all picture of infidelity patterns. Should be followed by reading the article in *Playboy* by Hunt.

———. "The Future of Marriage." *Playboy*, August, 1971, pp. 116–118, 168–175.
A fine synthesis and source, however brief. The most recent summary of impressions from a long-time study of marriage.

———. *The Natural History of Love.* New York: Alfred A. Knopf, 1959.
Readable and informative history of love in the Western world.

Huxley, Aldous. *Island.* New York: Bantam Books, 1963.
Huxley classic forecast of human sexual behavior in utopia.

Jeannière, Abel. *The Anthropology of Sex.* New York: Harper & Row, Publishers, 1967.
The preface to this book by a pioneering French Jesuit psychologist is especially worth reading. Daniel Sullivan nicely probes love and body/soul in the context of sexuality.

Jones, R. C. "Uses of Artificial Insemination." *Nature* (London), February 19, 1971, pp. 534–537.
A fine review of the techniques, social implications, and problems involved in a more extended use of artificial insemination.

Joyce, Mary and Robert. *New Dynamics in Sexual Love: A Revolutionary Approach to Marriage and Celibacy.* Collegeville, Minnesota: The Liturgical Press, 1970.
Detailed exposition and argument for the celibate, or celebrational, marriage.

Kassel, Victor. "Polygyny after Sixty." In Herbert A. Otto, Ed., *The Family in Search of a Future.*

Kennedy, Eugene. *What a Modern Catholic Believes about Sex.* Chicago: Thomas More Press, 1971.

Kirkendall, Lester. *Premarital Intercourse and Interpersonal Relationships.* New York: Gramercy Publishing Co., 1961.
Dated but worth skimming.

Kirkendall, Lester, and Whitehurst, Robert N., Eds. *The New Sexual Revolution.* New York: D. W. Brown, 1971.
A distinguished group of authors offer a responsible guide to sexual morality, yet one based on the ideal of sexual liberation.

Kovach, Bill. "Communes Spread as the Young Reject Old Values." *New York Times,* December 17, 1970, pp. 1, 84.

Levett, Carl. "A Parental Presence in Future Family Models." In Herbert A. Otto, Ed., *The Family in Search of a Future.*
Discussion of professional and third parents.

Lewis, C. S. *The Allegory of Love: A Study in Medieval Tradition.* Oxford: The Clarendon Press, 1936.
The classic in-depth study of courtly love.

Love, Nancy. "The '70s Woman and the Now Marriage." *Philadelphia,* February, 1970, pp. 55–58, 84ff.
A popular but basically valid account of flexible monogamy and swinging.

Lutheran Church in America. "Sex, Marriage, and Family." A social statement adopted at the Fifth Biennial Convention, Minneapolis, Minn., June 25–July 2, 1970.
A very traditional statement, with marriage being interpreted as "ordained by God as a structure of the created order," hence unchanging and unchangeable.

Mace, David R. *The Christian Response to the Sexual Revolution.* Nashville, Tennessee: Abingdon Press, 1970.

——. "The Employed Mother in the U.S.S.R." *Marriage and Family Living*, November, 1961.

Macklin, Eleanor. "Heterosexual Cohabitation Among Unmarried Students."
An unpublished paper delivered at the May, 1971, Groves Conference.

Macmurray, John. *Reason and Emotion*. New York: Appleton-Century-Crofts, 1936.

——. *The Structure of Religious Experience*. New Haven, Connecticut: Yale University Press, 1936.
A pioneering statement of what amounts to situation ethics, based on emotional fidelity rather than legalisms.

Marshall, Donald S., and Suggs, Robert C., Eds. *Human Sexual Behavior: The Range and Diversity of Human Sexual Experience Throughout the World as Seen in Six Representative Cultures*. New York: Basic Books, 1971.
A fascinating and very informative comparison of customs in Africa, South America, Polynesia, and the poor of England, Ireland, and America.

Martin, Ralph G. *Jennie: The Life of Lady Randolph Churchill*. The Romantic Years 1854–1895, Vol. I. Englewood Cliffs, N.J.: Prentice-Hall, 1969.

May, Rollo. *Love and Will*. New York: W. W. Norton & Company, 1969.
Fundamental reading from one of the best modern psychologists. Well worth pondering.

McLuhan, Marshall, and Leonard, George B. "The Future of Sex." *Look*, July 25, 1967, pp. 56–60.
Available as a reprint. A provocative, creative, and controversial interpretation. Basic.

McWhirter, William. " 'The Arrangement' at College." *Life*, May 31, 1968, pp. 56–68.
A good survey of new patterns of life style among college students, with comments by Albert Rosenfeld on the tendency to more sex but less promiscuity and a report by Roger Vaughan on how liberal colleges cope with the new patterns.

Mead, Margaret. "Marriage in Two Steps." In Herbert A. Otto, Ed., *The Family in Search of a Future*.

——. "Women: A House Divided." *Redbook*, May, 1970, pp. 55, 59.
Argues for a "professional prestige" view of domestic work.

Mead, Margaret, and Metraux, Rhoda. *A Way of Seeing*. New York: The McCall Publishing Co., 1970.
A marvelous and rich collection of Mead's essays, edited by Metraux, including a dozen major essays on marriage, trial marriage, limiting family size, sex education, and women.

Milhaven, John Giles. *Toward a New Catholic Morality*. Garden City, N.Y.: Doubleday & Company, 1970.

Money, John, Ed. *Sex Research: New Developments*. New York: Holt, Rinehart & Winston, 1965.
Technical report of recent research, but not too difficult reading for those with a little biological background—some good insights into psychosexuality.

Nemy, Enid. "Group Sex: Is It 'Life Art' or a Sign That Something Is Wrong?" *New York Times*, May 10, 1971, p. 38.

Neubeck, Gerhard, Ed. *Extramarital Relations*. Englewood Cliffs, N.J.: Prentice-Hall, Spectrum Books, 1969.
A varied and excellent collection of essays dealing with different aspects of infidelity.

——. "Polyandry and Polygyny: Viable Today?" In Herbert A. Otto, Ed., *The Family in Search of a Future*.

O'Neill, William. *Divorce in the Progressive Era*. New Haven, Conn.: Yale University Press, 1967.

Orleans, Myron, and Wolfson, Florence. "The Future of the Family." *The Futurist*, April, 1970, pp. 48–49.

Otto, Herbert A., Ed. *The Family in Search of a Future: Alternate Models for Moderns*. New York: Appleton-Century-Crofts, 1970.
The essays in this collection, all by recognized and respected authorities, deal with a variety of alternatives and options for the family. Basic reading.

Packard, Vance. *The Sexual Wilderness: The Contemporary Upheaval in Male-Female Relationships*. New York: David McKay Co., 1968.
Five hundred pages of informative surveys of the present situation here

and abroad, with some assessments of and suggestions for future directions. Basic.

Parker, Robert Allerton. *A Yankee Saint.* New York: G. P. Putnam's Sons, 1935.

Peter, H.R.H. Prince of Greece and Denmark. *A Study of Polyandry.* The Hague: Mouton & Co., 1963.
A six-hundred-page sociological study of polyandry observed firsthand by the author, a respected anthropologist. Instances of strict plurality of husbands are detailed in various cultures of Tibet, India, Ceylon, Africa, and among some North American Indians. He also reports on customs of cicisbeism, where a woman is married officially to one man but his brothers or other male relatives are allowed occasional sexual relations with the wife.

Pittenger, William Norman. *Making Sexuality Human.* Philadelphia: United Church Press, Pilgrim Press, 1970.
An Episcopal theologian, open and middle road.

Poor, Riva. *4 Days, 40 Hours: Reporting a Revolution in Work and Leisure.* Cambridge, Mass.: Bursk & Poor Publishers, 1970.
Thorough study of a revolutionary shift in working patterns.

Presbyterian Church. *Sexuality and the Human Community.* Philadelphia: United Presbyterian Church in the U.S.A., 1970. A task-force document issued by the 182nd General Assembly.
A creative, pioneering, and balanced statement. Essential and enjoyable reading.

Quaker View of Sex, Towards a. Rev. ed. London: Friends Home Service Committee, 1966.
Though written ten years ago, still an outstanding position paper.

Rabin, Albert. "Kibbutz Children—Research Findings to Date." *Children,* September–October, 1958.

Ramsey, Paul. *Fabricated Man: The Ethics of Genetic Control.* New Haven, Conn.: Yale University Press, 1970.
Patriarch of Princeton's School of Religion and long-time student of ethics, Ramsey presents a good Protestant translation of a Middle Ages Roman Catholic reaction to reproductive technology.

Reiss, Ira L. "How and Why America's Sex Standards Are Changing." *Trans-Action,* March, 1968, pp. 26–32.

——. *Premarital Sexual Standards.* Discussion Guide No. 5. New York: Sex Information and Education Council of the U.S., 1967.

———. *The Social Context of Premarital Sexual Permissiveness.* New York: Holt, Rinehart & Winston, 1967.

Richardson, Herbert W. *Nun, Witch, Playmate: The Americanization of Sex.* New York: Harper & Row, Publishers, 1971.
A lively, masterful exposé of the psychological and historical forces behind today's sexual upheaval. Enjoyable and full of meat.

Riegel, Robert E. *American Women: A Story of Social Change.* Rutherford, New Jersey: Fairleigh Dickinson University Press, 1970.
A readable, light, but solid review of the birth of the American female as woman and person.

Rimmer, Robert H. *The Harrad Experiment.* New York: Bantam Books, 1967.
This classic novel-essay deals with six young people in an experimental coed college who end up in a group marriage after graduation. Harrad is typical of many college campuses today.

———. Ed. *The Harrad Letters to Robert H. Rimmer.* New York: The New American Library, A Signet Book, 1969.
A collection of letters written to Rimmer in spontaneous response to *The Harrad Experiment* and his other two novels. Fascinating.

———. *Proposition Thirty-one.* New York: The New American Library, A Signet Book, 1969.
Story of two California couples who enter a four-party marriage. Revealing and realistic fiction.

———. *The Rebellion of Yale Marratt.* New York: Avon Books, 1967.
A lengthy, often philosophical, and deeply psychological novel of a triangular marriage. Essential as an in-depth experience.

———. *You and I . . . Searching for Tomorrow.* New York: The New American Library, A Signet Book, 1971.
More substantial than *The Harrad Letters,* this collection contains more letters from people who have been experimenting for some time; also contains some position papers and a long, rambling preface by Rimmer

Roberts, Steven. "The 'Living Alone' Phenomenon: Signs of It Are Everywhere." *New York Times,* January 31, 1971, p. 56.
A pessimistic report on a growing way of life.

———. "Youth Communes Seek a New Way of Life." *New York Times,* August 3, 1970, p. 28.

Robertson, Constance Noyes, Ed. *Oneida Community: An Auto-biography 1851–1876.* Syracuse: Syracuse University Press, 1970.
An absolutely absorbing, fascinating collection of excerpts from the journals and diaries of the Oneida Community.

Robinson, John A. T. *Christian Freedom in a Permissive Society.* Philadelphia: The Westminster Press, 1970.
Some scattered insights on sexual morality by the author of *Honest to God.*

Roosens, Eugeen. "Louvain Colloquium on Sexuality: Anthropological Approach." *IDOC-International* (North American Edition), October 31, 1970, pp. 61–65.

Rorvik, David M. "Taking Life in Our Own Hands: The Test-Tube Baby Is Coming." *Look,* May 18, 1971, pp. 83–86.
Details on Shettles' historic transplant of a human embryo from one woman to another.

Rorvik, David M., and Shettles, Landrum B. *Your Baby's Sex: Now You Can Choose.* New York: Dodd, Mead & Company, 1970.

Rosenfeld, Albert. *The Second Genesis: The Coming Control of Life.* Englewood Cliffs, N.J.: Prentice-Hall, 1969.
Dated but still useful over-all survey of the biological revolution in reproduction, organ transplants, and mind control.

Roy, Rustum. "New Dilemmas in Sex." Unpublished.

———. "The Obsolescence of Marriage, American-Style." Unpublished.

Roy, Rustum and Della. *Honest Sex.* New York: The New American Library, A Signet Book, 1968.
The original statement and argument for flexible monogamy, the option of comarital relations, and a carefully balanced and Christian ethic guiding this radical modification of couple marriages.

———. "Is Monogamy Outdated?" *The Humanist,* March–April, 1970, pp. 19–26.
Also in Lester Kirkendall and Robert N. Whitehurst, Eds., *The New Sexual Revolution.*
Note: Of all the writings on modifications in family and marital life, I find those of the Roys most provocative and balanced. If I were to single out one or two basic readings, it would be the writings of the Roys and the Rimmer novels.

Royden, Agnes Maude (Shaw). *A Threefold Cord*. New York: The
    Macmillan Company, 1948.
    A marvelous, wonderfully open, enjoyable autobiography of a modified
    triangular relation between an important Episcopal minister and two
    women, 1901–1944.

"Rules and Regulations for Test-Tube Babies." *Nature* (London),
    May 14, 1971.
    An editorial with perceptive comments on embryo transplants.

Sackerman, Henry. *The Crowded Bed*. New York: Bantam Books,
    1968.
    A satirical novel of a girl with two husbands. A good point is lost amid
    the farcical treatment.

Schur, Edwin. *The Family and the Sexual Revolution*. Blooming-
    ton, Indiana: Indiana University Press, 1964.

Sex and the Yale Student. New Haven: Student Committee on
    Human Sexuality, 1970. Also New York: The New American
    Library, A Signet Book, 1971.
    Informative and undoubtedly pioneering as a college approach to basic
    facts of reproduction, intercourse, and contraception. But limited to
    this.

Shope, David. "Virgins Make Happier Marriages." *Marriage*, Octo-
    ber, 1969, pp. 2–7, 58–61.
    A biased but useful study because of the implicit assumptions about
    conformity and happiness.

Simon, William, and Gagnon, John. *The End of Adolescence: The
    College Experience*. New York: Harper & Row, Publishers, 1969.

"Single Motherhood." *Time*, September 6, 1971, p. 48.

Snoek, C. Jaime. "Marriage and the Institutionalization of Sexual
    Relations." In Franz Böckle, Ed., *The Future of Marriage as
    Institution*.
    A German Redemptorist takes an open view of premarital sex, trial
    marriages, and group marriages, but hesitates on comarital relations

Stannard, Una. "Adam's Rib, or the Woman Within." *Trans-
    Action*, November–December, 1970, pp. 24–32.
    A fascinating article loaded with absorbing details from the history of
    man's not-so-hidden maternal instinct and woman's traditional lack of
    same.

Sylvin, Francis. *Test-Tube Father*. New York: The New American Library, A Signet Book, 1967.
Second-rate novel of a couple who resort to artificial insemination, and the psychological problems this creates.

Toffler, Alvin. *Future Shock*. New York: Random House, 1970.
An unexcelled survey of the real psychological shock we all are experiencing and ways of coping with it. The chapter on "The Fractured Family" is very well done for a brief study. Indispensable.

Tracy, Phil. "Fidelity: Forbidden Topic." *National Catholic Reporter*, December 11, 1970, p. 13.
Maintains that sexual exclusiveness is an obstacle to any kind of serious relationship with any other member of the opposite sex.

"Unisex in the Laboratory." *Time*, September 6, 1971, p. 49.
Mount Sinai psychologist finds a shift to unisex reactions in comparing reactions of patients in the 1950s with similar patients in 1970 with the Rorschach ink-blot test.

Updike, John. *Couples*. New York: Fawcett World Library, Crest Book, 1969.
A Christian novel of marital infidelity in the suburbs.

Valente, Michael F. *Sex: The Radical View of a Catholic Theologian*. New York: Bruce Books, 1970.
Valente offers an unusually cogent argument for the acceptance of two ethics, one for procreation, the other for non-procreative sexual intercourse and behavior. The latter, he argues, must be person-focused and show concern for growth and communication.

van der Poel, Cornelius. *The Search for Human Values*. Paramus, New Jersey: Paulist/Newman Press, 1971.
An open, easy-to-read Catholic survey of moral theology.

Watson, James D. "The Future of Asexual Reproduction." *Intellectual Digest*, October, 1971, pp. 69–74.
A good review of cloning prospects by a Nobel Laureate geneticist.

——. "Moving Toward the Clonal Man." *The Atlantic*, May, 1971, pp. 50–53.
A cautionary survey of the possibilities of asexually reproducing man.

Watts, Alan W. *Nature, Man, and Woman*. New York: Random House, Vintage Books, 1970.
Valuable insights and perspectives from the oriental traditions coupled with a deep insight into the nature of male and female.

Wells, Theodore, and Christie, Lee. "Living Together: An Alternative to Marriage." *The Futurist*, April, 1970, pp. 50–51.

Whitehurst, Robert. "Extramarital Sex: Alienation or Extension of Normal Behavior." In Gerhard Neubeck, Ed., *Extramarital Relations*.

Williamson, John. "Project Synergy." December, 1970.
An unpublished outline and abstract of the rationale behind the Sandstone Foundation for Community Systems Research, Inc., a very promising experiment in an engineered environment with open "cool sex."

———. "Sexuality and Social Stability."
Abstract of a presentation delivered at a 1970 Kirkridge conference on new life styles and a changing community. The author is a key figure in the Sandstone experiment in Topanga, California.

Willingham, Calder. *Providence Island*. New York: Dell Publishing Company, 1970.
An interesting novel of a man and two women marooned on an island, with a temporary triangle developing.

Wilson, M. J. "Celebrities Typify New Permissive Attitude—Unwed Mothers." Newsweek Feature Service, 1971.

Winick, Charles. *The New People: Desexualization in American Life*. New York: Pegasus, 1968.

Wohl, Burton. *The Baby Maker*. New York: Bantam Books, 1970.
Very well-handled novel and movie about a childless couple who hire a substitute mother to carry a child for them.

"Woman Problem, The." *Life*, August 13, 20, and 27, 1971. A three-part series.
An excellent, readable, historical overview of man's centuries-old distortion of woman.

Woodbury, Richard. "High-School Pregnancy." *Life*, April 2, 1970, pp. 34–39.

Zweig, Ferdynand. *Israel: The Sword and the Harp*. Rutherford, New Jersey: Fairleigh Dickinson University Press, 1969.
Chapter Four deals with the kibbutz.

Index